Laughter in the Dark

Alan Ayckbourn. (Photo by Clare Clifford)

Laughter in the Dark

The Plays of Alan Ayckbourn

Albert E. Kalson

Rutherford • Madison • Teaneck
Fairleigh Dickinson University Press
London and Toronto: Associated University Presses

Associated University Presses
440 Forsgate Drive
Cranbury, NJ 08512

Associated University Presses
25 Sicilian Avenue
London WC1A 2QH, England

Associated University Presses
P.O. Box 39, Clarkson Pstl. Stn.
Mississauga, Ontario,
L5J 3X9 Canada

PR
6051
.Y35
Z74
1993
Feb. 1995

Library of Congress Cataloging-in-Publication Data

Kalson, Albert E.
Laughter in the dark : the plays of Alan Ayckbourn / Albert E. Kalson.
p.   cm.
Includes bibliographical references and index.
ISBN 0-8386-3479-6 (alk. paper)
1. Ayckbourn, Alan, 1939–   —Criticism and interpretation.
I. Title.
PR6051.Y35Z74   1993
822'.914—dc20   91-58958
                                                             CIP

PRINTED IN THE UNITED STATES OF AMERICA

For Fran and Beudi, Angelo and Mary

Contents

Preface

Ian Watson concludes the preface to the second edition of his *Conversations with Ayckbourn* (1988) by quoting from a letter from the dramatist: "I rather enjoy being the least documented playwright of the twentieth century." Ready or not, Mr. Ayckbourn, that statement is about to become passé.

Despite the fact that Ayckbourn is Britain's most prolific, most successful dramatist since George Bernard Shaw, there have been, until now—apart from Watson's valuable *Conversations*—only two books on his work, one by a British journalist/drama critic, the other by an American professor. There are also a handful of journal articles as well as the usual interviews and pieces one finds in newspapers shortly before a play's first performance. In 1991, a collection of essays by professors of English and theater was published in the United States. Inevitably, more will follow, as his reputation among academics was enhanced when he was named the Cameron Mackintosh Professor of Contemporary Theatre at St. Catherine's College, Oxford University, for 1992.

The British have recognized Ayckbourn's importance as something more than a farceur, a provider of light entertainments, for some time. Four years before the dramatist established a relationship with Britain's National Theatre, now the Royal National, Peter Hall, about to assume its leadership, attended a performance of *Absurd Person Singular* at the Criterion Theatre, a commercial West End house. He wrote in his diary: "It is a hard, beautifully constructed play. But because it is commercial, it tends to be unregarded. I think Ayckbourn is much more likely to be in the repertoire of the National Theatre in fifty years' time than most of the current Royal Court dramatists" (*Peter Hall's Diaries*, 28 August 1973, 55). According to the playwright, a London critic once said, "We've got to stop depending on filling our theatres with Agatha Christie and Alan Ayckbourn!" And for a time Hall had to defend himself from the attacks of those who considered Ayckbourn's work too frivolous to be housed at so august a venue as the government-subsidized National (351). Now, however, after six of his plays have been staged there, the only complaints come from commercial managers painfully aware that they are losing money any time a sure-fire box-office success eludes them.

Respect for Ayckbourn as a serious writer has been late in coming in the United States. Here he has been mistakenly regarded as Britain's Neil Simon, a comparison that puzzles the dramatist, who admires Simon, and has directed some of his plays. "I don't see any connection," Ayckbourn told me. "I think the linkage is primarily due to the financial success of the body of work rather than the content." Although Ayckbourn's plays have become staples of America's regional theaters, until recently the few that have been presented in New York have not duplicated their London success. That too is changing: the two drama critics of the *New York Times*, Frank Rich and Mel Gussow, have become his champions. Both of them make a point of seeing the latest Ayckbourn play in London's West End on their annual visits there. On occasion one or the other travels to Scarborough in Yorkshire for the premiere of an Ayckbourn work at the Stephen Joseph Theatre in the Round, where the playwright serves as Artistic Director and presents his work before its London production. In a piece entitled "Bard of the British Bourgeoisie," Gussow places him at "the pinnacle of his profession, someone who has earned his position alongside Harold Pinter, Tom Stoppard, and a very few others" (*New York Times Magazine*, 28 January 1990, 23). Rich suggests Ayckbourn stands alone: "At a time when England boasts very few dramatists as vital as the dominant American playwrights of this decade, Mr. Ayckbourn is a one-man renaissance" (*New York Times*, 22 June 1989, 13).

Such strong statements have forced other American critics to rethink their estimates of Ayckbourn's worth and producers to reexamine the body of work. In New York in 1991, *Taking Steps* and *Absent Friends* had highly successful concurrent runs, albeit limited ones because of the similar policies of the production companies, Circle in the Square Theatre and the Manhattan Theatre Club. Lynne Meadow, artistic director of the latter, who had already presented *Woman in Mind* in 1988, has announced that there will be more American premieres of Ayckbourn plays in her company's future beginning with a Broadway production of *A Small Family Business* in 1992.

This study will not attempt to categorize or compare British comedy with American comedy, nor will it attempt extended definitions and comparisons of *comedy* and *farce*. Ayckbourn himself used to label his plays as one or the other, but abandoned the practice in 1981 after the publication in a single volume of *Sisterly Feelings* and *Taking Steps*. To his dismay his labeling the former a comedy and the latter a farce provoked "much lengthy and somewhat tedious discussion" as to where and when "the boundaries should be drawn between" the two. For Ayckbourn, comedies "are straight plays with a sense of humour, often saying much the same thing only more enjoyably and therefore to a wider audience." Farces "set out to be, and often are, funnier than comedies, though in order to achieve this, the author has necessarily had to jettison one or two things like deep character analysis or Serious Things. Good farce explores the extreme reaches of the credible and the likely. It proceeds by its own immaculate internal logic." Resolving never again to provide descriptions of his work, for, "ultimately, what matters is whether the play is good or not," he declared that "henceforth, they will all be plays. I will leave others to brand and pigeon-hole them if they want to" (preface, xii–ix).

Sunday Times critic John Peter seconds Ayckbourn. Reviewing the first production of *Body Language* at Scarborough, he wrote: "If you think that definitions are essential, take early retirement. Is Alan Ayckbourn's new play a farce, a comedy-farce, a black comedy or a tragical-comical psycho-medical entertainment? The one categorical imperative in Ayckbourn country is that on your way in you must leave your categories in the cloakroom" (27 May 1990, E5). Having myself been wary of the prestige that rightly or wrongly accrues to any play labeled a "tragedy," I too have long since given up the labeling game in the classroom. Comedy and tragedy spring from the same creative impetus. It is possible, after all, to cry at *Twelfth Night* and laugh at *King Lear*. Here I will use—loosely perhaps, but conveniently—the generic terms *comedy* and *farce*. Future critics may find it necessary to add *tragedy* to the as yet unwritten Ayckbourn plays. I was tempted to do so with some we already have. Ayckbourn's own words on the matter of labeling, it seems to me, ought to be heeded.

What I am attempting here is an exploration of the Ayckbourn canon, demonstrating wherever possible that character, situation, theme, and technique derive from the persona of the author, his experience with every facet of the theater, and his awareness of a bewildering world. That his concerns and his world, despite his characters' British circumlocutions and customs, are immediately recognizable everywhere (his works have been translated into thirty languages and are produced throughout the globe) makes the study of Ayckbourn's plays worthwhile, perhaps even essential, as his vision—like his world and ours—perceptively darkens.

Acknowledgments

I must first of all acknowledge a debt—one I share with anyone who ever has or ever will delve into the work of Alan Ayckbourn—to Ian Watson. He pointed the way for the rest of us with his article, "Ayckbourn of Scarborough," in *Municipal Entertainment* in 1978; his Ayckbourn "bibliography, biography, playography," *Theatre Checklist No. 21* for TQ Publications in 1980; and his indispensable *Conversations with Ayckbourn*, first published by Macdonald Futura in 1981 and published again in an expanded edition by Faber & Faber Ltd. in 1988. I have derived much useful information from the last, particularly about Ayckbourn's early career. Many persons have interviewed Ayckbourn, myself included, but Watson has drawn out the elusive dramatist as no one else has.

I am grateful to Faber & Faber Ltd. for permission to quote extracts from Watson's book and the following Ayckbourn plays: *Body Language, A Chorus of Disapproval, Henceforward . . . , Invisible Friends, Man of the Moment, The Revengers' Comedies, A Small Family Business,* and *Woman in Mind*. I wish to thank as well Chatto & Windus for granting me permission to use extracts from the following Ayckbourn plays: *Absent Friends, Bedroom Farce, Joking Apart, Just Between Ourselves, The Norman Conquests, Sisterly Feelings, Taking Steps,* and *Ten Times Table*. The extracts from *Absent Friends, Bedroom Farce,* and *The Norman Conquests* are from editions published by Grove Press Inc.; Grove Weidenfeld has also approved their inclusion here. Margaret Ramsay Ltd. has granted me permission to quote from Ayckbourn's *Absurd Person Singular, Family Circles, Intimate Exchanges, Relatively Speaking, The Square Cat, Time and Time Again,* and *Way Upstream*. All rights whatsoever in Ayckbourn's plays are strictly reserved, and application for performance, etc., should be made before rehearsal to Margaret Ramsay Ltd., 14a Goodwin's Court, St. Martin's Lane, London, WC2. No performance may be given unless a license has been obtained. The Peters Fraser & Dunlop Group Ltd. has kindly granted me permission to quote from J. B. Priestley's *Bees on the Boat Deck* and *An Inspector Calls* as published by William Heinemann Ltd.

A small part of Chapter Two of this volume was first published as

"Old Friends Reminisce," in *The Pinter Review: Annual Essays 1989* of the University of Tampa; the genesis of Chapter Three is my piece, "On stage, off stage, and backstage with Alan Ayckbourn," in *Themes in Drama, 10: Farce,* edited by James Redmond and published by Cambridge University Press in 1988. Having first published on Ayckbourn in *Dictionary of Literary Biography, Volume Thirteen: British Dramatists Since World War II,* a Bruccoli Clark Book (1982), I wish to thank the editor, Stanley Weintraub of Pennsylvania State University for starting me off on the journey that led to this volume.

I thank as well Doris and Jim Claiborne, Joan F. Dean, John Drake, Allen and Ruth Hayman, Jon Lawry, Mary Pat O'Kelly, and Stanley Sellers for fetching materials from England for me; Betty Thomas and Wendy Tigchelaar for their help in duplicating materials; A. A. De Vitis for his encouragement and invaluable suggestions as the manuscript, like an Ayckbourn "alternate" play, underwent countless permutations, all of which he read; Maydene Crosby for typing the manuscript, all the while reminding me of long-forgotten rules of grammar.

I extend my gratitude to the staff of Ayckbourn's agent, Margaret Ramsay, who enabled me to read some of his unpublished work, and to the staff of the Stephen Joseph Theatre in the Round, particularly Robin Herford, a fine actor, director, and former company administrator, for making my visits to Scarborough comfortable as well as profitable in the best sense. Most especially, I am forever grateful to Heather Stoney, sometime actress and a good one, better known for her role as Ayckbourn's aide, abettor, and protector, as she shields him from the likes of academics like myself and others who would intrude on his valuable time, for allowing me some access to the man himself as well as his current work.

Laughter in the Dark

1
A Chorus of Approval

In his *Diaries*, Sir Peter Hall describes an incident that took place in the country home of Denys Lasdun, architect of the National Theatre: "The living room has a wonderful door knob on it, honest iron. . . . A screw had come out. So four times, to the great architect's increasing rage, Sue Lasdun pulled the whole door knob off and it fell onto the boards with a resounding crash. Denys got pinker and pinker. He kept asking her to be careful and to jam it in. Later in the evening he pulled it off himself." An amused Hall, enduring at the time the frustrations of building delays and cost overruns as a vast theater complex was being constructed on London's South Bank, calls it "a scene out of Alan Ayckbourn."[1]

From such seemingly run-of-the-mill domestic setbacks, Britain's most widely produced living dramatist, Alan Ayckbourn, has forged an extraordinary career in the contemporary theater. An Ayckbourn play frequently centers on an ordinary mortal, not architects of world renown, who ought to be able to cope with minor irritants but cannot. A typical, easily recognizable Ayckbourn character is Dennis in *Just Between Ourselves* (1976), who would like to sell his wife's car but cannot move it out of the garage. The up-and-over door is stuck, totally defeating a man who regards himself as a do-it-yourself whiz. And on whom does Dennis take out his frustration? His wife Vera, neglected and depressed, quietly enters a state of catatonia at center stage as her oblivious husband continues to putter at odd jobs at his workbench. Is this the stuff of comedy? Alan Ayckbourn has made it so in such ordinary, everyday scenes that occur in most of his plays, now numbering more than forty, all of them comedies, many of them farces.

If the laughter at the final curtain of *Just Between Ourselves* is hesitant, just a little nervous, there have been hearty guffaws along the way. A man exiting the theater commented to the author on a scene in the first act in which Vera breaks down at the tea table: "If I'd known what I was laughing at at the time, I wouldn't have laughed."[2] And Ayckbourn prides himself on just such an ambiguous response.

Shortly after *The Revengers' Comedies* was first produced in 1989—his thirty-seventh play according to his staff at the Stephen Joseph Theatre in the Round in Scarborough, Yorkshire—the dramatist, once considered a spinner of gossamer boulevard comedies, told Mel Gussow of the *New York Times* that his ideal was to write "a serious comedy that will lead audiences to 'laugh, gasp, laugh, gasp.'"[3] It would seem that with *A Small Family Business* (1987), *Henceforward . . .* (1987), and *Man of the Moment* (1988), as well as *The Revengers' Comedies*, all of them hilarious comedies that leave audiences devastated, Ayckbourn had already achieved that goal.

As one might expect, the entry under profession on his United Kingdom passport reads "writer." Yet, oddly enough, Ayckbourn considers himself to be first of all a director. He spends only a week, two weeks at the most, writing his yearly new play. But Ayckbourn, the workaholic, is busy throughout the other fifty weeks of the year not only administrating a company and raising funds for its operation, arranging its touring program, and participating in its educational services, but also in directing plays written by others and, each season's high point, directing his own new one as well at the theater in Scarborough for which he serves as the artistic director but for which he is in fact the raison d'être. He has often admitted that the Stephen Joseph Theatre in the Round exists, in fact thrives, because he has chosen to live and work in the North Country's most popular, middle-class seaside resort. That Ayckbourn prefers life in Scarborough to life in London, where one would expect a phenomenally successful playwright and acclaimed director to work, reveals much about the man. More significantly, insight into the character of the man and some awareness of the path he took to achieve his unique position in an always precarious profession sheds light finally on what matters most—the plays themselves.

"In a sense," Ayckbourn revealed to Gussow, "one is the sum of one's characters."[4] The typical Ayckbourn male character who considers himself on top of every situation only to be defeated by the bewildering universe around him derives from the persona of the writer himself. The typical Ayckbourn female character fights a sometimes losing battle to maintain her sanity as she suffers indignity, embarrassment, even neglect as her mate calls the tune. The male cannot always cope, but he seems always to be in charge, like Ayckbourn himself, directing others. I was present at the Scarborough theater when the writer failed to meet with a London producer after a performance. While Ayckbourn sulked at home, an embarrassed Heather Stoney, his assistant who shares that home, had to make his excuses: the writer was having a bad night; the word processor, one of the many electronic gadgets and toys that obsess him, on which he depends as he writes, had betrayed him by losing a good idea, had chewed up some effective dialogue in its mysterious innards and was instead spewing out nonsense syllables! Yet another Ayckbourn scene. . . . In that lost scene Ayckbourn was no doubt, as he has said to Gussow, "living the life of his characters." To put it the other way round, perhaps the characters were living the life of Ayckbourn.

If it is the female who sometimes loses the thread of reality—like Vera in *Just Between Ourselves*, Eva in *Absurd Person Singular* (1972), and Susan in *Woman in Mind* (1985)—that too may be a side of the playwright's own complex character. Says Ayckbourn, who thinks of himself as having "a reasonably well controlled multiple personality," "My greatest fear is to be psychoanalyzed—or cured. A doctor would say, 'You've got a whole load of personalities, let's get rid of some of them. Then you'll be this very sane, balanced person.' And I'd say, 'Oh, no, it's my insanity that allows me to write.'"[5]

Born in Hampstead in 1939, Ayckbourn acquired the acting bug genetically; his maternal grandparents were music-hall performers, and his father was the deputy leader, assistant concert master, of the London Symphony Orchestra. As a very small child Ayckbourn remembers being taken to rehearsals and an occasional concert. He still loves full-bodied classical music, with Prokofiev a favorite, unlike his father who preferred light music to Beethoven once he was away from the concert hall. When Ayckbourn was five, his parents divorced; when he was eight, his mother, Irene Maud Worley, remarried. His stepfather, Cecil Pye, was a bank manager whose work necessitated the family's frequent moves from one Sussex town to another, from Billingshurst to Haywards Heath to Lewes to Uckfield. Despite his working years in the north of England, his plays are rooted in the south, his characters' habits and speech patterns reflecting his upbringing.

The major influence in his formative years was his mother. Known by her pen name, Mary James, and often earning more than her second husband, she wrote several popular volumes of romance fiction as well as countless short stories on a portable typewriter in the kitchen. For some years her son believed that typing was the primary function in Sussex kitchens, and soon he was doing it too, writing stories and poems. What she seems to have passed on to her son was an ingenious flexibility that enabled her to solve any problem as she kept within the moral code of each magazine: "In *Woman's Own*, at that time . . . your girl heroine could fall in love, but not with a married man; then in another magazine, you could have a married man, but they must have an unhappy ending."6 One magazine would initiate a project by sending illustrations around which she would then construct a plot. Had she traded typewriter for computer, Mary James might have been as prolific as Barbara Cartland, or at least as prolific as her son.

Now as playwright and director, Ayckbourn still proves himself as adept as his mother with each new play. As he writes, he must bear in mind the make-up of a changing company and the possibilities of an unchanging stage—his in-the-round theater allows only three doors. So many of his plays stem from what at first might appear to be insurmountable obstacles for which he himself is responsible. Why not write a play in which the three floors of a Victorian house are on a single stage level, the only level an arena theater allows? In *Taking Steps* (1979) he did so. Why not flood the playing area and set a play on a boat that actually moves through water? In *Way Upstream* (1981) he did so. Having solved all the problems presented by three interrelated plays in which the onstage action of one is the offstage action of the other two in *The Norman Conquests* (1973), Ayckbourn tested himself with a monumental challenge: why not reduce the theater's budget for actors by having a season in which two performers play ten characters in eight related plays stemming from an identical opening situation, with each variation having alternate endings—sixteen versions in all? *Intimate Exchanges* (1982–83) was his answer. For mother and son, the readiness is all.

Although he seems himself to have authored the tall tale about never having written a play before he was a member of a professional provincial repertory company, Ayckbourn actually turned dramatist of sorts as a schoolboy. His mother recalls that her self-dramatizing son "started this acting lark by bullying other children to take part in plays which he put on in the garden shed. I think he charged them a ha'penny to get in, but God knows what they acted in there because normally all you could hear was Alan's screaming, hysterical voice."7 Playwriting thus began with the urge to act, more specifically, to direct, but the director generally kept the most actable part, the character that got all the laughs, for himself.

These were not years in which a youngster consciously planned a future, and his prep school days were undemanding at the boarding school in Sussex that is no longer in existence. In his last years there the headmaster and mistress were packing it in. They had had enough, and Ayckbourn was one of only a handful of boys there for the final term, which was conducted more like a holiday camp than a school. The experience, however, would serve him well, as the headmaster and his wife provided the raw material for characters in several plays. Ayckbourn speaks of *Intimate Exchanges,* his most intricate "alternate"-versions play, as "a tremendous exercise in nostalgia. . . . Most of the characters are drawn from my childhood and it's set around my prep school. Toby and Celia are images of my old headmaster and his wife."[8] What he remembers most vividly about them—with affection rather than misgivings—was their continuing sweetness to the boys, who were diminishing in number from eighty to five, as they had "terrible rows around the school." That unpleasant aspect of marriage was underscored on weekends at home. With his mother's marriage unraveling, the rows at home were even more tempestuous than those at school. Yet Ayckbourn does not consider himself nor his younger stepbrother, who attended another school, to have been unduly upset or marked for life. Spending more time at school than at home, they could adapt to any situation, but Ayckbourn does remember wondering at the time why his mother had remarried.

At Haileybury, a good public school to which he won a bank scholarship, Ayckbourn vaguely considered a career in journalism as he edited the house magazine and wrote the end-of-term revue. Eventually, however, acting became his primary interest in his five years there, from the age of twelve to the age of seventeen when he left school. The man responsible for sustaining that interest was the school's French master, Edgar Matthews, a friend of the Shakespearean actor-manager Sir Donald Wolfit. Matthew's daughter was for a time Wolfit's secretary. The schoolmaster exercised his own passion for Shakespeare by directing the boys in plays that toured the continent during school holidays. Ayckbourn began by playing Peter in *Romeo and Juliet* and progressed to the role of Macduff on a month-long tour of cities along the east coast of the United States and Canada. He had hoped to play Macbeth, a role judged by Matthews to be unsuitable for "a six-stone weakling,"[9] but the excitement of the whole experience, including trips across the Atlantic on the *Queen Mary* and the first *Queen Elizabeth* more than compensated for the disappointment of not playing the lead. The point was that acting was fun, and that it might even keep on being fun in the real world.

In 1956 Ayckbourn left the school that would later honor him by naming its new theater after him, armed with a decent education, some experience on the cricket field (another lifelong passion), and a letter of introduction to Donald Wolfit that resulted in his first job in the professional theater as actor (a sentry) and ASM (assistant stage manager) for a three-week season at the Edinburgh Festival. The play was Fritz Hochwalder's *The Strong Are Lonely.*

Just before the London rehearsal period began, Ayckbourn was shocked to discover his mother, whose marriage had further deteriorated, in an extreme state of depression. The son may have saved his mother's life by taking her to London and finding her a job as an assistant to a writer, and soon she herself was writing again. By the time he returned from Scotland, she had made a remarkable recovery. A renewed zest had made her look twenty years younger. That brief dark period in his mother's life had an indelible effect on a young man not yet out of his teens. The mental and physical harm an unhappy, unhealthy relationship can cause a person has been a constant theme to be explored and expanded in many of his plays. In her resilience Ayckbourn's mother was more fortunate than most of the characters for whom she would seem to have been the inspiration. Only Eva, suicidal in act 2 of *Absurd Person Singular,* bounces back to take charge of her failed architect husband's career in act 3. Today Ayckbourn and his mother maintain a close relationship as she lives near him in Scarborough.

The three weeks with Wolfit, the model for the old actor past the peak of his powers in Ronald Harwood's *The Dresser,* convinced Ayckbourn that he had found his niche. He had no driving ambition at the time, no illusions about conquering the world of the theater, no deep-rooted feeling that apart from that world life would be pointless; but he felt comfortable there, at home both on stage and backstage. And the offstage hours he spent listening to the experienced actors telling wonderful stories and seeing many festival offerings without having to buy a ticket really were fun. Of Wolfit he said: "His performances were majestic and huge, and they were all about acting, they weren't about anything to do with the character." But there was a lesson to be learned from the old actor-manager who gave the audience what they wanted: "Theater is show business."[10] It was a lesson Ayckbourn would never forget as, always entertaining his audience, he would find the way to offer them something richer than they could have expected.

After his stint with Wolfit, Ayckbourn toyed with the idea of attending a drama school but instead took on a series of jobs for a year as ASM, minor actor, and general factotum. Supported by his mother, he worked without salary in a repertory company in Worthing along with the yet unknown Daniel Massey, Michael Bryant, Ian Holm, and Elizabeth Spriggs. Then as ASM he moved on to Leatherhead for a princely £12 a week, but there he had the opportunity to extend his range as actor in more substantial roles, such as the boy, Jim Curry, in N. Richard Nash's *The Rainmaker.*

The next year would prove a momentous one for the nineteen-year-old Ayckbourn, determining both his domestic life and his professional career. He married Christine Roland, the vicar requiring his mother's written permission, and would soon have a family to support. Asked by Rodney Wood, the Leatherhead stage manager, if he would like to be part of the stage team at Scarborough, Ayckbourn, without even knowing at the time the location of the town in which he would be spending most of his life, agreed. His less-than-ideal marriage together with the lives of friends and neighbors, even the nameless but hardly faceless inhabitants, some 50,000 of them, and visitors on the streets, on the beaches, in the fun fairs, even in the lobby, bar, and auditorium of a theater in a northern holiday town provide the truly comic yet comically true ingredients of an extraordinary body of work. Christine Ayckbourn, an artist and illustrator, separated from her husband and living in Leeds where she raised their two sons, Steven and Philip, asserts that "she would be among the richest women in the world if she claimed royalties for all the fodder she has provided for his bitter, biting domestic comedies."[11] Unknown to them, many Scarborough residents have contributed the raw materials out of which the plays that have entertained them at their local theater have been formed. But the sometime Scarborough resident whom Ayckbourn considers his mentor, the man who may have metamorphosed into a recurring Ayckbourn character type, was Stephen Joseph, the founder and director of the Scarborough repertory company, whose fanatic dream it was to turn the world into a theater-in-the-round.

Joseph, the son of Hermione Gingold and Michael Joseph—curiously enough, the sometime publisher of the works of Mary James—operated an on-again, off-again theater company wherever, whenever he could find a suitable space. Economy was only one aspect of his attraction to arena-style staging. More important was the truth in performance derived from the proximity of actor and audience. Joseph eschewed the word "intimacy" so often used to describe the special effect of his preferred style: "It is not a word I like in this context. It implies a domestic, if passionate, relationship while I want to emphasize a theatrical relationship in which there shall be passion indeed but not quite, I think, contact."[12] What happened one night in Scarborough during a performance of *Just Between Ourselves*—as Dennis exited leaving Vera on stage in hysterics, a man in the audience caught the actor's sleeve and said, "I wouldn't go if I were you, she's awfully upset"[13]—was not Joseph's ultimate aim; the truth that evoked that response, however, was. "As I see it," Joseph has written, "the open stage, by putting actors and audience into one architectural volume, provides proximity between actors and audience over a homogeneous range that includes three-dimensional perception. . . .

The actor can be seen to be a three-dimensional being, belonging to a three-dimensional world. . . . Behind a frame, on an enclosed stage, even the best of actors is flattened. On the open stage even the worst of actors will be fully exposed."[14]

In arena staging the actor must *be;* he cannot rely on performing. A valuable lesson that Joseph was to teach Ayckbourn and anyone else who ever worked with him was that the dramatist reaches the audience "through the actor, and if you don't get your actor right, there's very few dramatists who can actually survive."[15] The intermediary is the director who takes from the dramatist, gives to the actor, who, in turn, gives to the audience.

Paradoxically, the Library Theatre in the Round in Scarborough and the Victoria Theatre in Stoke-on-Trent, the two companies founded by Joseph, were thought of by those in the profession as writers' theaters. Whereas Joseph's quarrel with the West End had little to do with the kinds of plays that were presented there—his own favorite play, to the embarrassment of his company that performed it, was Laurence Housman's *Victoria Regina*—he believed strongly that new writing talent had to be encouraged, and that young writers needed to see their works performed. As a result his company presented early works by then unheralded playwrights, such as Harold Pinter's *The Birthday Party* and James Saunders's *Alas, Poor Fred.* Joseph worked most closely with David Campton, best known for his one-act plays, "Mutatis Mutandis" and "Soldier from the Wars Returning," urging him to develop such relevant themes as nuclear holocaust, and even suggesting scenes of dialogue. The director thought of Campton as the source of serious plays with a Pinter-like air of menace that he admired, while other fledglings would offer light entertainment to fill the seats. Ayckbourn's first playwriting efforts beyond his school days were encouraged by Joseph, not so much because he recognized immediately an extraordinary talent—the first Ayckbourn works were hardly remarkable—but because the founder of the Scarborough theater encouraged everyone in his company to be familiar with every aspect of the theater. Actors worked the box-office; actors worked sound and lights; actors wrote plays.

Despite his ability to inspire love and loyalty, to take a disparate group of theater people and transform them into a family-company, Joseph was himself an inept actor. As a director he frequently lost interest in the actors, allowing them to go their own way—fortunately they could not stray very far on an arena stage—as he became obsessed with a production's technical problems. Frequently the actors had to ask him to stop hammering away at onstage props, even auditorium seats, as they tried to rehearse. It was his encompassing passion for the theater that fueled the young company. Having begun in a temporary theater, he molded a company that would become a vital part of the life of the town. Unfortunately, although he spent hours drawing up and modifying plans for what he hoped would one day be the ultimate theater-in-the-round, he did not live long enough to see the company move to permanent quarters in a converted school, the theater that now bears his name.

The first production directed by Joseph that Ayckbourn ever saw, Sartre's *No Exit* at the Mahatma Ghandi Hall in London, was his first experience of in-the-round theater. Overwhelmed by it, the young ASM was excited by the prospect of working with the innovative director. That there would be no shifting of heavy scenery by the stage crew occurred to him too, but the company's touring season when the crew surrounded a makeshift playing area with temporary seating on risers would make a mockery of that notion. Nonetheless, Ayckbourn and Joseph, both of them fascinated by the technical end of a production, hit it off immediately, and the older theater practitioner would teach the younger everything he knew. Together they built new light grids and discovered how to make the most of such newfangled equipment as tape recorders. Ayckbourn may have been better than Joseph at getting up and down ladders—Joseph had at least one serious fall—but he was in awe of the older man's instinct for discovering the flaw in the structure of a new play.

Perhaps the reason they got on so well was that they were basically so alike. Both were extremely shy, never quite at ease, always avoiding eye contact with any but their closest friends and colleagues.[16] But both of them knew what they wanted and what they needed. Inspiring confidence with their dedication and loyalty, they managed to win support and have their way. Both of them, seemingly conventional in manner, eyed authority figures with amusement and suspicion. They stood apart from the rest with a subtle air of anarchy about them, which, for Joseph at least, could at times become blatant. When the Oliviers marched down St. James's to save the St. James's Theatre, Joseph marched up the street, urging that it be pulled down. His sensible, unheeded plan was to build theaters in office blocks to pay the rates. If Ayckbourn could not quite bring himself to such overt anti-establishment action, he had to admire a man who wanted to make theater more accessible, whose heart was in the right place even if his actions were occasionally wrongheaded.

Discussing the character Mint, a piano tuner who never speaks throughout Ayckbourn's early play, *Mr Whatnot* (1963), in his book *Theatre in the Round* (1967), Joseph might well be describing himself and his effect on others: "The chaos caused by the dumb man . . . an impossible clown enlightened by absolute good sense, in the complete family, symbol of a stable society, caused the audience to feel an exhilaration as though they had had a glimpse of a new freedom. The play made a pointing gesture in the direction of anarchy."[17] The playwright himself says of the work: "I always think of the *Whatnot* theme as being the Id figure who bounds along, the one inside me that would like to up-end and destroy—not destroy gratuitously, just to up-end, really, and confuse a little, upset *status quos*. And I suppose Stephen was much of a oneness with that anyway."[18]

By the time of *Mr Whatnot*, enough of the Joseph personality together with his ideas had rubbed off on Ayckbourn so that it is difficult to determine whether it is his mentor or the playwright himself who inspired the character. Perhaps Mint owes something to both of them. What is certain is that the play's theme and its central character, who is sometimes aware of the chaos he causes and at times totally unaware of his effect on others, recur throughout the Ayckbourn canon: Leonard in *Time and Time Again* (1971), Norman in *The Norman Conquests* (1973), Colin in *Absent Friends* (1974), Trevor in *Bedroom Farce* (1975), Dennis in *Just Between Ourselves*, Tristram in *Taking Steps* (1979), Guy in *A Chorus of Disapproval* (1984), Jerome in *Henceforward . . .* (1987), and Douglas in *Man of the Moment* (1988).

At the end of Ayckbourn's first season at Scarborough he was lured away for a season at the Oxford Playhouse, where he got some good parts, even playing the romantic juvenile opposite Mai Zetterling. Yet when Joseph phoned him to ask if he would like to return to Scarborough, he said yes. When Frank Hauser, the director at Oxford who was impressed with Ayckbourn's work as an actor, tried to convince him to stay, Ayckbourn told him, "Well, no, I think I want to go back to Scarborough. I don't know why."[19] He knew at the time that Scarborough probably meant an emphasis on stage managing rather than acting. After all, "You can get any amount of bloody actors, but stage managers are terribly rare, and people who were actually able to understand all this machinery were like gold dust." Ayckbourn's fate was sealed.

He returned to Scarborough in 1959 and has been there ever since, except for the two years as a founder member, together with Joseph, of the Victoria Theatre in Stoke-on-Trent (1962–64); the six years he produced radio drama for the BBC in Leeds, during which he found time to write three plays for Scarborough (1964–70); and his two-year sabbatical from Scarborough, during which he directed his own company of actors at the National Theatre in London (1986–87), establishing once and for all with his productions of Will Evans and Valentine

[Pechey]'s *Tons of Money,* his own *A Small Family Business,* Arthur Miller's *A View from the Bridge,* and John Ford's *'Tis Pity She's a Whore* that he is one of the foremost directors in the English-speaking theater. In 1970 he became director of productions at Scarborough, Joseph having died in 1967, and in 1976 he oversaw the move to a year-round, permanent, 307-seat theater by the company, formerly known as the Library Theatre in the Round, now the Stephen Joseph Theatre in the Round. By 1991 Ayckbourn was contemplating a move to more spacious quarters, possibly Scarborough's local cinema.

Ayckbourn himself looks back on his early days, marveling at the way he moved almost effortlessly from one job to the next, all of them seemingly a preparation for Scarborough: "I never, in all my years of acting, was ever unemployed. Once I started at Worthing, I didn't stop: Worthing, Leatherhead, Scarborough, Oxford, Scarborough." Asked at what stage he started choosing his jobs, Ayckbourn told Ian Watson, "Well, I never chose anything. Things just happened. It's this divine inertia."[20]

Something similar had happened to Joseph. Looking for a suitable space in which to start a theater, he had spent a none-too-promising week looking around Scarborough. Discouraged, he was passing time in the library until his train departure when he began a conversation with the chef librarian, telling him of his frustration. The sympathetic librarian, William Smettem, convinced him to stay one more day, and put him up in his own home. In the meantime Smettem spoke to the chairman of the Scarborough Libraries Committee. The next morning Joseph had his space, the Concert Room and Lecture Room on the Library's first floor, and Scarborough had its theater.[21] What part had fate played in all this? Had it been chance or choice?

The role of chance or choice in all our lives, a major theme in his work, has always intrigued Ayckbourn, who is still somewhat startled by his phenomenal success. He still wonders how he got there, and the plays seem to be his own exploration of that process. "My plays are all to do with recognition," he told interviewer Janet Watts. That recognition is not merely the audience seeing the mirror image of themselves; it is as well the playwright seeing himself. He also told Watts, who noted that "he looks not unlike one of his characters— thinning hair, thickening waist, neatly casual clothes," that all his characters "contain bits of him. The indecisiveness central to his comedy is his own." And he added: "I don't think I've made a single decision in my life, except possibly not to have the soup. I didn't give up acting—acting gave me up; I didn't want to write—Stephen Joseph made me."[22] But Ayckbourn provoked Joseph to goad the writer in him. Displeased by John van Druten's *Bell, Book and Candle* and the

thankless role of Nicky that he was saddled with, a disgruntled actor
told a director who was fast losing patience during rehearsals that he
could write a better play. "Do it!" said Joseph, and Ayckbourn did—
or at least did try.

If Ayckbourn's *The Square Cat* (1959) cannot hold a candle to van
Druten's *Bell, Book and Candle,* it was a start. About a married
woman who wants to spend a weekend alone with a rock star but is
prevented by her family, the farce proves that the author had already
heeded the director's advice—but little else. According to Campton,
"Joseph believed that every beginning playwright should start by
digesting Brunetière's 'Law of the Drama.' Brunetière defined a
dramatic situation as 'the spectacle of a will striving towards a goal and
conscious of the means which it employs.' In other words, someone
wants something and someone or something is preventing them from
getting it," which was no news to him, claims Campton: "I seemed to
have known it all my life."[23] Chances are, the same can be said for
Ayckbourn. Aided in structuring the play by his wife, a member of
the company at the time, Ayckbourn fashioned for himself a role to
demonstrate his range as actor. Once out of the limelight, crude,
overbearing rock star Jerry Wattis is shy, sensitive, bespectacled
Arthur Brummage, a young man who prefers conservative suits to the
flamboyant garb his profession and his public demand. Throughout
the play Arthur quick-changes personality along with his costume.
Consciously or not, Ayckbourn may have been drawing on the two
sides of his own character, the diffident young man transforming
himself onstage into the brash, confident performer, always aware of
himself inhabiting a role.

Contrary to what was to become his habitual method of writing a
play in a few days, Ayckbourn labored over *The Square Cat,* rejecting
all of Joseph's suggestions for comic dialogue. Adopting the pen name
Roland Allen, a combination of his wife's name and his own, he was to
use it for his next three plays, none of which has been published. "I'm
trying to destroy all known copies," he told an interviewer.[24]

During this apprenticeship, Joseph tried to get his two most prom-
ising writers to collaborate on a Christmas show, *Dad's Tale* (1961), a
process that began with a synopsis by Campton derived from a Mary
Norton novel, *The Borrowers,* that Ayckbourn finally had to reject as
he completely overhauled the piece. After an idea suggested by
Joseph, who wanted him to deal with the problem of overpopulation
by setting a play on Venus, proved unworkable for him, he wrote
Standing Room Only (1961), a futuristic farce about a family struggling to maintain a normal existence while stranded on a bus in
Shaftesbury Avenue during a twenty-year-long traffic jam. Ayckbourn

realized how he had to write a play. He was not a collaborator, a conclusion underscored years later by the failure of *Jeeves* (1975), with Andrew Lloyd Webber, his one attempt at a large-scale musical, and his plays had to come not from earthshaking problems but from personal experience. "I think you should stick to what you know," he says.[25] Even his later plays that mirror his country's worsening social and economic situation—corporate profiteering adding to the widening rift between rich and poor, increasing the numbers of the homeless—stem from a highly personal reaction to Britain's current political scene.

For Ayckbourn the writing process itself, coming after a long period of cogitation, must be rapid-fire, with rehearsal and production following immediately. His method resembles that of Pirandello, who was said to brood over an idea for a long period before actually getting it down on paper in a short time. Italy's master dramatist claimed to have written nine plays in one year, one in three days, another in six.[26] He likened the process to a washerwoman in his native Sicily giving birth at the river's edge, then continuing her work five minutes later. For Pirandello, creative work that had real worth had to come easily. Here Pirandello and Ayckbourn part company. Ayckbourn works as quickly, producing a complete play in four or five days, but for him the actual composition, the writing itself, is so painful that in the past he procrastinated until a week before the rehearsal period. Without a deadline there was no play; yet, though it was often a near thing, he always met the deadline.

After the failure of *Mr Whatnot*, his first play to be mounted in London's West End, Ayckbourn took refuge with the BBC, "that great paternalistic womb for the wounded to crawl into,"[27] producing radio plays in Leeds. When Joseph asked him to write a play for Scarborough that "would make people laugh when their seaside holidays were spoiled by the rain and they came into the theatre to get dry before trudging back to their landladies," what seemed to Ayckbourn "as worthwhile a reason for writing a play as any,"[28] he agreed, but no play was forthcoming. Joseph, getting more and more nervous, kept after him, wanting to see at least an act of the play, only to be told that it was progressing—slowly—even though not a word had yet been written. But with the play announced, posters printed, and the cast ready to rehearse, the script for *Meet My Father* (1965), now known as *Relatively Speaking*, appeared as if by magic; the magician, however, had just spent three or four sleepless nights getting the rabbit to come out of the hat. Ken Boden, who managed the theater between the Joseph years and the Ayckbourn years, tells an almost identical story concerning *How the Other Half Loves* (1969), and later on the same procedure would be repeated numerous times with Ayckbourn the writer making excuses to Ayckbourn the director. Since writing *A Small Family Business* (1987) for production at the National Theatre rather than his own, he now manages to complete his scripts, still written with astonishing rapidity, well before the start of the rehearsals.

Ayckbourn soon found himself facing two cold facts about life in the theater: (1) despite the occasional tailor-made role, he was not the actor he thought he was; (2) with his work finished the author is ignored; it is the director who brings the play to life. Abandoning acting for directing, the playwright who had fashioned for himself as actor a spectacular vehicle in *The Square Cat,* now offered himself as director an equally showy opportunity. *Mr. Whatnot,* the first of his plays he directed, presents anyone daring enough to undertake it some impossible tasks: many settings; frantic action—even car chases; a character who, losing control, spins round and round on the end of a crank as he tries to rev up a motor; and a hero who remains mute throughout the havoc that he himself, like his creator—Ayckbourn— is actually initiating.

Stephen Joseph describes the achievement of the play and its production orchestrated by the man who conceived it:

> The play had just enough substance to provide a beginning, middle and end. But it was written for performance without scenery and changed scene frequently, including several journeys—across acres of garden, down dark passages and even in speedy vehicles along the highway. Real properties, phoney properties and mime properties all enriched the scene, ranging from a genuine steering wheel to represent a car, to an entirely imagined piano that was played furiously. Here actors found unending opportunities for creating the substance of reality from the merest hint of its existence. The stuff of drama. . . . The acting, too, showed what vitality and joy can come from the efforts, freely contributed, individually chosen, and carefully selected, of individual artists, each creating what he believes to be right, each choosing for himself, yet at the same time matching the intentions of others, helping others, with tremendous singleness of purpose. All very paradoxical. And splendid. Dismiss the play as trivial by all means, but give it credit for showing at least some people a vision of possible human behaviour; far more worthwhile than a dozen of your serious dramas or poetic tragedies.[29]

Thanks to the ingenuity and imagination of the director, the author himself, the production gave meaning to the whimsy. In a later, expanded London production (1964) prettified to the point that it had no point, and, significantly, *not* directed by its author, *Mr. Whatnot* was dismissed out of hand, one of the critics calling it "appallingly cute."[30] Nonetheless, in 1963 with the first performance of *Mr. What-not* in Stoke-on-Trent, where he was briefly associated with a company at the Victoria Theatre, as writer-director, Ayckbourn was on his way.

Some years would pass before West End producers, quick to snap up an Ayckbourn play after the success in another director's hands of *Relatively Speaking* in London, would trust the author himself with the direction of his own work. Choosing to offer *Bedroom Farce* at the prestigious National Theatre in 1977, a move that startled many in the profession, Peter Hall co-directed it with him. After the very respectable eleven-month West End run of *Ten Times Table*, the first of his plays that Ayckbourn directed by himself in London, in 1980 Hall once again named him co-director, this time with Christopher Morahan, of his second play at the National, *Sisterly Feelings* (1979). Having already been responsible for a production of the complex four-part play that satisfied him as well as his Scarborough audience, Ayckbourn accepted the London compromise with good grace. Since then he has achieved acclaim as sole director of a company of his own for a season at the National, and he is now invited to continue in that capacity there and elsewhere. In 1991 he returned to the National to direct one of his children's plays, or, as he prefers to call them, his "plays for the family," *Invisible Friends*, which was first performed in Scarborough in 1989. Except for directing productions of *Way Upstream* and *Absent Friends* in 1982 and *Henceforward . . .* in 1987 at the Alley Theatre in Houston, Texas, he has declined other offers. He prefers to remain in Scarborough to premiere each new work before overseeing its production himself a year or two later in London.

Scarborough, firmly established as his professional base, offers him the ideal working conditions that perhaps no other British playwright has enjoyed since Shakespeare—his own theater, his own company, and an ideal audience that welcomes his growth as writer-director just as he has enabled them to expand their own artistic sensibilities and understanding. Of that audience, part local Yorkshire people not easily pleased, part vacationers eager to be pleased, he has said that somewhere among them, "the Scarborough middle class, the local youngsters and the influx of amazingly varied holiday-makers during the summer season, can þe found the key to a universal sense of humour."[31] What that diverse audience as an entity demands from him is that they be entertained. And Ayckbourn considers that their right.

In 1836 Eugène Scribe told the French Academy that "you go to the theatre for relaxation and amusement, not for instruction or correction."[32] Ayckbourn has said much the same: "My duty is to entertain,"[33] and he has since clarified that duty as he sees it: "If I tell my stories terribly solemnly and seriously . . . nobody wants to see them. I've really got to make them entertaining . . . so that people say, 'Golly, I was held from beginning to end.' And it's up to me to employ whatever technical resources I have; but I always try to be extremely careful that the technical resources do not deny the characters their true destinies."[34] In his address to the Academy Scribe said: "What most amuses you is not truth but fiction. . . . The theatre is therefore rarely the direct expression of social life . . . It is often the inverse expression."[35] This Ayckbourn cannot accept. He is uneasy in his awareness at times of a laughing audience's "faint sense of guilt that there is something called enjoyment going on. Should we, people seem to be asking, be sitting here laughing like this?" Ayckbourn would prefer the laughter to signal an audience's recognition that what it is witnessing, though it may be painful, is an essentially honest reflection of life. A play "can be funny," he says, "but let's make it truthful."[36]

2

Other Dramatists, Absent Friends

The first of Ayckbourn's plays to be produced by Stephen Joseph's company was not the first to be written. After reading some of his young ASM-aspiring actor-novice writer's earliest attempts, Joseph had wisely advised him to put them away. Among these lost, forgotten, unproduced efforts was one that the mentor recognized as—and the protegé confessed to be—a Pirandello play, "the one that everyone writes, about the group of actors with a director, and they all take on the characters."[1]

The Square Cat (1959), the first work to receive Joseph's stamp of approval and a production by the company, with Joseph himself directing Ayckbourn in the principal role, is not quite a Pirandello play, but may be considered one once removed, Pirandello filtered through the sensibility of the continental dramatist that the Italian master influenced most obviously. France's Jean Anouilh has stated: "I have come from Pirandello, that's all. 'Six Characters in Search of an Author.' I haven't invented a thing since."[2] Recounting the plot of *The Square Cat* for Ian Watson in 1981, twenty-two years after he had written it—and getting some of its details wrong—Ayckbourn suddenly preceived what he had been consciously unaware of at the time, that his first professionally produced effort owed something to the work of another: ". . . a little Anouilh coming out there: there were a lot of definite influences in this play. In fact it's *Dinner with the Family*, I now realize!"[3]

After World War II, Anouilh's plays were produced with some regularity not only in London's West End but in provincial rep theaters as well. Even after the theatrical revolution of the Angry Young Men, the British audience still enjoyed seeing plays about the French upper classes set in the rarefied atmosphere of a chateau in the country, still enjoyed the comic possibilities inherent in the staple of the Feydeau farce, the typical French triangle of man, wife, and mistress. Setting and situation recalled a way of life that had passed—had it ever existed—in England, a way of life that had set the tone for the plays of Somerset Maugham, Noël Coward, Frederick Lonsdale, and Terence Rattigan. More bitter, more pessimistic in tone, Anouilh's comedies served as transition for the British who were beginning to cope with the grimmer aspects of life brought to the fore in the plays of John Osborne, John Arden, and Arnold Wesker.

Critical response to an Anouilh play was often not as favorable as spectator response. Audiences appreciated Anouilh's insistence on entertaining them even as he probed the death of love, the incompatibility of man and woman locked into an officially sanctioned relationship, or—a dominant theme borrowed from Pirandello—the multiplicity of the self. For Anouilh, as for Pirandello before him and Ayckbourn after him, theater and life were interchangeable. The Frenchman thought of the theater as a place for games, for playing at playing. Plays had to be written as actors needed something to act. What they acted might or might not be serious, but they had to be daringly theatrical, often employing the metaphorical use of theater as life. Theater for Anouilh, for Pirandello, for Ayckbourn is the ultimate reality.

An Anouilh play, like Ayckbourn's later work, is not easily labeled. Mood changes; spirit changes. Fantasy and reality overlap. The happy ending, satisfying in itself, is not always convincing nor is it meant to be. John Harvey notes that critics have misgivings about what he calls the "patently false ending" of *Le Rendez-vous de Senlis*, written in 1937, first performed in 1941, produced in London in translation as *Dinner with the Family* in 1957, two years before Ayckbourn wrote *The Square Cat*. "No one is duped," Harvey writes, ". . . for were there but another scene, this 'pièce rose' would turn into a 'pièce noire.' In fact, *Le Rendez-vous de Senlis* is a perfect illustration of Schopenhauer's generalization that comedy must always drop the curtain swiftly at the moment of joy, so that no one may see what comes after."[4] For many critics Anouilh was too frivolous to be taken seriously, a charge that Ayckbourn too would have to face. For both playwrights, however, there was compensation—the approval of their audiences. That both eventually came to be the directors of the plays they wrote afforded them an extra share of that approbation.

Anouilh's *Dinner with the Family* begins playfully enough with its Pirandellian element at first a mere theatrical game involving actors learning about the new roles they are to play, not on a stage, but in the drawing room of a rented house in the country, twenty-five miles from Paris. Georges, actually a car salesman deeply in debt, is turning life into theater by hiring two professionals to pretend to be his parents for the benefit of Isabelle, who has been invited to dine at what she believes to be the ancestral home of the man she loves but hardly knows. Georges, however, is in fact married to Christine, a wealthy woman he does not love, but who keeps him and his actual parents in grand style, even enabling Georges to hire his best friend as his secretary while he keeps his friend's wife as his mistress.

Pretense abounds. Even the dinner that the host says is being prepared by his servants is something other than it seems: it has been catered by a Parisian firm that has supplied employees to cook and serve it. Georges plays dutiful husband to Christine, unattached suitor to Isabelle, and faithful lover of Barbara, his mistress, whose real name is Jeannette. Georges's friend in fact hates and envies him but pretends to be loyal. Georges's true parents seem concerned about their son's welfare and his future, but their real anxiety is for their own fate should Georges and Christine divorce.

As the play progresses, the Pirandellian element deepens as Anouilh explores the mystery of identity and the multiplicity of the self, a theme he had already introduced in his previous play. In *Traveler without Luggage (Le Voyageur sans bagage*, 1936), Gaston, an amnesiac, a protagonist often used by Pirandello, learns the truth about himself as Jacques, something of a monster, nothing like the gentle person he has been since his memory loss. Gaston finally rejects his former self by choosing a new identity as a little boy's only surviving relative, which he knows to be false, leaving those who had recognized him as Jacques in a state of confusion, uncertain even of their own convictions. Paradoxically, the assumed identity is true to the self that Gaston has become. In *Dinner with the Family*, Georges realizes that he has been playing roles just as the hired actors do. He must finally decide which man he is to be, for his several contradictory roles now disgust him. Barbara's Georges cannot be Isabelle's Georges. "He's not at all a nice young man, my Georges," Barbara tells her innocent rival. "He's everything you must hate. He's sad, he's never sure of anything. He's unfair. He's cruel," to which Isabelle responds, "You're lying."[5]

Georges chooses what he knows will not be easy to accomplish—to make the momentary happiness he experiences in four minutes with Isabelle last a lifetime: "Four minutes gone! Doesn't time fly! I was wondering where this confidence, this comfort, this feeling of peace had crept in! Of course, we've reached the stage of calm and tender affection—our golden wedding already" (76). But Georges's perception of the relationship of Barbara and her husband, his parents' relationship, as well as his own with the wife who does not appear are all indelible reminders of inevitable change, of the evanescence of joy and rapture, of the disenchantment of longtime commitments. The theater metaphor returns at the end of the play as the actors instruct Barbara and her husband how to make an effective exit as Georges and Isabelle, together with his pretend-parents, go off to the dining room to have at last their "family dinner."

The basic elements of *The Square Cat* are the same. Alice Glover, a married woman with two adult children, has become so infatuated with rock star Jerry Wattis that she determines to spend some time alone with him. Borrowing a relative's large country house in Surrey that she will pretend is her ancestral home, she invites him for a weekend. Unsure of her motives—perhaps she merely wants to offer him maternal affection; perhaps she wants something more—Alice is certain, however, that her marriage to Sidney Glover has turned to dull routine. Pretending to be single, she is in search of glamor, adventure, romance. Having intercepted letters between "Jerrikins" and "Cuddly Bunch," Sidney, along with his son Steve, gets to the country house before his wife. His daughter Sue is to arrive shortly too. "The way to head him off, drive this Wattis fellow out of our home," Sidney tells Steve, "is to present a solid family front. You must play the devoted son, I the loving husband."[6] Steve's plan is to remold his father's image and even directs him briefly in a new but for Sidney unworkable role with an Elvis Presley smile and drawl. Alice is infuriated by her family's intrusion but cannot persuade them to leave.

After a long wait for the rock star's first entrance—author Ayckbourn has done all he can for actor Ayckbourn—Sidney and Steve as well as the audience are stunned by his appearance. Instead of the confident, outgoing, flashily dressed performer they had expected, a reticent, conservatively dressed young man, tentative and unsure of himself, appears. Jerry Wattis is actually the professional name of Arthur Brummage, who is the exact opposite of the invented persona that has provided him with sudden fame and fortune. Throughout the play, however, Alice, upstairs at the time of Arthur's arrival, only gets to see her idol Jerry; for Arthur, having been insulted by Sidney, determines to stay to offer Cuddly Bunch whatever she wants of Jerrikins. Thinking that the shy young man can be no threat to his marriage and that the family crisis is over, Sidney is startled at the end of the first act when Arthur, who has left the room to change, returns as Jerry—in full regalia, brandishing his guitar. At the climax of the first act of his very first play—there are no quick curtains in arena staging, only a sudden blackout—Ayckbourn delivers the first of the countless memorable theatrical coups that will heighten much of his work.

Within minutes of meeting Sue, Arthur—again as Arthur—knows that he has met the girl with whom he wants to spend the rest of his life, and Sue, more sensible than her giddy mother, finds herself attracted to the quiet, courteous young man, not the loud, boorish rock star. Even as Anouilh in *Dinner with the Family* contrasts the idealized Georges-Isabelle relationship as yet untouched by time with the sordid Georges-Barbara relationship and the unfulfilling Georges-Christine marriage as well as the relationship of his unloving parents, Ayckbourn contrasts a young couple falling in love at first sight with a disillusioned pair who have been together for years. The Glovers' relationship has not always been what it has now become. Sidney, strumming Jerry's guitar, tells his son about his romantic honeymoon on the night boat to Ireland when he sang a charming French love song, *"Je raconte une histoire triste,"* to his bride. Now, however, the Glovers do more screaming than singing:

> *Mum:* You are the most possessive man.
> *Dad:* Certainly I'm possessive.
> *Mum:* And selfish.
> *Dad:* I deny that.
> *Mum:* You won't allow anyone to have any sort of amusement. . . . Twenty years. I've wasted twenty years of my life on a man like you.
> *Dad:* What do you mean waste? I've always been completely fair by you, Alice.
> *Mum:* Every morning I've sat and watched you grunt your way through your breakfast. I've put up with your moods and your shocking temper.
> *Dad:* I have never lost my temper. I have always been completely calm even under the most catastrophic circumstances. And let me tell you, Alice, if I'd been half the man I am I'd have walked out on you a long, long time ago.
> *Mum:* Go on, then. I don't want you.
> *Dad:* I'm not going to give you the satisfaction.
> *Mum:* You brute. You callous, self-centred brute.

In the few surviving typescripts of this unpublished play, the last three lines—too strong for a small farce that demands an arbitrary happy ending with the reconciliation of the Glovers—have been crossed out. The relationship of a long-suffering, discontented wife and a husband indifferent to her moods, her needs, and her problems would soon become a crucial element in the Ayckbourn canon. Within months of *The Square Cat*, the novice playwright wrote a bitterly comic one-act play that gives the lie to the critical cliché that all his early works were lighthearted farces. In "Countdown" (1959), performed ten years later in London as part of *Mixed Doubles* (1969), a collection of playlets by nine authors, a couple married for twenty years barely communicate after supper.[7] Like the characters of Eugene O'Neill's *Strange Interlude*, however, they speak aloud their

grim private thoughts. Everything her husband does—carrying the
tea tray, reading the newspaper to her, telling a pointless, unfunny
joke—irritates the wife who can still remember the happy laughter
that accompanied their courtship, a laughter chillingly stilled by the
death of love.

A wife's discontent becomes something ever more serious for
Diana, on the verge of a breakdown in *Absent Friends* (1974); for
Vera, who does suffer a breakdown in *Just Between Ourselves;* for
Susan, who actually crosses the line into madness in *Woman in Mind*.
Alice in *The Square Cat*, searching for an escape from a humdrum
existence, attempts to stage a play of sorts, coupling herself with an
actual performer in what she hopes will be an ideal situation in a
romantic setting. She is like Georges in *Dinner with the Family* who
gathers the ideal family around him by hiring actors to perform as
perfect parents. Ayckbourn eventually develops the situation he initiates in *The Square Cat*, with the assistance of Anouilh, into a state of
mind for Susan in *Woman in Mind* that enables him to break the
bounds of the naturalistic theater to lure his audience into the imaginary world of a woman losing her grasp of reality. Susan creates an
idealized family to solace her in her domestic unhappiness once she
has lost control of her real family. But even the imaginary members of
her family overwhelm and betray her, turning sinister and destructive
as her aberration deepens. A key situation in the mild, harmless farce
of *The Square Cat* evolves into the core of a play, *Woman in Mind*,
technically a comedy, that carries its unsuspecting audience to the
brink of tragedy.

The very center of *The Square Cat*, a protagonist who cannot
comfortably coexist with part of himself, who would deny that part of
himself, is another element on which Ayckbourn builds throughout
his career. Arthur Brummage, like Anouilh's Georges and Gaston,
finds himself disgusted, even appalled by a part of his identity that is
at odds with what he considers to be the true self. Arthur cannot live
with his alter ego, despite the fact that the world demands his
transformation into Jerry Wattis. Only when he discovers that Sue
prefers Arthur to Jerry can he come to some accommodation: he can
be Jerry in his public life with Sue's loving support the basis of
Arthur's private life.

At the end of the first scene of the second act, before Arthur meets
Sue, comes a telling moment that Ayckbourn eventually judged to be
too dark for a play he himself labeled "a cool comedy." Steve leaves a
disconsolate Arthur alone on stage, saying, "Cheer up—half the
world's mad about you," to which Arthur responds, "Not me—Jerry
Wattis." Once Steve exits, Arthur picks up a photo of his other self and

speaks softly: "I'll kill you one of these days." In the typescript the line and the stage direction that follows—"*He knocks the photo onto the floor and gazes sadly as lights dim*"—have been crossed out.

Always at odds, Arthur Brummage and Jerry Wattis, in various personifications of the straitlaced square and the sly cool cat, supply the conflict of many Ayckbourn plays, but the playwright, honing the drama, divides the split personality in two. Protagonist and antagonist become two clearly differentiated characters, not a single tormented being struggling with himself. And the mood of the Ayckbourn play darkens to the point where the square will not merely triumph over the cat, as does Alistair over Vince in *Way Upstream* (1981), but eventually he will do what Arthur could only think about until the author exed the thought right out of the script. In *Man of the Moment* (1988) shy, introverted, law-abiding Douglas Beechey not only plays a major role in the life of Vic Parks, boorish ex-criminal turned TV talk-show host, but a more significant role in his death.

Along the way the contrasting characters in conflict reappear as mild Ed and domineering Tony in *The Sparrow* (1967); unemployable Leonard and exasperated Graham in *Time and Time Again* (1971); bumbling Bertie Wooster and overbearing Sir Roderick Spode in *Jeeves* (1975); introvert Neil and extrovert Dennis in *Just Between Ourselves* (1976); leftwing Eric and rightwing Tim in *Ten Times Table* (1977); imperfect Sven and perfect Richard in *Joking Apart* (1978), mild-mannered Tristram and bullying Roland in *Taking Steps* (1979); inept Stan and threatening Wolfie in *Making Tracks* (1981); Guy, out of his element, and Dafydd, a director very much in charge, in *A Chorus of Disapproval* (1984); and gentle, ineffectual Stanley and his tyrant brother-in-law Austen in *Wildest Dreams* (1991).

On occasion the two conflicting characters are of opposite sex— Norman and Sarah thwarting one another throughout the three parts of *The Norman Conquests* (1973), Henry and Karen doing the same in the two-part *The Revengers' Comedies* (1989). Some of the plays have in pivotal roles contrasting female personalities, a mousy young woman offering the mildest of challenges to the woman who flaunts her femininity: Evie and Julie in *The Sparrow;* Kitty and Elizabeth in *Taking Steps;* Caroline and Joanna in *Suburban Strains* (1980); Rachel and Belinda in *Season's Greetings* (1980); Emma and Fleur in *Way Upstream;* and the obedient robot and the termagant Corinna in *Henceforward . . .* (1987). *The Revengers' Comedies'* termagant Karen is not only contrasted with accommodating Henry but with sweet-natured Imogen as well. In *Making Tracks* one of the contrasting women, Susan Brown, insecure and less attractive than the other, Lace, becomes the inverse of Arthur Brummage-Jerry Wattis. She would like to transform herself into pop star Sandy Beige but is not talented enough to make the grade.

The pattern can be varied in other ways. Uncharacteristically, Ayckbourn turns the two contrasting characters back into a single self in one of his most disturbing works. In *A Small Family Business* (1987) the writer, in his most pessimistic vein, transforms his protagonist from a scrupulously honest citizen who will not tolerate even the theft of a paper clip into an unscrupulous entrepreneur not averse to dealing in drugs, a movement for a single character, in Ayckbourn's words, "from small English businessman to Mafioso *capo*."[8] At his boldest in *Body Language* (1990), Ayckbourn takes two very different women, a stunning model and an obese radio reporter, and makes the two one—or nearly. As a result of a bizarre helicopter accident the two literally lose their heads. Each becomes part of the other as a brilliant if careless surgeon saves their lives but attaches the wrong head to the wrong body.

Ayckbourn had already been moving toward this moment of supreme black farce in a children's play, *Mr A's Amazing Maze Plays* (1988) in which a sinister character steals sounds from animals and voices from people, interchanging them so that the wrong words come out of the wrong mouths. The vocal interchange is itself a variation on *Henceforward . . .* in which Jerome, a composer, records the words people speak and reduces them to synthesized sounds. Needing an ideal family to convince his estranged wife that his home is a suitable place for his young daughter to visit, Jerome, recalling Georges in Anouilh's *Dinner with the Family*, hires an actress to play the perfect fiancée. When the actress rejects the role and leaves, Jerome, who has recorded her words, programs them into the mechanical voice of Nan 300F, a robot that will assume the role of the perfect mate, as man and machine become interchangeable.

Returning in *Henceforward . . .* to the initial situation of Anouilh's *Dinner with the Family*, which he had already used in *The Square Cat* and varied in *Woman in Mind*, Ayckbourn demonstrates how he can take something from the work of another writer yet can finally make it his own. If the mock household of *The Square Cat* is less intriguing than Anouilh's mock worlds, Jerome's nightmare household, his eerie inhuman music, his interchanging of human and robot are elements inconceivable to a Jean Anouilh. Alan Ayckbourn, despite the borrowings, in effect owes less to Anouilh and to those writers who have stimulated him than William Shakespeare owes to Raphael Holinshed, Thomas Lodge, Matteo Bandello, and Giraldi Cinthio. Thomas Bishop's thoughts on the Pirandello-Anouilh relationship apply as well to the Anouilh-Ayckbourn relationship: "If Anouilh's theater is . . . thoroughly imbued with Pirandello, it must not be assumed that his plays are copies of the latter's." Pointing out, as have other critics, influences beyond Pirandello—Gérard de Nerval, Jean Giraudoux, and Alfred de Musset—Bishop concludes: "Anouilh is no imitator. His theater is original, but, of course, no playwright writes in a vacuum. . . . It is proof of Anouilh's originality that he has been able to weld such different antecedents into a new entity bearing his own individual stamp."[9]

A writer learns his craft, then develops a voice of his own. Ayckbourn's credo, "I think you should stick to what you know,"[10] extends beyond his personal experience with family and friends to his experience as reader, as theatergoer, and as actor and ASM. Influenced by an abundance of theatrical riches the maturing dramatist moves from imitation to innovation. Others before Ayckbourn, Noël Coward for one, have traveled the same course. Of his *Easy Virtue*, an early work written in 1924, Coward has said, "The form and tone and plot of a Pinero play was exactly what I had tried to achieve."[11] When Shaw read another early Coward piece, *The Young Idea* (1922), and recognized its similarity to his own *You Never Can Tell*, first performed in 1899, he wrote to the younger dramatist cautioning him not to see or read any more plays by GBS: "Unless you can get clean away from me you will begin as a back number and be hopelessly out of it when you are 40." The advice was sound, but, as John Lahr has observed, "Coward had to absorb his influences before he could discard them."[12] The same can be said of Ayckbourn.

Of his first West End success in 1967, *Relatively Speaking*—a title that may owe something to Coward's *Relative Values*—Ayckbourn writes:

> . . . the people who liked this play . . . remarked that it was "well constructed"; those that didn't called it old-fashioned. If the latter is true, then I suppose it's because, as the song goes, I am too. As to whether it's well constructed, well, in a way I hope it is, since I did set out consciously to write a "well made" play. I think this is important for a playwright to do at least once in his life, since as in any science, he cannot begin to shatter theatrical convention or break golden rules until he is reasonably sure in himself what they are and how they were arrived at.[13]

Relatively Speaking concerns Greg, like Leonard in the later *Time and Time Again*, a young man who cannot hold down even the simplest job. He has entered into an affair with the more employable Ginny, who holds her job by the practical means of sleeping with the employer, the older, well-to-do Philip, about whom Greg knows

nothing. Once Greg asks Ginny to marry him, Ginny must get Philip
to stop telephoning, to discontinue the gifts of flowers and chocolates
that have aroused Greg's suspicions, in short, to leave her alone.
When Ginny goes off for a day in the country, supposedly to visit her
parents but actually to confront Philip, Greg decides to follow her.
Once the scene shifts to the country Ayckbourn contrasts, as he had
done in *The Square Cat*, as Anouilh had done in *Dinner with the
Family*, the intensity of a new relationship with the disenchantment
and boredom of a relationship of long standing.

Arriving at Philip's home before Ginny, Greg asks for her hand from
the man he believes to be her father, Ginny's now confused former
lover, who mistakenly believes that the strange young man is asking
for the hand of Sheila, Philip's even more befuddled wife, who has no
idea what is taking place. Once Ginny arrives, she forces Philip to
play the role of father. Meanwhile, Greg believes that Sheila, who is
still in the dark and has never laid eyes on Philip's employee-lover, is
Ginny's mother. Eventually, in the English idiom, the penny drops for
Sheila. She fathoms the Philip-Ginny relationship, makes sure that
Philip will never again bother Ginny and Greg, and triumphantly
adds fuel to Philip's suspicions concerning the possibility of the existence of her own on-the-side lovers.

Slight as this may seem, Ayckbourn mixes the comic ingredients
into what has been called a "superbly constructed meringue of a
play"[14] by choosing as his model what may be the most perfect of all
well-made comedies, Oscar Wilde's *The Importance of Being Earnest*
(1985). Anouilh too appreciated Wilde's play, even translating it (with
Claude Vincent) as *Il est important d'être aimé* and had already used
its familiar elements of nineteenth-century melodrama and farce—
unexpected arrivals in unfamiliar surroundings, mistaken identities,
and verbal misunderstandings—in many of his plays, including *Dinner with the Family*, the inspiration for *The Square Cat*. Ayckbourn
hardly needed Anouilh to introduce him to Wilde, but the
Frenchman had already demonstrated how effective those elements,
which Ayckbourn honed in *Relatively Speaking*, could be.

Whereas all the complications in the Wilde play are set in motion
when Algernon leaves town for country to engage in a new relationship, the initiating circumstance in Ayckbourn's play is Ginny's
movement from a London flat to a house in the country to put an end
to an established relationship. Just as Algy learns of Cecily's existence
by means of an inscription on a cigarette case, then overhears her
address—The Manor House, Woolton, Hertfordshire—Greg finds the
address to which Ginny is off for the day written on a cigarette
packet—The Willows, Lower Pendon, Bucks (the playwright's first

mention of Pendon, the setting for many later plays). Wilde ends his first act with Algy reading the address that he had already written on his shirt cuff, and Ayckbourn ends his first scene with Greg glancing again at the cigarette packet as he goes out the door to begin, like Brummage-Wattis, a Bunburying expedition of his own.

What characterizes both plays are the standard ingredients of the well-made play: secrets known to some but withheld from others, quid-pro-quo conversations in which two speakers, actually at odds, believe they are discussing the same person, and, of course, assumed identities. As in all well-made plays, both *Earnest* and *Relatively Speaking* are neatly and reasonably resolved; in both the denouement involves a prop brought onstage at a climactic moment. As Algy arrives before Jack, so Greg arrives before Ginny. As Gwendolyn and Cecily believe they are engaged to the same man who is in fact two men, Jack in Gwendolyn's case and Algy in Cecily's, so Philip believes Greg to be audacious enough to be asking him for the hand in marriage of his own wife. As Jack reluctantly pretends to be Algy's brother, Philip must play Ginny's father. As Cecily has written love letters to herself, supposedly from Earnest, Sheila may also have written letters to herself in hopes of making her husband jealous.

Even the question of illegitimacy arises in both plays: for a time Jack believes Miss Prism to be his mother, whereas Greg believes that Sheila is denying her relationship to Ginny because she is too embarrassed to admit the circumstances of Ginny's birth. When the infamous handbag is produced in *Earnest,* the truth is out, just as in *Relatively Speaking* the light dawns for Sheila about Philip and Ginny when Greg opens his luggage to produce the slippers he had found under Ginny's bed. That the slippers may not be the ones that Sheila had bought for Philip affords Sheila an insight into the younger woman to which the men are blind: there is a third man in Ginny's hyperactive life.

Echoes in dialogue abound. When Philip, under the misapprehension that Greg wants to marry Sheila, is told by Ginny that she has received a marriage proposal, he comments: "Infectious, this marriage epidemic. I seem to be the only one who's developed immunity" (52). Told of the impending marriages of Jack and Gwendolyn, Algy and Cecily, Lady Bracknell makes a pronouncement: "I do not know whether there is anything peculiarly exciting in the air of this particular part of Hertfordshire, but the number of engagements that go on seems to me considerably above the proper average that statistics have laid down for our guidance."[15]

Therein lies the greatest difference in the plays. Wilde dazzles with wit, the polished epigram and aphorism, whereas Ayckbourn offers the serviceable joke. When Greg looks around and discovers "No Ginny," Sheila says, "No, I'm afraid not. There's some sherry, if you like" (32). Asked what prize she won in school for Memory and Elocution, Sheila replies with a matter-of-fact "I've forgotten" (34). Yet the situation in *Relatively Speaking* is so fraught with comic possibilities that the audience continues to laugh at lines that are in fact not so much witty as cleverly arranged within an amusing dramatic context, a talent that Ayckbourn shares with Coward, that Coward has himself explained: "To me, the essence of good comedy writing is that perfectly ordinary phrases such as 'Just fancy!' should, by virtue of their context, achieve greater laughs than the most literate epigrams. Some of the biggest laughs in *Hay Fever* occur on such lines as 'Go on,' 'No there isn't, is there?' and 'This haddock's disgusting.' There are many other glittering examples of my sophistication in the same vein."[16] As spoken by Maggie Smith in the National Theatre's revival of *Hay Fever* in 1964, directed by the author, Coward's last example brought down the house.

Relatively Speaking offers lines in a similar vein. When Philip loses his temper over something Sheila chooses not to understand, she berates him: "I've never seen or heard such extraordinary behaviour in my life. Really. Whatever's come over you? I really think you ought to go and do some digging. And work a little of it off. Whatever it is" (29). When Greg admires her garden saying, "They're huge. How do you get your delphiniums that size?" Sheila answers, "Oh, well . . . constant practice, really" (30), little wit perhaps but clever enough to evoke waves of laughter when spoken by Celia Johnson in the play's first London production, and more original than the exchange in *The Square Cat* when Steve, who had inadvertently shut off the water supply and has corrected the problem, suddenly enters saying, "Dad—the water's on," to which Dad replies, "I know," at the moment that his wife, arguing with him, bursts into tears.

Humor arising from the plot, learned from Coward, sets Ayckbourn apart from a comic gag writer like the American Neil Simon, who, the British writer insists, pursues a different comic ploy: "If you dropped a play of his in the street and the pages fell out in any old order, you'd still be laughing as you picked them up. If you dropped a play of mine, too bad. As a writer, he's highly verbal whereas I'm situational."[17] Kenneth Tynan identifies Coward as the playwright who "took the fat off English comic dialogue,"[18] perhaps a matter of necessity for both Coward and Ayckbourn. Although both eschew the gag, neither is capable of Wildean wit. Nonetheless, each has made a virtue of linguistic limitation, Ayckbourn at times provoking laughter at a character's inability to express himself: "Well. It seems to me—that we ought to find a way of—well—sorting out our relationship—if we have one—to such a degree that we—come together more or less on a permanent basis. Temporarily at least."[19]

Coward's influence on Ayckbourn goes beyond an approach to dialogue. As Ayckbourn interweaves elements of Wilde's *Earnest* into the fabric of his own *Relatively Speaking*, his later comedy, *Season's Greetings* (1980), gains an added fillip for the knowledgeable, aware theatergoer who recognizes its relationship, here a diametric opposition, to Coward's classic comedy of bad manners, *Hay Fever* (1925). The relationship of the Ayckbourn play to the Coward work is yet another example demonstrating that the younger playwright is by no means guilty of plagiarism. Ayckbourn's method of borrowing, perhaps more accurately termed his building upon pre-existing drama, is to offer his audience an added resonance in his work by suggesting mutually reflexive comparisons and contrasts to the work of others. Because Ayckbourn attempts to reach and to entertain a popular British audience that has remained loyal to him, that understands his plays as comments on their own lives, he makes no demand that they prepare themselves for an Ayckbourn play by brushing up on the history of world drama. But the added meaning that can be derived from a recognition of the interdependence of drama is there for the taking.

In *Hay Fever* an assortment of weekend houseguests are completely ignored by the actress and her family who have invited them as the family carries on with its usual, self-absorbed eccentricities. The guests take the only refuge available to them. They pack their bags and steal away—unnoticed. Not unnoticed is Clive, a writer in *Season's Greetings*, who is invited by Rachel, a thirty-eight-year-old spinster, to spend Christmas with her family. While the male members of the family generally ignore him, Rachel, her sister Belinda, and Belinda's sister-in-law Phyllis cannot leave him alone. Attempting to escape unscathed, Clive packs his bag to steal away in the middle of the night only to be shot by Uncle Harvey who thinks he is looting the presents under the tree. Saved by the suitcase that cushions the impact, Clive must nevertheless be taken to a hospital, as another family member comments, "You can't go around shooting your guests, you know, whatever you might think of them."[20] Whereas Coward points out the indignity of the ignored houseguest, Ayckbourn makes clear that being ignored is preferable to being maimed.

Confirming some of the influences on his work, Ayckbourn told an interviewer in 1976: "I've got an awful lot of Congreve and Oscar Wilde, I've also got a good collection of Chekhov. I think one starts by copying other people. There were one or two people at the time I started, like Rattigan and Coward . . . and then very early on in my career the new wave lot happened."[21] That the elliptical patter of the Pinter play originated in the dialogue of Coward, as Tynan claimed, is debatable[22]; that Pinter too has influenced Ayckbourn in shaping dialogue is a matter of record. For Ayckbourn the most intriguing playwright among his contemporaries is Pinter, specifically for his unique way of "distorting the everyday phrase, slightly bending it."[23] He has frequently related his first experience of a Pinter play when he was working as an actor in Joseph's Scarborough company. Joseph, always the promoter of new writing, had invited Pinter to direct *The Birthday Party* there soon after its London failure in 1958. Most of the company were either bewildered by the play or simply rude about it, laughing at its seemingly banal dialogue. Ayckbourn joined in the fun at the author's expense, but after the amazing response on opening night that surpassed everyone's expectations, laughter turned to awed admiration. Ayckbourn now likens his introduction to a Pinter play to the extraordinary experience of hearing for the first time the music of Schoenberg.[24]

"What I liked when I first came into contact with his work as an actor was, I suspect," Ayckbourn recalls, "that the way you understand him is as a poet. He writes rather like poets in that his use of words is very specific."[25] He is especially impressed by the effects Pinter achieves through repetition. A clichéd phrase like "whole hog" or the coupling of oddly juxtaposed words like "slum slug," amusing on first hearing, take on a terrifying resonance in *The Collection* (1962) when they are repeated. As an example of repetition in his own work, Ayckbourn offers a line from *Just Between Ourselves:* "It's quicker to walk really. And then there's the parking and all that. It's very bad these days trying to park. Dreadful. *(Slight pause)* And then, well really I found I didn't really enjoy driving really."[26] On first reading the line the actress was sure that the repeated "really"s were a misprint in her script, but the author, always wary of actors rewriting his lines, insisted it was exactly as he had written it and got the effect he wanted—an early indication of the character's lack of confidence, her growing mental anguish.

Ayckbourn's *Absent Friends,* a play in which stage time equals actual time as it details the comically disastrous events of an afternoon tea, ends with a closing speech about old friends that might have been written by Pinter himself: ". . . oh, look at us. Honestly. All drooping about like wet weekends . . . still, why shouldn't we, I say. There are worse ways of spending the time. Than sitting peacefully with your friends. Nice to sit with your friends now and again. Nice . . ."[27] If the speech, reproduced here exactly as written, seems oddly punctuated, Ayckbourn, obviously aware of the well-known Pinter pause, explains his use of the full stop, which he admits his English master would not have approved: "There is no point in putting a semicolon in the script, an actor doesn't know what it's there for, whether it's a long pause or a short pause. . . . I tend to write in straight fragmented ways in order to bring over a sense of the dialogue, which I hope, rather like a musician might read, an actor can read."[28]

Punctuation and pauses may not be the full extent of Pinter's inroads on Ayckbourn's sensibility. The metaphoric "weasel under the cocktail cabinet,"[29] Pinter's own phrase for the vague, unseen threat that pervades much of his work, may well be lurking in the junk-filled flat shared by Tony and Ed in another early Ayckbourn play never produced in London and never published. *The Sparrow* (1967), which some critics likened in spirit to Ann Jellicoe's *The Knack* (1961),[30] approaches, if it does not achieve, the claustrophobic shape and menacing air of a Pinter play. Its atmosphere is nearly that evoked, at Stephen Joseph's urging, in several plays by another Scarborough writer, David Campton. In fact *The Lunatic View,* Campton's collection of one-act plays, subtitled "Comedies of Menace," was performed in Scarborough in 1957, the same year Pinter's first play, *The Room,* was performed at Bristol University, a year before the first London production of any work by Pinter. *The Sparrow,* written seven years after the success of *The Caretaker* (1960), resembles the Pinter play in its conflict: two men in a room in disarray are involved in a contest of wills for control of a third party, a girl invited by one of them to spend the night. Ayckbourn's undefined threatening air is closer to that of the usual Pinter work than the Campton plays in which the menace has a clear social, political basis. In *The Sparrow* Tony, a car salesman, convinces his bus-conductor friend Ed's pickup, Evie, that he is a successful wheeler-dealer of high-powered business deals. Tony's actual motive is to demonstrate to his estranged wife Julia and to Ed, who have had a brief fling, his authority, sexual and otherwise, over them all. Tony and Julia are finally reconciled to a relationship that will be a permanent, literal battle of the sexes, while Ed and Evie go off to the pub for a drink that will reinforce their pipedream of building boats, perhaps one day owning a shipyard. That the author is uncomfortable, thus unconvincing at drawing characters at the lower end of the economic scale may be responsible for the brief flight of *The Sparrow,* a play that may be considered Ayckbourn's own comedy of near-menace. As a writer Ayckbourn is more at ease with those he knows best, those higher up on the social scale, if far from its apex, people closer to the characters of *Absent Friends,* "the 'tea in the front room' class of people lately promoted out of that into a vaguely monied status."[31]

Absent Friends is Ayckbourn's daring attempt, artistically a success, to extend his capabilities as a writer of comedy. Following as it does the technically exhilarating three-part *The Norman Conquests,* it is a return to a straightforward, one-set domestic play, like *Time and Time Again,* with, for Ayckbourn, the innovation of a continuous time scheme. After what the author considers "the most robust and . . . the most overtly funny" first part of the *Norman* trilogy, *Table Manners,* he had consciously adopted for the second part, *Living Together,* "a tempo far slower than anything I had written before" that encouraged him "to slacken the pace in a way I had never dared to do in a comedy" (12). That slowing pace, necessitating further development of "small detailed action" and of characterization in depth continues in *Absent Friends,* making it, in Ayckbourn's opinion, "a play for a small intimate theatre where one can hear the actors breathing and the silences ticking away. It was a terrifying risk when it was first produced. I'd never pitched anything in quite such a low key before" (8). More effective perhaps in the round in Scarborough than in a large conventional West End house, although he has since directed a successful production in Houston's large Alley Theatre, *Absent Friends* was Ayckbourn's most underrated work until its acclaimed production in a small off-Broadway theater in New York in 1991.

In the first scene of *Relatively Speaking* Greg says: "When I got up just now. . . . I fished with my feet under the bed for my slippers. One of my habits, that is, one of my idiosyncracies—it helps me to recognize myself when I'm half asleep. I always think that's important, don't you? That the first thing you do when you wake up in the morning is to make sure you know who you are. I have a terror of that, losing my identity in the night" (13). Critics who are now thoroughly conscious of the darkening mood and themes of the plays in the Ayckbourn canon suggested when *Relatively Speaking* was revived in Greenwich in 1986 that those elements were already distinguishable in the very early work, yet Greg's line is surely intended as a joke, shedding light on the character's already muddled mind. Sensibly guided by Gwendolyn's observation in *The Importance of Being Earnest* that metaphysical speculations have "very little reference at all to the actual facts of real life, as we know them" (557), Greg's observation is not seriously explored in *Relatively Speaking*. It serves rather to introduce a vastly amusing, highly inventive case of mistaken identities. Yet metaphysics does crop up again, seriously albeit comically, in *Absent Friends,* a play that centers on a theme vital to the works of

Pirandello and Anouilh, that is at the very core of *Old Times*, a Pinter play first performed in 1971, three years before *Absent Friends'* Scarborough premiere.

In *Old Times* the relationships of three characters are scrutinized in light of shifting memories of past events as each attempts to establish dominance through contradictory, ephemeral truths. Rather than the past establishing the present, in Pinter's world the present creates the past. "Was she your best friend?" Deeley asks his wife Kate, as they await a visit from Kate's friend Anna who is already present on stage in the shadows of the room. Kate responds with another question: "Oh, what does that mean?" "What?" asks Deeley, and Kate explains what it is she is questioning: "The word friend . . . when you look back . . . all that time."[32]

Old Times's most frequently quoted line—"There are some things one remembers even though they may never have happened. There are things I remember which may never have happened but as I recall them so they take place" (31–32)—may well serve as epigraph for *Absent Friends*, like so much of Ayckbourn's later work, a play that evokes laughter despite its bleak tone. Unlike the genial, comforting *Relatively Speaking*, *Absent Friends* is a comedy of pain and loss probing marital relationships as well as friendship. Colin, visiting the town where he used to live, is invited to tea by Diana. According to Diana, Colin and her husband Paul were once inseparable best friends who even courted Diana and her sister Barbara together, although who was courting whom is later subject to Pinter-like shifts of memory when all the guests reminisce about old times. Before Colin's arrival, an annoyed Paul attempts to set straight the matter of friendship as he sees it. "Excuse me," he says to his wife, "he is not a friend of mine. . . . I just happened to know him, that's all" (111). When Evelyn, like Julia in *The Sparrow* in having had an unpleasant sexual encounter with Paul although she is the wife of another reluctant guest, John, says to her husband, "I don't know why you came. . . . You said you didn't like him," John corrects her. "I didn't mind him," he says, to which Paul adds, "I didn't like him" (119). Nonetheless, on Colin's entrance Paul greets him with a warm, welcoming embrace: "Colin, my old mate, how are you?" (123). A third friend, Gordon, is at home ill in bed, but his wife Marge dutifully attends the tea, checking on her husband by phone every few minutes.

Diana's real reason for inviting Colin is to cheer him up, for two months earlier Colin's fiancée Carol had drowned. Colin will be unhappy, Colin will be mired in gloom, Colin will be reticent to speak of his intended, or so the others think. Not so. Colin will speak of nothing else. A few minutes after his arrival he goes out to his car and returns with a large candy box containing a photo album and an envelope of loose snapshots. He passes around pictures of Carol— Carol with Colin, Carol with her dog, Carol with her mum. In the midst of five miserable people trapped in disintegrating marriages, there is one contented being—Colin. All his memories are happy ones. He reminds the others of an outing the friends had taken together:

> *Colin:* . . . it was a marvelous day, wasn't it?
> *John:* Was it?
> *Colin:* Oh, it was a great laugh—sorry, Evelyn, this must be boring for you, love—
> *Evelyn:* Yes.
> *Colin:* Remember that fabulous picnic?
> *Diana:* All I remember is running from one car to the other in the rain with the thermos flask.
> *Colin:* And we found a great place for tea.
> *Paul:* Where they overcharged us.
> *Colin:* It was great. I'll always remember that.
> *John:* Yes.
> *Colin:* What a marvelous day that was.
> *Diana: (doubtfully)* Yes.
> *Marge:* I suppose so, yes.
> *Colin:* You missed something there, Evelyn.
> *Evelyn:* Sounds like it. (140)

Colin's entire life is wonderful, and he does not begrudge his friends their happiness, he tells them, because he has had, with Carol, the perfect relationship, as Ayckbourn suggests that the perfect relationship, all a matter of memory and the mind, need not stand the test of time. Death has made Colin a happy man.

All six characters are isolated beings seeing the others through their own sensibilities; all of them are oblivious to the pain they are causing. Diana, who knows about Paul and Evelyn, becomes increasingly hysterical as the party progresses. Finally she can take no more. She pours a jug of cream over her astonished husband's head and has a nervous breakdown at center stage. As she goes to pieces in front of the others, she recounts in a long speech the dreams and disappointments of her youth. She had wanted to join the Royal Canadian Mounted Police, but "little girls don't join the Mounted Police. Little girls do nice things like typing and knitting and nursing and having babies. So I married Paul instead" (147). The speech might be described as Ayckbourn doing a Pinter parody of Eugene O'Neill's

Mary Tyrone. Funny and horrifying at one and the same time, it is what Ayckbourn does best—revealing the pain of life through laughter.

Two Ayckbourn plays that can stand alone but that achieve fuller effect when audiences are aware—and Ayckbourn insists on that awareness by actually using scenes from the works that inspired them within his own—are *A Trip to Scarborough* (1981) and *A Chorus of Disapproval* three years later. The former is a variation on Richard Brinsley Sheridan's play of the same name (1777) that is itself a redoing of John Vanbrugh's *The Relapse; or, Virtue in Danger* (1696), the latter a play about an amateur company rehearsing a production of John Gay's *The Beggar's Opera* (1728). Whereas a case could be made for *The Rehearsal* by George Villiers, itself a burlesque of heroic drama like John Dryden's *The Conquest of Granada,* as well as Henry Fielding's *Tom Thumb* and Sheridan's *The Critic; or, A Tragedy Rehearsed,* both of which parody eighteenth-century theatrical fashions, the most significant influence here, especially for *A Chorus of Disapproval,* may lie elsewhere. Anouilh, like Pirandello, frequently used the framework of a play within a play. Perhaps his most effective work in this vein is *La Répétition ou l'amour puni* (1950), in which guests at a dinner party rehearse scenes from Pierre de Marivaux's *La Double Inconstance* (1723), which parallels their own situation. That Anouilh is again Ayckbourn's guide is suggested by the fact that Ayckbourn once performed the central role of the Count in a production of the work, known in translation by the same title as Villiers's play, *The Rehearsal.*

The obvious attraction for Ayckbourn of *A Trip to Scarborough,* Sheridan's politer version of Vanbrugh's play, is the title itself. Vanbrugh had set *The Relapse* in both town—London—and country. Sheridan's moving the locale entirely to the Yorkshire spa, the site of Ayckbourn's own theater, makes the work, which the modern writer probably never intended for production beyond Scarborough, irresistible for his company, the townspeople, and the tourists who flock there in season. Sheridan, diluting Vanbrugh's bawdier excesses of language and situation, retained the theme of role-playing and pretense. Several characters play at supposed amorous involvements actually aimed at making jealous the true objects of their affections. The liveliest part of the play involves Tom Fashion convincing Sir Tunbelly Clumsy that he is his own brother, Lord Foppington—yet another Bunburying expedition, relatively speaking—to take advantage of a sizable dowry for Miss Hoyden, Sir Tunbelly's daughter. The principal character true to himself throughout is Foppington, who is, was, and always will be the fool.

Ayckbourn retains the Fashion-Foppington plot but invents others as he sets the entire play in the foyer of Scarborough's Royal Hotel, turning it into a Grand Hotel along the lines of the setting of Vicki Baum's novel and better-known film. He outdoes Baum, however, in the juggling of various plot strands by also playing with time. The play takes place at once at Christmas in 1800, in 1942, and in the present year. It begins with Miss Hoyden, a teenage girl in eighteenth-century costume, seated on the divided staircase, singing a refrain that will be repeated as the play progresses:

> Through all the drama—whether damned or not—
> Love gilds the scene, and women guide the plot.[33]

At this point she appears "a rather pale ghostly figure. . . . as if some vision not yet fully materialized," but she will come into focus in the 1800 scenes. The time changes to World War II and soon after to the present, then moves fluidly from one temporal frame to another, the audience initially understanding the scheme by the characters' costumes. Yet as the play continues and there is to be a costume ball in the hotel, more and more characters appear in eighteenth-century dress as, in a motif that Ayckbourn will later develop in his "alternate" plays, *Sisterly Feelings* and *Intimate Exchanges,* all time is one time.

Allusions to Sheridan crop up throughout. Two young executives attending a conference are with Brinsley International. Some of the characters attend a performance of the Sheridan play at the Scarborough Opera House. Another group becomes involved in the sale of what may be the eighteenth-century author's original manuscript. There is pretense in all the time frames. A man goes off to the theater with his wife and returns with another woman, insisting she is the same one. The manuscript is at the center of a scam involving proliferating con artists. For some the war provides a means of making money, as in Gogol's *Dead Souls,* by keeping the dead on the payroll.

If one strand of the interwoven plots, concerning a woman awaiting news of her missing flyer husband, seems out of place in mood and theme, that the others conspire to comfort her by suggesting the situation may be less serious than she believes aligns it with the rest. The World War II section with flyers on a recuperative binge between dangerous missions provides the play with its funniest interlude. Three buddies launch into a comic rendition of the Andrews Sisters' signature song, *"Bei Mir Bist Du Schön."* When the spectacle is interrupted by the entrance of Wing Commander Tunbry (played by the same actor who also takes the parts of Sir Tunbelly Clumsy and Sir George Tunberry—a three-part casting scheme extending to most of the company), one of the flyers calls the other two to attention. Catching sight of his commanding officer, the drunkest of the three exclaims, "Good lord, it's Vera Lynn." In Scarborough's Royal Hotel, nothing is what it seems to be.

A Trip to Scarborough is unquestionably entertaining and highly theatrical. Its diffusion, however, relegates it to a minor position among Ayckbourn's plays. *A Chorus of Disapproval*, a more focused use of another play, is something more as it follows the onstage as well as the offstage fortunes of members of an amateur theatrical company rehearsing, then performing John Gay's ballad opera. The songs from *The Beggar's Opera* serve as comic counterpoint as a newcomer to the company works his way during the rehearsal period from walk-on to the plum role of Macheath by opening night. But Guy's rise to stardom has little to do with thespian talent and more to do with backstage maneuverings and backstabbings involving every aspect of contemporary life in the United Kingdom, from sexual liaisons to big business land deals. *A Chorus of Disapproval*'s juxtaposition of time, ingenuity of setting, and engaging comic action pointing to its author's deepening political concerns all coalesce into a work of major significance, demonstrating, as in Tom Stoppard's *Rosencrantz and Guildenstern Are Dead*, what may be gained by interweaving a new play with an older, known work.[34]

A Chorus of Disapproval depends on and grows out of *The Beggar's Opera*. British novelist-dramatist Michael Frayn uses another method of acknowledgment, a homage, in his play *Benefactors* (1984), in which a character says, "What was that girl in Ibsen called?. . . . The one who made the old boy climb up the scaffolding?. . . . Inspired by her youth and vitality, he climbed to the top of his new high-rise. . . . And fell off and broke his neck."[35] With this line the playwright directs his audience to compare David, Frayn's architect-protagonist, a well-meaning, socially committed good man who strives to help others, who never actually builds the tower he is planning, to Ibsen's Master Builder, Halvard Solness, the egocentric architect who relies on mystical helpers and servers to do his bidding, whose eventual fall from his completed tower ironically signals his ultimate triumph. David, a confused contemporary man, dares no one, leaves nothing behind. Solness, the strongwilled nineteenth-century Übermensch, dares his God, and his tower is his monument.

Like Frayn, who has himself charted a theater company's disintegration in the farce *Noises Off* (1982), Ayckbourn has become a pessimist, his view of mankind—what happens backstage, what happens beyond the surface of complacent middle-class life—growing progressively bleaker. From a sunny comedy of mistaken identity,

Relatively Speaking, he has moved on to madness in *Woman in Mind* and even murder in *A Small Family Business* and *The Revengers' Comedies*. His darkening vision parallels that of another British writer, J. B. Priestley, whose novels are still widely read in Great Britain and whose plays receive frequent West End revivals. Priestley first attracted attention with an early picaresque novel, the sunny *The Good Companions* (1929), in which he suggested that mankind working in harmony, in community, as a family, could overcome all obstacles and achieve success. By the end of World War II, however, Priestley, calling himself "a cautious optimist," was not so certain.

Priestley typifies the hearty, straightforward, no-nonsense Yorkshireman that Ayckbourn, a more indirect, shyer southerner, had to learn to live with once he threw in his lot with a theater company in Scarborough. Priestley's works may very well have been his key to understanding the Yorkshire character since he is well-versed in those works as director and, earlier on, as actor. In recent years he has directed, among other Priestley plays, *Time and the Conways* (1937) and *Eden End* (1947). Significantly, one of the roles he has performed is that of Eric Birling, the son in *An Inspector Calls* (1945).

Ayckbourn has acknowledged being intrigued by Priestley's unusual handling of time, the end returning to the beginning in *Dangerous Corner* (1932) and *An Inspector Calls*, the precognitive second act of *Time and the Conways*, inspired by the time theories of J. W. Dunne, that thrusts the family eighteen years forward in time only to return in act 3 to the earlier setting of act 1. The split-time scenes of *Suburban Strains* and the movement in time in *A Trip to Scarborough* may be outgrowths of his immersion in Priestley as is the remarkably fluid structure of *Time of My Life* (1992), in which characters on stage together move through individual, differing time schemes simultaneously. Ayckbourn, like Priestley, in a phrase the older writer has applied to himself, is a time-haunted man. The setting of *Way Upstream*, an allegorical ship of state, echoes that of the Yorkshireman's own political satire, *Bees on the Boat Deck* (1936). With the expressionistic *Music at Night* (1938) and *Johnson over Jordan* (1939), Priestley shattered the conventions of the then staid British theater as Ayckbourn continues to do in play after play.

Just as Ayckbourn has at times spoken with Priestley's voice in his plays, the younger writer has been known to do an uncanny imitation of the older man's deep-voiced, deliberate speech patterns, so familiar to Englishmen from his radio "Postscripts" during World War II. Ayckbourn vividly conjures up Priestley's jowly face with its piercing eyes as he recounts his one meeting with him. One night after the opening of a Priestley play, Ayckbourn was introduced to the author.

The prolific writer nearing the end of his career said to the newcomer on the scene, "You write very good plays," then after a pregnant pause tempered the compliment: "So I've heard." The "youngster" tells the story with obvious affection and admiration, for, as a role model, Priestley had earned Ayckbourn's respect and served him well.[36]

Three years after A Chorus of Disapproval, another work demonstrates Ayckbourn's most incisive, perhaps intuitive structuring of the new upon the old. In Ayckbourn's A Small Family Business, the newly appointed managing director of a furniture manufacturing firm says of another character, "Do you know what that man was trying to do? I'll tell you. He was attempting to blackmail me. . . . Employ me and I won't prosecute. Can you believe that?"[37] Although a central situation may call to mind a parallel situation at the core of Ibsen's A Doll's House, Ayckbourn, unlike Frayn in Benefactors, does not underscore what in this case could be an incidental similarity. In more obvious ways as well as in what may be some deliberate marked contrasts, the play owes more to Priestley than to Ibsen. An Inspector Calls, unacknowledged within the younger writer's play, serves as pentimento for Ayckbourn's A Small Family Business. As Lillian Hellman has redefined the term, which refers to old paint on canvas that sometimes becomes transparent suggesting that the painter "repented" or changed his mind, "Perhaps it would be as well to say that the old conception, replaced by a later choice, is a way of seeing and then seeing again."[38]

When An Inspector Calls was first performed in London in 1946, many critics dismissed it as a conventional melodramatic family thriller. When Ayckbourn's A Small Family Business opened in London in 1987, most audiences viewed it as yet another hilarious family romp with the familiar Ayckbourn ingredients, mental and marital breakdowns. Yet anyone who had attended the coincidental revival of the Priestley play just a week before the opening of the Ayckbourn work might well have noted, as at the time London's drama critics did not, certain structural and thematic elements suggesting that both Priestley and Ayckbourn's focus on one man's family insists inevitably on the family of man, or, more precisely, on the failure of that universal family. For Priestley, his play, set in 1912, was "an attempt to dramatise the history of the last thirty years," the disastrous social climate that led to two world wars.[39] Looking back at the idyllic years of his youth before the first World War, Priestley probed the possibility that the seeds of man's destruction had already been planted. Echoing Priestley's play and its growing pessimism, while allowing aware spectators to make the connection themselves, Ayckbourn in A Small Family Business, still providing comic charac-

ters in comic situations, carries the family forward to the routine
horrors of Mrs. Thatcher's Britain. In the Ayckbourn play the size of
the family's business is diminished just as their social status is
lowered, but their potential for destruction has become limitless.

At a quiet, elegant family dinner party in an industrial city in the
North Midlands on a spring evening in 1912, the Birlings in *An
Inspector Calls* are celebrating the engagement of their daughter
Sheila to Gerald Croft. The coming marriage is especially fortuitous as
it signals the merging of Birling and Company and Crofts Limited.
Instead of competing, the rival firms may soon be "working to-
gether—for lower costs and higher prices."[40] But the family celebra-
tion of marriage and merger is interrupted by an enigmatic Inspector
Goole, new to the district, who informs them that a young woman,
Eva Smith, has swallowed a strong disinfectant and died in agony in
the Infirmary. Goole's questioning of the family reveals that Mr.
Birling had sacked the girl for her part in a strike at the factory.
Sheila, annoyed by her supposed impertinence, had had her
discharged from her next job in a dress shop. Changing her name to
Daisy Renton, Eva Smith had become Croft's mistress until the
arrangement proved an inconvenience. She had then taken up with
young Eric Birling and become pregnant by him, but Eric could only
support her by taking money from his father's firm. Rather than
accept stolen money, the girl had asked for assistance from the
Brumley Women's Charity Organization but had been denied by the
interviewing committee, chaired by Mrs. Birling, who felt strongly
that the man who got her into trouble should shoulder responsibility
for her fate. Having "been turned out and turned down too many
times" (302), she had ended her life.

Before his departure, Goole, the play's moral center, forcefully
states the theme which has emerged from the family's steadily mount-
ing denials, charges, countercharges, and confessions—that Eva
Smith and the Birlings are intertwined. "We don't live alone," he
says. "We are members of one body. We are responsible for each
other. And I tell you that the time will come when, if men will not
learn that lesson, then they will be taught it in fire and blood and
anguish" (311).

At Goole's departure, Mr. and Mrs. Birling, more concerned with
reputation than responsibility, learn that there is no new man on the
district police force, and no one has died in the Infirmary that night.
Convincing themselves that an elaborate hoax has been played on
them, that their involvements have all been with different girls, not a
single one, and that nothing calamitous has occurred, they resume the

evening's celebration until a phone call interrupts them. "That was the police. A girl has just died—on her way to the Infirmary—after swallowing some disinfectant. And a police inspector is on his way here—to ask some—questions—" (323), a dumbfounded Mr. Birling reports to his family as the curtain falls.

If Priestley was suggesting in 1945 that the fire and blood and anguish had not yet run their course—that it could all happen again— Ayckbourn, four decades later in *A Small Family Business*, a play with no moral center, suggests what may seem at first a calamity on a smaller scale—there is no world war on the horizon—but finally an even more devastating future for the prosperous middle class of Mrs. Thatcher's Britain. In *An Inspector Calls* the family has in fact not broken a law or committed a crime other than Eric's stealing some money from his father, and their victim is a person apart from themselves. In *A Small Family Business* the family, guilty of committing actual, horrible crimes, is in the process of destroying one of its own, thus destroying itself.

Like *An Inspector Calls*, *A Small Family Business* begins with a family celebration. Jack McCracken has just left a position as manager of a frozen food firm to take over as managing director of Ayres and Graces, a furniture manufacturing company founded by his father-in-law, which also employs his brother-in-law, his own son-in-law, and his own brother. Jack, a thoroughly honest, well-intentioned man, tells the others he will introduce into the firm "one simple concept. And that concept is basic trust." "I'm talking about establishing the understanding that so far as every individual member of that firm is concerned, working there is no longer going to be purely a question of take, take, take . . . whether it's raw materials from the shop floor, an extra fifty quid on our car allowances or paper clips from the office," he tells the others. "Let's try and put across the idea that many of us believe in it so strongly that we are even anxious to put something back in. Effort. Hard work. Faith. . . . We're a small family business. . . . There's no them and us about it. . . . All the lads we have working for us; all the girls in the office. They're practically family themselves" (8).

Jack's ideals are soon shattered. The party is interrupted as an inspector of sorts, far more ghoulish than Priestley's Inspector Goole, calls—at the back door. Benedict Hough is described by the author as *"an unimpressive, unmemorable man of indeterminate age—probably in his mid-thirties* (18). But as Ayckbourn himself directed actor Simon Cadell who played him in the first production, Hough is memorable indeed. Twisted in posture as well as spirit, in ill-fitting clothes, with a shuffling gait, insinuating voice, and unpleasant leer, Hough announces himself, not as a representative of the local police, but as a private investigator for a security firm.

Hough has caught Jack's sixteen-year-old daughter Samantha, who has given her name as Imogen Gladys Braithwaite, shoplifting a "family-sized bottle of Clearalene medicated shampoo and a stick of Little Miss Ritz waterproof eye-liner. Total value, one pound eighty-seven p" (22). Although Hough suggests, almost gleefully and with frightening relish, that his own solution would be corporal punishment, he insists that Samantha must be prosecuted unless Jack can see his way clear to hiring him as investigator for Ayres and Graces. But a principled Jack refuses, only to be amazed by his immediate family's plea that he go along with Hough's plan, that, in fact, everybody steals. "Am I the only one left with any moral values at all?" Jack asks his family, adding, "Well, that's one down, isn't it? Nine to go. Next! Thou shalt not kill, what about that then?" (30–31). The breaking of that commandment comes later in the play.

When Jack's father-in-law informs him that the company's designs are being copied and manufactured by an Italian firm that is outselling them despite the Italians charging higher prices (who can resist a foreign label?), that an insider is committing industrial espionage, Jack loosens his principles just a bit—the first of many times in the play—for the sake of his daughter and hires Hough.

Soon Hough, who does know his job, discovers that the Italians are in fact selling Ayres and Graces pieces that they are getting directly from the firm, that all of Jack's relatives are getting rich by robbing their own firm blind. The workers are in on the fiddle and will threaten to strike if told they can no longer swindle the firm that employs them. In *An Inspector Calls* only the son was guilty of stealing, and the workers at Birling and Company had threatened to strike for an additional two-and-a-half shillings a week, a mere living wage.

Does the family in *A Small Family Business* need the extra money that it comes by unlawfully? Jack's brother Cliff tells him, "Before you leave, have a look out there in the front drive. You'll see a black Porsche 944S Coupe, brand new registration, personalized number plates. That I love. Just through there, I have over three thousand quids' worth of sound gear and a couple of hundred compact discs. That I adore. Just outside Chichester I have a small sailing boat that I would willingly lay down my life for. I am even in love with my new liquid-crystal display digital wrist computer" (50). With so much passion spent on his material possessions, how much love has Cliff left for his wife Anita? None, it seems, but Anita does not mind. She has closets full of clothes to keep her happy and warm as well as a room full of sexual paraphernalia with which she entertains five Italian brothers, the Rivettis (played by a single actor), who are on the receiving end of the firm's goods. And Jack's brother-in-law Des, son of the firm's founder, has put away enough on the side that he will soon be able to disappear to Minorca where he will open his own restaurant. Des will not be taking his wife Harriet along, because Harriet, another disintegrating Ayckbourn housewife, does not share her husband's obsession with food, has in fact become so nauseated by the very thought of food, that she can no longer bring herself to eat.

To save the family Jack must buy off Hough, who knows too much. When the investigator's demands become outrageous, the men of the clan gather to plan on getting rid of Hough at the same time that Jack's wife and two daughters are in the actual process of doing just that. What is "very satisfying" to Ayckbourn about the play's bizarre turn of events, the dramatist himself admits, is the irony inherent in the situation, that Jack "should have involved his wife and daughters, whom he set out to protect, in the really ultimate crime."[41] Fighting with Hough to keep him from getting his hands on a briefcase full of pound notes, Mrs. McCracken and her daughters shove the outman-ned—or rather outwomanned—Hough into a bathtub, cracking his skull. In perhaps the most daring scene Ayckbourn has ever devised, the dramatist offers his first onstage death in such a way that he proves his point about the very collapse of civilized society, underscores its sickness, with his audience's reaction: Hough's demise evokes up-roarious laughter. With astonishing finesse Ayckbourn indicts his audience, finding them, in conniving with the McCracken women by spurring them on, guilty of conspiracy to murder.

More horror is in the offing. The action of *An Inspector Calls* is continuous at a single dinner party with the end returning to a point near its beginning. *A Small Family Business* moves forward in time but ends as it began with another family celebration, this time to honor the firm's founder on his seventy-fifth birthday. As the party progresses, Jack learns that the Italians will dispose of Hough's body, but for a price. Cliff tells Jack, "It appears tht they could find a use for our domestic furniture distribution network for the circulation of urgent medical supplies" (107). So involved in the business that he has paid less and less attention to his family, Jack has not yet noticed that some of those urgent medical supplies are already being used by his daughter Samantha, who, throughout the play, appears more and more withdrawn. Her petty thievery at the beginning of the play gives way to theft on a larger scale: compact disc players for resale to support her growing drug habit.

In act 1 of *An Inspector Calls,* just before Goole interrupts the
party, Birling offers advice to his son and future son-in-law:

> I don't want to lecture you two young fellows again. But what so many of
> you don't seem to understand . . . . is that a man has to make his own
> way—has to look after himself—and his family too, of course, when he has
> one—and so long as he does that he won't come to much harm. But the
> way some of these cranks talk and write now, you'd think everybody has to
> look after everybody else, as if we were all mixed up together like bees in a
> hive—community and all that nonsense. But take my word for it, you
> youngsters—and I've learnt in the good hard school of experience—that a
> man has to mind his own business and look after himself and his own—
> (273–74)

A Small Family Business takes Ayckbourn's audience—and Priestley's too—full circle. As the family party continues, Jack raises his
glass: "I'd simply like to propose this toast. . . . Here's to us. Here's to
the family. And finally, here's to the business. We've had our share of
troubles and we've seen them off. And together, I can promise you
this, we will continue to see them all off—whoever they are and
wherever they come from. Ladies and Gentlemen, I give you—the
family business!" (111–12). Acknowledging the innuendo, the others
respond, "The family business!" as the lights dim on the party scene.
Only one spot of light remains on the stage, on the one family
member not celebrating with the rest. Samantha sits alone in the
bathroom, blankly staring ahead of her. The last light fades. Finita la
commedia. Ayckbourn's despairing comedy can stand alone. Together
with *An Inspector Calls,* however, it completes the tragic arc of the
moral blight of the twentieth century.

The author of more than forty plays continues to build—sometimes
directly, sometimes indirectly—on foundations provided by others to
produce plays which are finally and all at once the side-splitting,
disturbing, unmistakable work of Alan Ayckbourn. His early unpublished piece, *Love After All* (1959), written under the pen name
Roland Allen, unmistakably borrows the plot of *The Barber of Seville,*
resetting it in the Edwardian era. Possible sources of his recent work
are sometimes more obscure. His *The Revengers' Comedies,* a contemporary equivalent of Jacobean drama with its tangled web of
unbridled passions and unspeakable crimes, pays special homage in
its title to Cyril Tourneur's little known *The Revenger's Tragedy*
(1607). Ayckbourn's play opens on London's Albert Bridge where two
characters, strangers from widely different classes, accidentally meet
as each attempts suicide and fails. In the first scene of Murray
Schisgal's comedy *Luv,* a Broadway hit in 1964, now neglected, two

acquaintances who have not seen one another in fifteen years meet again by chance on a bridge in New York where one is about to jump to his death. The other, stopping him, soon decides he too should end it all, but perhaps the solution to his problem is to introduce the friend to the wife he is trying to rid himself of. Whereas British audiences are unlikely to remember *Luv*, they may recall, and are perhaps meant to do so, the cross-motive murder scheme to which only one of two parties agrees in Alfred Hitchcock's comically macabre film, *Strangers on a Train* (1951), as well as the inventive murders in the classic film comedy, *Kind Hearts and Coronets* (1950).

Reviewing the Scarborough premiere of *Body Language*, the play in which heads are switched, John Peter has commented on Ayckbourn's wide-ranging use of possible sources with shrewd insight: "This is not an inherently funny subject; and indeed it forms the theme of one of Thomas Mann's most haunting stories, 'The Transposed Heads.' It doesn't matter in the least whether Ayckbourn has ever read it; what matters is that the subject which drew from Mann a tale of tragic, melancholy irony has inspired Ayckbourn to write an edgy, sardonic, boisterous play, funny and distressing, fantastical and realistic—in other words, deeply and sardonically English."[42] That Ayckbourn's seemingly insular plays are produced in every society in which theater exists, that in translation "his words are heard in Walloon, Serbo-Croatia and Urdu,"[43] makes clear that while the English may be singular in their peculiar thirst for warm beer, their stronger passions together with their needs, their dreams, and their pain are emphatically universal. Ayckbourn's subject is humankind, his boundary-shattering plays, however inspired, uniquely his own as they underscore the continuing life of the drama and the need of the artist to experiment and create anew.

3

Exchanges, Intimate or Otherwise

In the preface to *The Norman Conquests*, Scarborough's resident dramatist describes the Yorkshire resort as "a holiday town, which means that a large proportion of the potential audience changes every week of the summer. On Saturdays, the roads in and out of the town are scenes of mile-long queues as visitors leave and arrive" (10). Ayckbourn is indeed intrigued by, has even been inspired by gridlock, setting one of his first plays, *Standing Room Only* (1961), in a traffic jam that lasts a quarter of a century on Shaftesbury Avenue, the heart of London's theater district. Since then much of his work has depended on the dramatist's highly conscious, very deliberate manipulation to avoid traffic jams by carefully maneuvering his actors through the intricacies and obstacles of both onstage and offstage theatrical space. This element of his work enables audiences to recognize in an Ayckbourn play the idiosyncratic guiding hand of an iconoclast who refuses to be restricted by conventional concepts of what the theater can and ought to be, an aspect of his craft that reveals the extraordinary impact on Ayckbourn the playwright of Ayckbourn the director.

An Ayckbourn play does not always read well, nor need it, for it has been designed by an experienced theatrical practitioner to achieve full effect in performance. Robin Herford, for many years a pillar of the Scarborough company who has been in more original productions of Ayckbourn plays than any other actor, admits that an initial reading may prove disappointing.[1] A case in point for Herford is *Ten Times Table* (1977), a single-set play that moves forward in chronological time, bending no conservative bounds. The actor found it mildly amusing at first reading, but "nothing too special." In the hands of the author-director, however, who had himself suffered through countless frustrating meetings like those in the play when he had served on the committee to relocate the Scarborough theater to a permanent home, *Ten Times Table* became something more—a highly rewarding comic experience for the Scarborough audience that saw it staged in the round. Its dominant piece of furniture is a conference table at center stage around which a committee splits into more and more unyielding factions as it plans a village pageant, and the play lost some of its intense focus behind the proscenium arch of a West End theater. This was a problem that Ayckbourn, always writing with his in-the-round stage in mind, has for the most part managed to solve as he continues to direct the London productions of his plays as well as their Scarborough premieres. That some actors as committee members had their backs to the audience in the heated confrontations around the table was both acceptable and effective in Scarborough. In the West End the actors within the proscenium angled toward the audience rather than facing one another squarely, allowing that element of "performing" that Stephen Joseph always warned against to enter the production, to some extent marring it.

Herford, himself an accomplished director with Stephen Mallatratt's adaptation of Susan Hill's *The Woman in Black* to his credit, was exhilarated by his first encounter with Ayckbourn as the director of his own work. He was amazed by "the depth of color and texture that he brought to the play as he fleshed out the skeleton of the text." Ayckbourn knew the number of actors available to him as he wrote the play, the make-up of the company, but that did not influence him as he developed his characters. In the rehearsal period, however, as the director, Ayckbourn made use of his actors' individual personality traits in helping them discover the characters' core. He also taught them, Herford feels, to capitalize on the intimacy of the Scarborough theater by experimenting with lines that might get the best response, the biggest laugh, by being thrown away in an offhand manner rather than addressed in full voice to another actor. Herford, in fact the entire company, learned at the author-director's hands that an Ayckbourn play is designed for ensemble performance, not for star turns. An obstacle to the success of *Ten Times Table* as well as some other Ayckbourn plays with new casts in their London productions was the breakdown of the ensemble as actor vied with actor for the spotlight. In theater-in-the-round the veterans' trick of gaining attention by upstaging the rest of the cast is impossible; thus actors are more likely to allow themselves to be guided by the director in a more generous performance. When, as in Scarborough, the director is the author of the piece, actors willingly place their trust where it belongs—in the play. Says Herford: "As the director of his own work you know that even if it isn't on the page, he's got it in his head. The more we let Alan help us, the better we are all going to seem. We trust Alan and we desperately want the play to work."

Ayckbourn has earned his actors' faith in him by trusting them in turn. Having been in their position as actor, he understands what the performer is capable of bringing to a role, and he counts on his actors to make his characters live. In *The Square Cat,* the two-sided role of Arthur Brummage-Jerry Wattis was devised to showcase the actor—Ayckbourn himself—despite the fact that the author knew perfectly well that the performer was hardly an accomplished singer and was incapable of playing more than a single chord on a guitar, the play's essential prop. The author, however, trusted the actor to metamorphose convincingly into a popular rock star. The play's manuscript cannot begin to convey the striking effect achieved by the author-actor at the surprise ending of the first act. What did the trick was not a line of dialogue but the actor's stance, his costume, the one chord, and a quick black-out—the magic of performance.

Many of Ayckbourn's plays are more complex in structure than such straightforward works as *Ten Times Table, Absent Friends,* or *Just Between Ourselves,* as the dramatist manipulates time and space in innovative ways. His actors, finding themselves in ever more delicate and precarious positions as the plays depart from a simple setting and a linear development, must trust the play—and each other—implicitly. Ayckbourn's confidence in his company is revealed by his insistence in much of his work on a double focus—the actors at one and the same time as characters *and* performers, the unique aspect of an Ayckbourn play that compels the audience to react in what may seem an oxymoronic manner: (1) they must identify with the characters and lose themselves in the dramatic situation, (2) yet they must maintain a consciousness of the intricacies of what is unmistakably a theatrical performance taking place not merely on stage in front of them, but occurring offstage and, more remarkably, backstage as well, rarely an area of concern for a playwright.

Farce frequently depends on an enclosed stage space as setting to which access is provided by several doors. The joke of such a Feydeau play as *Occupe-toi d'Amélie* (1908) is that a character within a theatrical setting, expecting a second character with whom he is hoping to form an alliance, is suddenly confronted with a third character who poses a threat to the new relationship. A man expecting his mistress, for example, is startled by the appearance of his wife. But there is always another door proffering escape. Within a fixed setting, the relationships remain in flux as doors swing open only to be slammed shut. The audience's delight, however, is determined not so much by the agility of the performers, which may be noted in direct proportion to the speed with which they enter and exit, but by the cleverness of the situation, the plot in which performers lose their identities as actors and transform themselves into characters. In the Feydeau farce, it is the characters with whom an audience becomes involved.

This is true too of such an early Ayckbourn play as *Relatively Speaking,* in which the author spins out a case of mistaken identity with a skill equal to that of Feydeau or even Wilde whose *The Importance of Being Earnest* seems to have been its model. By the time he wrote *How the Other Half Loves* four years later in 1969, however, he had developed a means of adding to a farcical concoction what might be termed the A-effect, or Ayckbourn effect, in part related to, yet finally diametrically opposed to Bertolt Brecht's *V-effekt,* the well-known alienation effect that prevents an audience's identification with the characters. *Verfremdungseffekt* distances an audience with its emphasis on theater as theater. The audience recognizes that the actor is an actor, commenting on the situation of the character he is representing in order to lead the spectator to think about that situation, even to consider alternatives to it. There is a terrible comic irony in Mother Courage leading her children to their doom, but the audience is made aware of every wrong turning she takes, knows an alternative route could have been hers. As Azdak, the rascal-judge of *The Caucasian Chalk Circle,* dispenses his droll justice, the audience cannot fail to see that the laws of man, oftentimes indifferent, even inhumane, serve the system rather than the individual. Brecht's plays may entertain incidentally, but they are didactic in intention. By contrast the A-effect, Ayckbourn's means of distancing, enhances an audience's pleasure in his early works. As Ayckbourn's vision grows bleaker in the later plays, he may offer alternatives, yet none are palliative measures. The audience is not urged to take to the streets to protest the status quo. In the words of Beckett's tramps, there is "nothing to be done."

In *How the Other Half Loves,* Ayckbourn begins to play the role for which he is best known today—the documentor of the maddening rituals of suburban life, the social chronicler. Yet the play, while foreshadowing the more serious tribulations of daily life which take center stage in the later works, is, like *Relatively Speaking,* light-hearted entertainment meant to evoke an audience's guiltless laughter. Bob Phillips is involved in an affair with his employer's wife, Fiona Foster. Inventing a marital break-up of the socially backward Featherstones as an excuse for coming home in the middle of the night, he unwittingly sets off a chain of misunderstandings which nearly wreck three already unstable relationships. Before mate is reunited with proper mate, Teresa Phillips and Frank Foster learn the truth and forgive their wayward spouses, but hapless, innocent Mary and William Featherstone are not quite reconciled to what they now perceive to be a sterile relationship.

What sets *How the Other Half Loves* apart from any number of mindless West End farces about marital mix-ups is a telling contrast of social and economic status made evident by the play's complicated but ingenious setting which makes the A-effect possible. It is Ayckbourn's masterstroke to place the living-dining area of both the tasteful Foster home and the cluttered, uncared-for Phillips home on stage together, not side by side as one might expect from a conventional playwright presenting two locales, but actually superimposed. The expensive Foster period reproduction furniture shares a one-room stage with the modern, trendy Phillips pieces. In the West End production the sofa was even sectioned into Foster cushions and Phillips cushions. Yet, by means of clashing styles and colors, the audience has no difficulty in discerning who lives where, once the actors establish their roles.

In *Run for Your Wife* (1983), a witless albeit entertaining, long-running West End farce, Ray Cooney adapted Ayckbourn's two-household setting juxtaposed into one but failed to put it to telling use. The setting added little to the fun of Cooney's piece and never became an integral part in building to the farcical climax. Ayckbourn, originator of the inventive setting, uses it significantly in yet another remarkable innovation that makes possible one of the most hilarious scenes in modern comedy, capping any single action of a Ben Travers Aldwych farce. The single enclosed theatrical space, already accepted by the audience as two distinct locales, is viewed as existing in two distinct moments of time—Thursday night at the Fosters and Friday night at the Phillipses. Two calamitous dinner parties take place simultaneously at one extended dining table where the Featherstones are at once the guests for an elegantly formal meal replete with linen napkins and crystal goblets, and a less-than-casual supper with paper napkins and glass tumblers. The scene ends with poor William Featherstone wringing wet—hit with the soup which an enraged, drunken Teresa throws at Bob on Friday in the very spot, seemingly at the very same time, where the Fosters' upstairs loo suddenly leaks through the ceiling on Thursday.[2]

Variations on the farcical action appear in later Ayckbourn plays. In *Absurd Person Singular,* Sidney, whose wife Jane, caught in a downpour, makes a disheveled entrance at a Christmas party in act 1, emerges in act 2 from under a sink he has attempted to repair during a lull at another Christmas party, drenched in dirty water (68). At an afternoon tea in *Absent Friends*, during which nothing has gone quite right, Diana, the hostess, on the verge of breaking down, picks up a cream jug and pours it slowly over her husband Paul's head (144). At another disastrous dinner party in *Suburban Strains,* Caroline, near hysteria, takes up the soup tureen and deliberately ladles soup down the back of Joanna's dress.[3] After having a jar of mayonnaise spilt on her dress during lunch with the vicar's wife, Celia in *A One Man Protest*, the seventh in the series of related plays that comprise *Intimate Exchanges*, suffers the further indignity of being splashed with a bucketful of water as her husband puts out a fire in their garden shed.[4] Effective as these later moments are, none has the added dimension, the breathtaking ingenuity, of events occurring in two separate places on two different days which have become one time, one place.

The space, ingeniously and imaginatively utilized, provides *How the Other Half Loves* with yet another dimension, one beyond the visual. The audience is not kept in a state of apprehension as in Feydeau's *La Puce a l'Oreille* (1907) or Travers's *Rockery Nook* (1926), wondering which character will be revealed next as doors open and close. In fact Ayckbourn has commented on what to others might seem a limitation of arena staging: "I couldn't have written *Rookery Nook* even if I'd wanted to, because I haven't got any doors."[5] The suspense in *How the Other Half Loves* transcends plot in involving the audience's appreciation of the characters as actors negotiating the onstage traffic to which they must appear oblivious. Actors portraying characters supposedly miles apart occupy the same space as they circle one another, seemingly on a collision course, then veer to relative safety to the audible sighs of relief from an audience savoring the illusion, willing it to be maintained. This aspect of the play that the dramatist suggests offhandedly in a single-sentence stage direction—"The characters in their different homes will often pass extremely close but without ever actually touching" (2)—might be overlooked by a reader of the play. But *How the Other Half Loves* is a joyous experience fraught with vicarious danger for the theatergoer who gasps in the midst of laughter as two actors, blind to one another, come within an inch of making contact. A single brushing of one against the other would burst the illusionary balloon, end the suspense, the fun, the very play. *How the Other Half Loves* thus depends as much on the ingenuity of its director as on the ingenuity of its author. Perfect timing matters at least as much as plot or language. Added delight comes from the realization that Ayckbourn's special form of distancing requires that that dimension be supplied finally by the actors themselves. Through his management of space, Ayckbourn has manipulated his audience to identify not merely with his characters, but also with his performers.

In *Taking Steps*, a farce written a decade later in 1979 and set in a symbolically decaying Victorian house which a drunken bucket manufacturer is considering for purchase, Ayckbourn attempted a similar manipulation of space that once again thrust his actors into the lime-light as actors. The title wittily refers to more than theme, describing in fact the staging on which much of the action depends. Having written the work originally for the single-level stage of Scarborough's theater-in-the-round, Ayckbourn makes frequent use of flights of stairs to accommodate slapstick pratfalls, somersaults, and general frenzy. But in *Taking Steps,* the stairs are flattened, merely indicated, so that three levels supposedly exist on a single stage floor, which means that actors rushing about the attic or the first floor actually move in close proximity to, and are in danger of colliding with, other actors on the ground floor.

Reminiscent of the superimposition of two households in *How the Other Half Loves,* the device makes perfect sense in the theater for which it was designed. On the proscenium stage of a West End theater that could in fact accommodate various levels if called for, and in the hands of a director other than its author, it reduced to pure gimmickry, assuring laughter without providing the telling social counterpoint of the earlier play. Behind the proscenium arch, *Taking Steps* never worked quite as well as it did in the round in Scarborough, where the audience's laughter on the first night added seventeen minutes to the play's running time.[6] Yet with Ayckbourn as the director making the transition from one type of staging to another with a finesse lacking in the London production, which became something of a star turn for Dinsdale Landen as the bucket king, the Scarborough company toured the play in conventional theaters with great success. What was missing in the West End that the original Scarborough company provided their audience was an intricately worked out, perfectly timed ensemble performance in which the double focus of the A-effect on actor-as-character led to sheer delight.

Eight years later in *Henceforward . . .,* first performed in Scarborough in 1987 in a period in which the darker concerns of his plays were brought to the fore, Ayckbourn found a way to make the A-effect do more than entertain his audience. In a comic yet highly disturbing fantasy that never lets an audience forget the horrors of the present, the focus on the performer underscores a terrifying theme: in losing his ability to love, man is metamorphosing into machine.

Henceforward . . ., after *Standing Room Only,* is the dramatist's second excursion to a future world. In the first act Nan (short for Nanny) 300F, a defective limping robot, is revealed as housekeeper for Jerome, a composer, who has been separated from his wife and daughter for four years, a period in which his artistic creativity has been blocked. Jerome desperately wants to win the right to have his thirteen-year-old daughter Geain, pronouncd Jane—not Gaelic, "just pretentious"[7]—visit him. To do so he must convince Mervyn Bicker-dyke of the Department of Child Wellbeing as well as his no-nonsense wife Corinna that he is a fit father living a normal life in a suitable environment.

Into the windowless, sparsely furnished studio-home filled with sophisticated electronic equipment, not unlike the gadgetry that fills Ayckbourn's own home, limps a very human Zoë. Hired by Jerome to enact the role of his fiancée, she has just been mugged by the Daughters of Darkness who roam the unprotected area of the futuristic North London suburb where the composer lives and works. Temporarily employed by an escort service, Zoë is an out-of-work actress who lists among her credits Hedda Gabler, Queen Margaret, Madame Arkadina, and the mad Mrs. Rochester—all of them women who have either lost their children, ignore them, or detest the thought of bearing them. Zoë is immediately attracted to Jerome and, soon after, seduced by him, but leaves in disgust on learning that he has recorded the sounds of their love-making on a digital audio system to be synthesized into a musical composition. She is thoroughly unimpressed by his explanation that he wants to express the feeling of love in an abstract musical form in such a way that those hearing it will respond by relating it to their own feelings of love, augmenting the world's supply of the precious commodity. "How could you ever possibly, ever, in a million years," Zoë asks, "conceivably describe something you can't even recognize?" (51). Poor Jerome, who, until Zoë's arrival, had had almost no face-to-face contact with another human being "since they fully automated the hypermarket" (37), has no recourse but to reprogram Nan 300F as fiancée, a crazed variation on the *Dinner with the Family* plot device which Ayckbourn so often reinvests with startling originality.

Only Geain recognizes that Nan, who scrubs the face of anyone with whom she comes into contact in her never-ending search for a child to care for, is a machine. Using the language of a truckdriver, Jerome's unwashed daughter, who crossdressses in a leather jacket studded with the words "Sons of Bitches," the name of her gang, curiously enough responds to the robot's maternal quality, something she has never discerned in her own mother who is incapable of disciplining her.

By the end of the play Jerome and Corinna are to be reunited and prepare to flee the bunkerlike flat in the lawless no-go area that the Daughters of Darkness—some of them even women, and a rival gang to the Sons of Bitches—are about to attack. When Jerome, overwhelmed by a sudden urge of creativity, hangs back as the others leave, he uncovers more and more machines that take up the entire stage. He is to use them in the process of synthesizing the word "love," as uttered by Corinna, into a symphony of eerie, electronic sound. As the all-encompassing, uncomfortably amplified music engulfs Jerome and the audience, the machines give off a blinding light show as well. The artist is at last fulfilled, but the audience is painfully aware that he is alone. He has so fragmented the sounds that make up the word "love" that it can hold no meaning for anyone but the self-indulgent creator of meaningless madness. His search for love, his attempt to reestablish a relationshp with the daughter he no longer recognizes, has only been a means to an end—to process human relationships through bloodless machines.

What gives added dimension to a play that is both horrifying nightmare and delightful comic romp is the A-effect by which the audience is at one and the same time beguiled by the character and the performer. Ayckbourn has so structured *Henceforward . . .* that it becomes feasible, in fact necessary for the theme of the play, for two performers to play three roles. Two actresses play the two live adult women in Jerome's life, Zoë and Corinna. But the two must share the performance of a third character, Nan 300F, the robot. The performer playing robot Nan in act 1 becomes the wife in act 2, while the performer undertaking the role of Zoë, a character who is herself an actress, plays Nan playing fiancée Zoë in act 2. In *Henceforward . . .* actors, like interchangeable mechanical parts, play characters who are interchangable with machines. (Later, in *Body Language* [1990] two actresses actually seem to exchange parts of their bodies.) *Henceforward . . .*'s protagonist Jerome, portrayed by an actor as a live person throughout, is revealed at last to be a human being with the soul of a machine. A work built on the standard ingredient of an early Ayckbourn farce, assumed and mistaken identities, *Henceforward . . .* entertains its audience with its hilariously inept robot with human, maternal emotions. At the same time the A-effect that insists at once on the audience's recognition of performer as character, of man as machine, affords the play, an all-too-real futuristic comic nightmare, a shattering depth.

Indicative of Ayckbourn's developing mastery of yet another aspect of theatrical space are two plays written before *Henceforward . . .*, actually coming between *How the Other Half Loves* and *Taking Steps*, which focus on what is occurring directly within the audience's view. In *Absurd Person Singular*, first performed in 1972, and *The Norman Conquests*, the following year, the playwright addresses the dramatic possibilities of offstage action that supplements, even causes the action on stage. In the preface to *Absurd Person Singular* he writes, "Very early on in my career as a dramatist I discovered that

. . . an audience's imagination can do far better than any number of playwright's words. The offstage character hinted at but never seen can be dramatically as significant and telling as his onstage counter-parts" (7). The impetus for that essential discovery may have come from Anouilh's *Dinner with the Family*, so influential on Ayckbourn's early work. The one member of the family who never appears in the play, the wife with whom Georges is locked in an unhappy marriage, is directly or indirectly responsible for every action in the play and is never out of the thoughts and words of all the others.

As important as is the actor in the scheme of an Ayckbourn play, the unseen character who is never physically embodied by an actor yet is nevertheless indelibly imprinted on the audience's imagination be-comes for Ayckbourn, as for Anouilh, a key performer. One might point to Carol, Colin's fiancée who has died before the play begins, as the central character of *Absent Friends*. Marge's ailing husband, Gordon, repeatedly telephoning his wife, is another absent friend whom the audience gets to know quite well in the course of the play. Douglas Beechey's wife Nerys, Vic Parks' long-ago victim in *Man of the Moment*, never appears, yet, as the catalyst for Douglas and Vic's first terrible encounter, she is never absent from the play as the two men meet again in preparation for a television show, *Their Paths Crossed*. One critic has noted that "absent children cast their nasty little shade on the stage" in "Mother Figure," the first of the five interlinked one-act plays that comprise *Confusions* (1974), and in *How the Other Half Loves*, "where we are continuously fed hair-raising information about Terry's son's devastating activities in the kitchen."[8]

Absent mothers matter too. The mother who has just died is a pervasive influence in both *Time and Time Again* and *Sisterly Feel-ings*. In *Wildest Dreams* the mother who deserted Rick and the mother whom Warren wishes would desert him—a woman who very nearly makes her way on to the stage—are absent presences throughout. The infirm mother in *The Norman Conquests*, unseen but hardly absent, is actually the initiator of the action in that the family gathers to look after her. The audience is constantly aware of her presence in the house in an unseen upstairs room and cannot overlook her influence on her children. They scurry to answer her bell, discuss her temperament and her condition, prepare her meals and her medicines, discover her on the telephone line, even remi-nisce about her past: "Do you remember Mother taking us on holi-day? Where was it? Weston-super-Mare. Were you old enough to remember? . . . . When she picked up that sailor? . . . . He kept throwing that ball half a mile down the beach. Trying to get us all to run after it. Run along, kids. Go and fetch it. Let me talk to your Mum" (38), a line amusing to the audience, but on first hearing rather startling for Ayckbourn's mother, unaware till then how much her son's plays grew from his own experience—and hers. A candid Mary James confessed to an interviewer: "It gave me an awful shock, because that was *me*. I thought Alan was too young to even know about it: he was only four. I think my God, what else does he remember?"[9]

Ayckbourn's comments in the *Absurd Person Singular* preface on unseen characters lead him logically to a consideration of unseen action as well: "Offstage action is more difficult. Unless care is taken, if the dramatist chooses to describe rather than show his action, the audience can rapidly come to the conclusion that they're in the wrong auditorium" (7). Shortly after beginning the play, which originally took place at three parties on three successive Christmas Eves in the sitting rooms of three different households, Ayckbourn came to the conclusion that he was in the wrong room: "Dick and Lottie were indeed monstrously overwhelming . . . and far better heard occasionally but not seen. By a simple switch of setting to the kitchen, the problem was all but solved, adding incidentally far greater comic possibilities than the sitting room ever held. For in this particular case, the obvious offstage action was far more relevant than its onstage counterpart." In the subsequent reversal of offstage and onstage action, the guests in act 1 seek sanctuary in the kitchen to avoid the awful jokes of the hearty, unseen Potters; in act 2 they are held hostage by George, a large unseen dog who has just bitten the still unseen Mr. Potter in the adjoining room; and in act 3 the Brewster-Wrights and the Jacksons hide unsuccessfully from the uninvited Hopcrofts. What matters in *Absurd Person Singular* happens in the kitchen, but what adds bite to this black farce about sexual incompatibility and class warfare is that the characters in each act are trapped on stage by the offstage characters, some of whom never appear, with whom the audience grows more and more familiar as the play progresses.

In *The Norman Conquests*, a trilogy comprising *Table Manners, Living Together*, and *Round and Round the Garden*, Ayckbourn exploits the ultimate possibilities of offstage action through a single set of characters in a house and its surroundings where Annie awaits her brother Reg and his wife Sarah. They are to relieve her of caring for their bed-ridden mother so that Annie may take a well-deserved holiday. Unknown to the others, who suspect she may be going off with her neighbor Tom, the local vet, Annie is in fact about to leave for a "dirty weekend" with Norman, who is married to her sister Ruth.

When over-eager Norman arrives too soon, complications multiply. Shocked upon learning the truth, Sarah forbids Annie to leave, summons Ruth, and takes over the household, forcing Reg, who is mainly interested in getting a square meal and trying out a game he has invented, to spy for her. Totally bewildered by what is happening around him, dull-witted Tom suspects that all the women have designs on his person, while Ruth, attempting without much success to retain her composure, sorts matters out. Through it all, exasperating, inept Norman remains the surprisingly irresistible shaggy dog whom all the women actually wish to cuddle. And all of them do—in a corner of the dining room in one play, on a rug in the sitting room in the second play, or in the bushes of the garden in the third. At one point Norman even gets to embrace Reg, clasping his brother-in-law's knees as he professes a platonic love for him. Ultimately, the entire household is frustrated as they are trapped in the rituals of a summer weekend—eating, drinking, storytelling, game-playing, wooing. The male-female relationship with its dream of blissful happiness is reduced in *The Norman Conquests* to the comedy of furtive groping and interrupted coupling.

In a recent theatrical development, what might be called the walkabout play, such as John Krizanc's *Tamara* (1984), about the peculiar goings-on in the unconventional household of Italian author Gabriele D'Annunzio, the audience, forewarned to wear comfortable shoes, follows the drama, housed in a large sectioned building—the Seventh Regiment Armory in New York—rather than a theater, by strolling from room to room. With something happening in various rooms simultaneously, the individual spectator chooses where to go, what to watch. In his *The Norman Conquests* trilogy, perhaps the inspiration for the walkabout play which pretentious producers might prefer to trace back to the medieval street dramas performed by craftsmen's guilds, Ayckbourn for the first time but not the last, forces theatergoers to make a choice concerning which part to see, whether or not to return for seconds, perhaps even for thirds. For maximum entertainment, the best choice is to take in all three, for the three parts ingeniously combine to enable the audience to know what every member of a basically average, normally befuddled English family is up to at any given moment in any part of the household. By choosing which part to see, theatergoers are actually choosing to watch the family in action in a particular part of the household. Rather than having to walk about, they are comfortably seated as they view one of three possible settings—dining room, sitting room, or garden. Significantly, in a comedy evolving from frustrated sexual couplings, the bedroom is not among the audience's choices. Ayckbourn leaves the onstage bedroom, or rather three of them, for his later *Bedroom Farce*, which, despite its titillating but ironic title, involves many characters in many beds, none of them engaged in a sexual act.

For the spectator who returns for one or two additional helpings of *The Norman Conquests*, a heady comic feast that can be begun with any of the three courses, the fun expands. As the three plays are taking place in three locales simultaneously, one audience member may be in on a joke that another, seated alongside, cannot appreciate as fully. When, for example, Sarah sends Reg from the dining room in *Table Manners* to fetch something, anything, from the sitting room in order to spy on Annie and Norman, and he returns foolishly carrying a wastepaper basket only to be berated by his wife for not having "found something a little more natural" (33), the audience is amused. But those who have already seen *Living Together*, in which an embarrassed Reg interrupts Annie and Norman in the sitting room and grabs the basket in confused desperation (101), have the heartier laugh. *The Norman Conquests* is the rare play in which some spectators enjoy a wider perspective than others, resulting in a curious response; although the entire audience is being entertained, the veterans among them are having a better time than the newcomers to the situation.

To bring off his prodigious feat, to be sure he knew where he was and where he was going in the plays, Ayckbourn wrote them crosswise. As he explains, he "started with Scene One of *Round and Round the Garden*, then the Scene One's of the other two plays and so on through the Scene Two's" (11). One hardworking critic, who has laid out the "precise programme" of the entire trilogy as if it were "a railway timetable," reveals that his "dogged search in the printed versions for some fracture points between the plots yielded . . . only two moments when the internal sequence within the single play was slightly at variance with the chronological sequence of the saga."[10] Because no three-part theater will ever be built specifically for an audience, seated in three different sections of a vast auditorium, to watch actors going about all of *The Norman Conquests* trilogy at a single performance on a mammoth stage divided into two rooms plus garden—a delectable if impractical prospect—the worldwide audiences that have now seen the play, either in theaters or on television, may never discover the discrepancies in the chronology of the playwright's incredible achievement. And, by chance, should they do so, Ayckbourn would surely be forgiven them.

Whereas Chekhov led his audience to a play's subtext, his characters' internal thoughts, Ayckbourn has devised three plays, of which any two may be regarded as the subtextual yet external offstage action of, or commentary on, the third. According to Ayckbourn, *The Norman Conquests* "to all intents and purposes was the end of my exploration of offstage action. Three plays, two of which were happening off stage simultaneously with the one on stage, were quite enough."[11] What the brilliantly innovative dramatist still had left to explore was the possibility of turning an audience's attention not so much to some fictional offstage action, but to place in focus once more the actor as actor, to invite an audience to follow imaginatively the actor moving from onstage theatrical space to the theater's unseen backstage area. Both Ayckbourn, and, to some extent Michael Frayn, who also utilized the A-effect in his *Noises Off* (1982) and less successfully in *Look Look* (1990), would discover further dramatic possibilities in the exploration of backstage theatrical space.

For Ayckbourn, the transitional work in this movement is *Sisterly Feelings* (1979), the first of what he regards as his "alternate" plays,[12] or plays that exist in more than one version, all versions of which are presented at various times but not all together at a single performance. The actual beginnings of the alternate play in its simplest form, however, with two versions of a single scene enacted at one performance, can be traced back to *Dad's Tale*, the Christmas show presented at Scarborough in 1960 in conjunction with a dance company. Originating as a collaboration between Ayckbourn and David Campton, the piece became Ayckbourn's own and was attributed, like the other early works, to the nonexistent Roland Allen.

Narrated by Martin, a young house painter awaiting his mate with the ladder, *Dad's Tale* is a very tall tale clumsily interspersed with three dances—a shopping ballet, a fairy-tale ballet, and, most unlikely of all, a crime ballet—about how Dad turned into a budgerigar one Christmas Day. Despite its epic theater frame of a narrated story, *Dad's Tale*, not surprisingly, owes very little to Bertolt Brecht. One slight yet significant Brecht-Roland Allen connection, however, is evident. Whereas the serious-minded Marxist attempted to turn an audience's thoughts to alternative actions for his characters, Ayckbourn, merely manufacturing Christmas tinsel, provided those alternatives at one point in the play. When Mr. Breakwater, Dad's neighbor, learns that his Christmas order from the grocer has been delivered next door by mistake, he reacts in different ways, depending on who is narrating at the moment, but both versions are performed for the audience. When Auntie gives Martin a rest and takes up the tale, warning the audience that her nephew is inclined to exaggerate, Mr. Breakwater is good-neighborliness personified. He is not the least disturbed at losing his Christmas dinner and compliments Auntie as a splendid cook. But Martin, reminding the audience that he had already cautioned them not to listen to Auntie, retells the incident another way. An angry Mr. Breakwater, not imbued with the holiday spirit this time, has a fit and insults Auntie with the accusation that, as usual, she has probably even burnt the stolen dinner. If Martin's seems the likelier version, the inane *Dad's Tale*, like a Pirandello play gone haywire, offers an audience two truths. The choice is theirs, but finally which one is accepted matters not a whit and has no effect on the ending of the play in which Dad indeed flaps his arms and leaves the stage as an oversized bird.

The far more sophisticated, skillfully crafted, wholly credible *Sisterly Feelings* only resembles *Dad's Tale* in that, despite its alternate middle scenes that are presented at different performances, it has a fixed opening and a single ending. The alternate scenes, however, lend the play an air of spontaneity, making it a milestone in the contemporary theater. Because the play illustrates its dramatist's theory of comic determinism by exploring the effect of chance or choice on his characters' lives, chance or choice plays upon the audience as well. *Sisterly Feelings* is a two-act comedy divided into four scenes which invert the cycle of life by beginning with a funeral and ending with a wedding at which the bride is pregnant. While act 1, scene 1 and act 2, scene 2, the first and last scenes, are the same in all versions, act 1, scene 2 and act 2, scene 1 each have alternate versions so that the play can be arranged in four different ways for presentation at four separate performances. Which of the alternate middle scenes are to be presented, changing the shape of the performance, is determined by a toss of a coin at one point and a performer's whim at another.

As an aid to an audience obviously unaccustomed to an arbitrary performance, the theater program provides a cast list in the form of a genealogy and a map suggesting the alternative routes this unique comic vehicle may travel. The genealogical table and the map underscore Ayckbourn's ingenuity, further proclaimed by his subtitle, "A Related Comedy," a pun, like *Relatively Speaking*, encompassing content, form, and theme. Nearly all the characters are about to be members of a single family; the incidents are intertwined; and, because variable scenes obviously exist, any one version suggests for the central characters only a relative truth.

Each version of *Sisterly Feelings* begins with a scene entitled "A Funeral." On the day of his wife's interment, Dr. Matthews takes his family to the spot where years before he had proposed to her on Pendon Common, the play's single setting that metaphorically suggests life's pitfalls: "There is no firm ground. We are standing in a marsh."[13] The doctor's three children are Abigail, whose husband

Patrick is a pompous business man; Dorcas, a local radio newscaster involved with Stafford, an unemployable poet; and Melvin, engaged to Brenda. The sisters both find themselves attracted to Brenda's brother, narcissistic, muscular Simon, home from Africa. When Patrick drives off early to attend a board meeting, one place is left in another car once the rest of the party, which includes the doctor's brother-in-law Len, a policeman, and Len's wife Rita, are accommodated. Simon flips a coin for the sisters, who are in effect vying for the opportunity to remain behind to walk home with him, to determine which of the two will occupy the remaining seat in the car. The one who loses the ride—actually the winner—stays and establishes a relationship with Simon, thus incurring not only her sister's jealousy but the displeasure of either Patrick or Stafford, one or the other of whom disrupts the next family outing a few months later in the play's second scene, which, depending on the coin toss, is either "Abigail's Picnic" or "Dorcas' Picnic." (In the first Scarborough performance during which the coin toss would actually dictate the course of the rest of the play in Ayckbourn's delightfully innovative theatrical coup, the coin miraculously landed on edge and rolled offstage, deflating the moment, as the actor playing Simon had to follow it off as well.)[14]

When a rainstorm abruptly ends the picnic, the sister (or rather the actress performing the role) who has ensnared Simon, has the choice of prolonging her affair with him or giving him up to her rival, thus initiating the third scene, either "A Day at the Races" or "A Night under Canvas." If Dorcas is with Simon after the picnic, she becomes a steward for the cross-country race which, Stafford's attempts at sabotage failing, Simon wins. If Abigail is with Simon after the picnic, the two go camping and endure interruptions first from Len, then from Patrick.

The variable scenes, initiated by chance—a coin toss—or choice—a performer's spur-of-the-moment decision—do not determine the outcome. *Sisterly Feelings* always ends with the same fourth scene, "A Wedding," in which the bride is neither Abigail, who resumes a conventional life with Patrick, nor Dorcas, who resumes her nursemaiding of unconventional, childlike Stafford, but bossy Brenda, now pregnant, who has been having her way with their docile brother Melvin. Neither chance nor choice has seriously interrupted life's flow. As Dorcas says, "The important thing is for us to *feel* we've made decisions" (146), voicing the play's theme.

According to Ayckbourn, the whole scheme "has the effect of stimulating actors, irritating stage managers and infuriating box office staff" (viii). In theory the audience too should be excited by the supposed spontaneity of the performance as they envision what must be taking place backstage—an entire theater company at the ready to move in one direction or another, to put in place one set or another, one series of props or another, to set in motion one series of actions or its alternates. In actual practice the excitement is diminished by pragmatism. After the first few performances during the London run of *Sisterly Feelings* at the National Theatre, the course of the play was predetermined, chance giving way to choice. The entire company knew beforehand the result of the coin toss, and the actress's whim was in fact dictated. Backstage chaos settled into theatrical routine as audiences, aware that the alternatives were already selected, concentrated on onstage action.[15] Successful as it was at the National, Ayckbourn told an interviewer that Peter Hall claimed "it would have run for a lot longer, except that no one could understand the leaflet!" British audiences were bad enough, but the dramatist claims to have seen American tourists in despair at the box office, "trying to work out what they'd seen and what they were seeing."[16] Once the confused Americans had purchased their tickets and taken their seats in the Olivier Theatre, they would have been highly entertained as their convictions about the eccentric English would have been reinforced through a dramatization of curious tribal customs and mating habits. They would have had no difficulty in following whatever version of *Sisterly Feelings* was being performed.

The same perhaps could not be said for the audiences who some years earlier coped with one of the rare Ayckbourn plays that never reached London. Although producers twice toured the play, first presented in Scarborough in 1970 under the title *The Story So Far* and revised in 1979 as *Me Times Me Times Me*, the closest it ever came to the West End was a production at the Orange Tree Theatre in Richmond in 1978, there retitled *Family Circles*. Its importance in the Ayckbourn canon is that it may be regarded as the seed for what would be a far more challenging, more intricately constructed alternate play than the four-version *Sisterly Feelings*. The theme as well as the form of the sixteen-version mammoth *Intimate Exchanges* is there in embryo in the earlier play with no alternate scenes or endings, but a complicated alternate pairing of its characters within the standard length of its final, single version as *Family Circles*, which was deserving of a better fate. Ayckbourn, known to have a weak spot for his works that were ultimately unsuccessful, says of the play, "It is probably not vintage, but it's got a few good laughs in it, the premise of the play being that, depending upon whom you marry, you become slightly different. And it's quite fun to watch."[17] The statement is basically accurate. The play may have even more than a fair share of laughs, but the too-convoluted working out of the premise bewildered

a part of the audience that mistakenly thought it had wandered into an
unpleasant play about wife-swapping. The failure of *Family Circles*
suggests that for once a brilliant playwright with a computer-like brain
had been too clever by half for an average audience that this time
could not catch up with him or even catch on to one of his most
entangled schemes.

Family Circles takes place over a weekend during which Edward
and Emma's daughters, along with their mates, come to celebrate
their parents' wedding anniversary. In the first scene, pregnant Jenny
is married to Oliver, Polly is married to David, and Deirdre has begun
a relationship with James. But something extraordinary happens in
the scene that follows. For once the reader of an Ayckbourn play may
be in a better position than the theatergoer. The stage business
invented by a gifted director will be missed, of course, but the
author's stage direction at the start of act 1-scene 2 makes clear the
form of *Family Circles*:

> *Scene: The same—a second later.*
> *Only the individual relationships have changed.*
>   *OLIVER is now married to DEIRDRE, DAVID to JENNY who is still*
> *pregnant, and JAMES has been invited down by POLLY. The relative*
> *physical positioning of each pair has correspondingly altered since the end*
> *of Act 1, Scene 1. The clothes, particularly the women's have also*
> *changed, reflecting the new relationships. They are all, though, basically*
> *the same people, merely altered by the different circumstances of their*
> *lives. DAVID and JENNY are poorer, since DAVID, under her influence,*
> *is more unsuccessful than ever. DEIRDRE is happily spending OLIVER's*
> *money and shows it. POLLY is more the bachelor girl making less compro-*
> *mises than ever. . . . EDWARD remains unfortunately married to*
> *EMMA.*[18]

In the play's third scene, mate switches mate once again with the
last of the possible permutations—Polly married to Oliver, Deirdre to
David, and the now unmarried but still pregnant Jenny keeping
company with James. Another essential stage direction in the last
scene, the most frenetic, and the most complicated for the unsophisti-
cated theatergoer who never quite comprehends Ayckbourn's plan,
comes to the aid of the reader:

> *Since in this scene, everyone, with the exception of EDWARD and EMMA*
> *appear in the various roles they played in the previous three scenes, they*
> *are numbered according to the scene in which their character first ap-*
> *peared. Thus the DEIRDRE in this instance is the one that first arrived*
> *with JAMES, known as DEIRDRE 1.*

The theatergoer must work his way through the skillfully prepared farcical denouement without the benefit of numbers appended to the performers.

Whereas *Family Circles*, hardly intended as a naturalistic piece despite a naturalistic performance, is designed to demonstrate that people change to some extent in accordance with the person they marry, what comes through even more strongly is an abiding Ayckbourn theme: married life is hell. None of the younger couples finds happiness in any of the play's permutations. But the older couple, Edward and Emma, who have reared three difficult daughters, have steadfastly remained together through a lifetime of trials and tribulations. Like the elderly couple in *Bedroom Farce*, they have made an accommodation with one another, hence with life. The irony on which the plot builds is that a neighbor has informed the girls that one of their parents is trying to do away with the other. The three younger couples, desperately trying to prevent a murder—a number of bizarre incidents support the possibility that the rumor may be true—are completely unaware that their own relationships are in far worse shape.

A later failed Ayckbourn work, perhaps this one deservedly so, *It Could Be Any One of Us* (1983), is another alternate play, a mystery with three possible solutions, for which not even its author seems to have much affection. Anticipating by two years a musical adaptation of Dickens's *The Mystery of Edwin Drood* for which Rupert Holmes supplied multiple solutions, it resembles *Family Circles* in that the anticipated murder never takes place. Instead, the owner of a decaying Victorian mansion, like *Henceforward . . .*'s Jerome an unsuccessful composer, is about to leave his property to a former student, not to his siblings who are failed artists like himself, one a writer and one a painter. What seem to be attempted murders, all unsuccessful and none as amusing as the accidents in *Family Circles*, occur at predictable intervals, yet the composer suffers nothing more than a severe bump on the head. A private detective comes up with the wrong solution, accusing the only character who cannot be the bona fide culprit of any of the three solutions; but none of the "correct" solutions proves to be intriguing. An unconventional whodunnit, as one might expect from Ayckbourn, in that there is no corpse, *It Could Be Any One of Us* is surprising only in its lack of invention, thus not much fun. Even the uninspired method of choosing the culprit—

This can be pre-decided and arranged—or, more interestingly, the card game at the end of Act 1 Scene 1 can be used to pre-select a killer at random—depending on, say, who gets a certain card[19]

—suggests that Ayckbourn's heart was never in this belabored exercise.

Intimate Exchanges (1982), Ayckbourn's marathon alternate play that dwarfs in scope David Edgar's adaptation of Dickens's *Nicholas Nickleby,* even Shakespeare's history tetralogies, appears to have been a labor of love for the author and the two performers, Robin Herford and Lavinia Bertram, the longtime members of his company who comprised the entire cast of the eight interrelated plays with many alternate scenes and sixteen alternate endings—some thirty scenes in all and fourteen hours of dialogue—presented in the round in Scarborough in 1982 and in proscenium theaters in Greenwich and the West End two years later. Allowing Ayckbourn time to demonstrate a thesis that could only be tentatively suggested in the single-version *Family Circles*—that one's character remains basically stable, but the direction of a life can be changed by various relationships—*Intimate Exchanges* further explores the role of chance or choice in our lives, the theme of *Sisterly Feelings*. Like the latter play when its performances were not predetermined, Ayckbourn's "ultimate in alternatives"[20] once again brings the frenzy of backstage action to the fore.

Each version of *Intimate Exchanges* begins with the same scene: alone in her garden, Celia must decide whether or not to have a cigarette before 6 p.m. This trivial decision leads to more and more complex decisions on her part and on the part of the man who joins her soon afterwards—Miles, the director of the board of the Bilbury Lodge Preparatory School for Boys and Girls, where her husband Toby is headmaster; or Lionel, the school's groundskeeper. In various versions Celia either continues or breaks off her relationship with her husband and enters into or discourages a relationship with one of the other two. The three men explore further relationships with either Rowena, Miles's wife, or Sylvie, Celia's sometime helper around the house. Other characters who appear briefly, sometimes tellingly, are Celia's mother, Lionel's father, a strident clubwoman, and a polite cricketer. Before all the versions have run their course, the audience gets to know well, even affectionately, others with connections to the school who never appear—Colonel Malton, the board's elder statesman; Terry Hogg, the PE instructor; and Rachel, Sylvie's bright, overweight sister, a scholarship student, nicknamed Tubsy.

Each version is played in four scenes, all the scenes having alternates based on decisions that have ever more serious consequences. The first scene in the garden moves in one of two directions: Celia is interrupted either by Lionel or Miles. Should she decide to smoke a cigarette, Celia hears Lionel ring the doorbell. Should she decide against the cigarette, she goes into the garden shed momentarily, thus missing Lionel, encountering instead Miles when she emerges. Her initial conversation with Lionel leads to the first two possible variations of the next scene five days later, her alternate conversation with Miles to the last two possibilities—four alternative second scenes in all, all in the garden. The third scene, five weeks later, has eight variations—four for the Lionel sequences, four for the Miles sequences; these are set in any one of several places: the school grounds, a hotel terrace, a vicarage garden, a meadow, a cricket field, a golf course, a deserted clifftop. The fourth scene, always taking place in a churchyard five years later, subdivides so that there are sixteen possible conclusions—eight in the Lionel sequences, eight in the Miles sequences. The occasion for the final scenes may be a happy one—a wedding, a christening, the school's anniversary, a midnight mass, a harvest festival—or a sad one—a memorial service or a funeral.

A small-scale play despite its gargantuan underpinnings, *Intimate Exchanges* avoids the sensational and the melodramatic, but in its examination of the inception and the sometimes disintegration of the tenuous relationship of any two human beings, Ayckbourn continues to ask the question that so intrigues him: are our lives guided by chance or choice? In *Sisterly Feelings* it seems finally not to matter because each version ends in the same way, suggesting that something within our characters guides us whatever we will. In *Intimate Exchanges* Ayckbourn is not so certain. Chance or choice rules, but the sixteen separate endings dictate that the terrifying question is best left unanswered.

Metaphysics aside, Ayckbourn has by no means lost the knack of entertaining his audience. To do so, in *Intimate Exchanges* he presents his actors with their greatest challenge, which in turn provides yet another dimension for his audience. Unlike *Sisterly Feelings*, the course of each performance is set in advance, enabling returning spectators to seek out a version they have not seen before guided by eight subtitles: *Affairs in a Tent, Events on a Hotel Terrace, A Garden Fête, A Pageant, A Cricket Match, A Game of Golf, A One Man Protest, Love in the Mist*. All the characters in all eight versions are played by two performers, one man and one woman. In only one version are there as few as four characters, two of them male, two of them female. The maximum number of characters in a single version is eight—four men, four women. This means that each time one of the two performers leaves the stage, the audience is in a state of suspense: will uptight Celia reappear as sophisticated, all-knowing Rowena, as Celia's dowdy mother Josephine, as slovenly Sylvie, or overbearing

Irene Pridworthy? Will dithering Miles return as angry, drunken Toby, or sullenly arrogant Lionel, or Lionel's doddering father Joe? As in *How the Other Half Loves,* the audience is not only caught up in the characters' relationships, but in the mechanics of the perform- ance; but this time they are directed to contemplate what must be happening backstage. How does the performer change costume, wig, even girth so rapidly? How does he or she get from exiting side to opposite entering side? The single female performer must quarrel with herself offstage, even come to blows with herself behind the curtain of a make-shift stage. The single male performer must do the same in a garden shed and a cricket hut.

The least complicated version to follow through in that it has only four characters throughout—two for the male performer, two for the female performer—is *A Pageant,* in which the audience early on witnesses Lionel pursuing a relationship either with Celia or with Sylvie. Should Sylvie be the one, when Lionel suggests that she has much to learn about life, she asks Toby to become her tutor, to play Higgins to her Eliza. Her next decision alters the course of events that follow. She can either become engaged to Lionel or follow the path to self-discovery as Toby's star pupil. Despite Toby's realization that his growing fondness for Sylvie cannot lead to a lasting relationship, Sylvie, also smitten, would like to try.

In one of Ayckbourn's most frantic demonstrations that what can go wrong generally does, Toby must decide to cast either his wife or his pupil as Boadicea (in this play of alternatives he prefers to call her Boudicca) in the local pageant he is directing. On a collapsible make- shift stage under which Lionel, its builder, hammers away angrily, both women, equally unsuited to the role, rehearse. The decision is finally taken out of Toby's hands by the women themselves who battle for the role as well as the favors of the director. In one of the entire scheme's best moments, the one female performer has a knock-down, drag-out fight with herself behind the pageant curtain with first Celia's head, then Sylvie's head popping out from under it as the one, then the other, gets the upper hand. The scene ends with the victress of the fisticuffs becoming Boadicea, the warrior queen, riding off in a chariot, more of Lionel's none-too-sturdy handiwork, pulled by a reluctant Toby. The scene of course has alternate endings: it may be Celia or it may be Sylvie who at last triumphantly proclaims:

> Let men stay slaves but be it known that I
> Mere woman do intend to fight or die. (1:185, 187)

The concluding scene of *The Pageant,* like all of the scheme's final scenes, has two possibilities. Should Sylvie win out, she and Toby, together now for five years, attend a harvest festival at the church, but their relationship is far from perfect. As Toby says to Sylvie about Celia: "I behaved appallingly to her for twelve years because I didn't love her. I'm behaving badly to you because I love you too much. There must be a happy medium somewhere" (1:191). Should Celia win out and hold on to her husband, the still discontented couple belatedly discover that they were in complete agreement only once in their seventeen-year life together: at Sylvie and Lionel's church wedding, Celia admits for the first time that their own wedding was "absolutely awful" (1:196).

An "Author's Note" in the prefatory material of the published texts reads: "These plays were written originally for a cast of two. They could of course be performed by a larger cast but the end result would, in my view, be infinitely less satisfying." The difference between a cast of ten and a cast of two is the difference between one more satisfyingly funny Ayckbourn play with serious overtones and a rare theatrical treat, an exhilarating tour de force, hilarious in its execution yet sobering in its theme. Besides, additional actors diminish the effect of the theme, the possibilities within the relationship of any two persons. A larger cast might have simplified the lives of Herford and Bertram over a period of two years, but the two delighted in the most challenging roles of their careers. Herford has admitted that there were a few nightmare moments when one of them could see panic in the other's eyes, as one or the other momentarily lost track of the scene being played, of which alternate scene followed.[21] Two splendid professionals, however, completely trusting each other as well as the author-director who had entrusted them with a unique opportunity in a unique play, forged ahead every night to the alternate, concluding churchyard scene. Ayckbourn once again has made use of the A-effect as he provides another theater piece with a double focus throughout. In its exploration of relationships, *Intimate Exchanges* is recognizable as life; in the frantic activity it demands backstage, it offers its audience some insights into a life in the theater.

To appreciate fully Ayckbourn's considerable achievement in *Intimate Exchanges*, an audience must do more than sample its parts. Only a complete viewing reveals its balance of craft and artistry, yet few theatergoers, not even the drama critics of the London press, returned more than once or twice. Ayckbourn is too shrewd, too practical a man of the theater to have expected that *Intimate Exchanges* would become a national pastime with theatergoers returning once a week for two months to experience its major permutations. Whether to consider it finally a virtuoso piece or a lunatic folly depends on how one determines success in the theater; nonetheless, *Intimate Exchanges* deserves to be a source of satisfaction for its creators—its author-director and its actors. Of additional importance is its role in generating the impulse for a later single-version play requiring a mere two hours of stage traffic, *A Chorus of Disapproval* (1984), one of the playwright's worthiest successes, whatever the standard of measurement, a success not repeated by the 1989 film version adapted by Ayckbourn but not directed by him.

If all of *Intimate Exchanges* insists on the audience's simultaneous awareness of events on stage, offstage, and backstage, the version that best exemplifies the whole scheme is *The Pageant*, in which there is a stage on the stage as a play within a play is being rehearsed. Characters as actors move on the stage, off the stage, and behind—even beneath—the stage. The achievement of *A Chorus of Disapproval* is that the metaphor of theater in its entirety is clearly maintained and thoroughly explored in a single play performed by actors whose profession it is to transform themselves into characters who in this case transform themselves into actors. *A Chorus of Disapproval*, moving in circles, is not about characters in search of an author—they already have a remarkable one in Ayckbourn—but about characters in search of themselves using the theater to make possible that fulfillment. Structured as a circle, like Priestley's *Dangerous Corner* and *An Inspector Calls*, *A Chorus* ends as it begins with the conclusion of *The Beggar's Opera* and the company's curtain call. What follows the call, however, differs. In the beginning the others shun Guy as Macheath after taking their final bow. The second time round, his fellow actors embrace each other as well as their leading man as Ayckbourn illustrates John Gay's concluding couplet:

> But think of this Maxim, and Put off your Sorrow,
> The Wretch of To-day, may be happy To-morrow. [22]

As he deconstructs *The Beggar's Opera*, Ayckbourn enables his audience to follow a play from audition through rehearsal to performance, all the while establishing the relevance of theater, the need for its mirroring function. Lonely, friendless Guy, a recent widower, auditions for hyperactive, insensitive director Dafydd, a messianic Welshman obsessed with the theater, during a rehearsal break. The Pendon Amateur Light Opera Societey, three months away from a performance of Gay's ballad opera, still needs bit players to complete the cast, and Dafydd is an old hand at persuading his victims that even the tiniest part is practically a lead. Guy's audition in *A Chorus of Disapproval*, not unlike the same process in the quintessential backstage musical, *A Chorus Line* (1975), in that the director is at times an unseen presence barking orders and firing questions at a quaking applicant, proves satisfactory. When Dafydd, actually a solicitor, learns that Guy is employed in Alternative Forward Costing for BLM, "a multinational company that's become extremely diversified" (38), he is especially eager to have him in his cast and under his thumb. Guy, he thinks, may be useful to him in his backstage maneuverings in a land deal with other members of the cast, all of them upstanding citizens of the local community. Those others are also eager to become Guy's friends, their wives something more. As in *The Beggar's Opera*, money and sex are the world's driving forces.

The ballads sung in their rehearsals act as counterpoint, as in Brecht's *Die Dreigroschenoper* (1928), to the offstage lives of Ayckbourn's characters. Gay's eighteenth-century Britain, Sir Robert Walpole at the helm, becomes interchangeable with Guy's Britain with Mrs. Thatcher controlling the purse strings. Gay's unsentimental triangle with Polly and Lucy battling over Macheath, paralleled by the headmaster-director's wife and pupil vying for his favors in *The Pageant*, is twice parodied in *A Chorus of Disapproval*. First Dafydd's wife Hannah and another woman create a scene in a restaurant, vociferously arguing over their rights to Guy or, rather, a stray pair of underpants that may or may not be his; then two younger women in the company come to blows over the young punk initially cast as Macheath, whom Guy replaces.

The interplay of theater and life is comically highlighted as Guy and Hannah attempt a private conversation on the deserted stage only to be interrupted by Dafydd directing his light man to refocus various lamps, all of which manage to spotlight the unhappy couple desperately trying to hide themselves as well as their relationship. A production of *A Chorus of Disapproval* by Chicago's Court Theatre presented in tandem with *The Beggar's Opera* (1990) cleverly involved the audience in the scene as the nervous light man on a grid directly over the auditorium dropped his colored gels right on the theatergoers' heads. Life in the theater may be as perilous for the audience as it is for the director, actors, and stage crew.

Theater reflects life, Ayckbourn tells his audience, but few care. Dafydd, like *Henceforward . . .*'s Jerome, considers himself an artist and has no time, like Ayckbourn himself perhaps, for domestic arrangements. Dafydd's twin daughters, seeing so little of their father, have a large, homemade, male rag-doll they call "Other Daddy" (31) or "Daddy-doll" (39). Committed to the theater, the director of the Pendon Amateur Light Opera Society involves himself in unethical financial deals to survive. The director of the Stephen Joseph Theatre in the Round, his small Scarborough company always in need of more financial assistance than it receives, must himself walk a tightrope between art and commerce. More professional and more ethical than the character of the Welsh director, Ayckbourn has put what must be his own thoughts, his own frustrations, into Dafydd's mouth: "Nobody really cares. Not in this country. Anything you want to mention's more important than theatre to most of them. Washing their hair, cleaning their cars. . . . If this was Bulgaria or somewhere we'd have peasants hammering on the doors. Demanding satisfaction or their money back. This place, you tell them you're interested in the arts, you get messages of sympathy. Get well soon" (76–77).

A Chorus of Disapproval demonstrates a society's need for the art of the theater, not merely as entertainment, but as a means of seeing the past in the present and the present in the past, thereby shedding light on age-old problems of existence. Whereas Ayckbourn's play, like Gay's, comments on the morality, or lack of it, on the part of a society's leaders, a primary concern here as elsewhere in his work involves chance or choice as life's determining factor. Which matters more in deciding the ultimate destinies of Macheath and Guy? Once again the question has no easy answer. Ayckbourn approaches the dilemma by inverting the career and fate of Gay's hero. Macheath is very much in charge as he shapes his own life, only to be betrayed by his "friends." Aware, finally, that he has no control over his destiny, he is about to be hanged when chance intervenes and he is reprieved by the whim of the Beggar-Author. Guy, Ayckbourn's diffident, complacent "hero," despite a meteoric rise through the ranks of the Pendon Amateur Light Opera Society, is never in control, never even aware of how he is being used, bribed, and betrayed by others in the corrupt land deal, as he moves from bed to bed and progresses from the minor role of Crook-Fingered Jack, to the supporting roles of Matt of the Mint and Filch, and finally to the principal role of Macheath. Supplying alternate endngs for *A Chorus of Disapproval* with one of those endings coming at its beginning, Ayckbourn suggests, as does Gay, that society may impose a system of seemingly just punishments for the unethical, but there is always the possibility of a deus-ex-machina proffering unmerited rewards. It would seem wise, however, not to pin all one's hopes on any man-made system of justice.

As he manipulates stage space and breaks theatrical boundaries, Ayckbourn is in his own way providing a new definition for the unities of time, place, and action, the Aristotelian tradition in which he is still immersed. In seeming to flail against that tradition, Ayckbourn actually aligns technique and theme. As Oedipus flailed against his pre-ordained destiny, Ayckbourn's characters desperately make their choices only to learn that chance too plays a role in the shaping of their lives. Ultimately the playwright himself must play God to his characters—first creating them, then directing the actors who embody them—but in arranging alternative possibilities Ayckbourn playfully allows the actors themselves, seemingly, to have a hand in their characters' destinies. If the Aristotelian tradition itself constrains fate within the bounds of one time, one place, one action, Ayckbourn's alternative scenes adhere to the same unities, but he has expanded them beyond the stage to the unity of the entire theater. In *How the Other Half Loves*, two times are one time; in *The Norman Conquests*, three plays in three places are one time, one place. In *Intimate Exchanges*, eight actions with sixteen conclusions are one action as each character explores all of life's relationships in a single, but expanding, pairing of the male and female. In *A Chorus of Disapproval*, 1728 is 1984 or any year as theater in all its aspects and dimensions mirrors life itself. As long as Ayckbourn's frantic performers manage to avoid a fatal collision in some part of the theater—on stage, offstage, backstage—he may continue to explore the limits of the Aristotelian tradition leaving his audience, as usual, helpless with laughter as they contemplate the mirrored traffic jams of their own none-too-blissful lives.

4
Women In and Out of Mind

"A lot of my plays," Ayckbourn has told an interviewer, "are generated out of the sheer excitement of working with actors." His own early career as a performer has, he knows, provided invaluable experience for him as dramatist and director: "I can understand how actors normally think and feel. . . . The old mistake that one still sometimes makes is to slightly underestimate what an actor can do with three words as opposed to thirty-five."[1] Having directed his own company in the Scarborough premiere of *A Chorus of Disapproval*, Ayckbourn had the unusual experience of directing two other companies in the same play within a matter of months, one for London's National Theatre, the other with a mostly new cast for the play's subsequent transfer to a West End house. A change of cast provides yet another kind of alternate for an Ayckbourn play, the author likening the *A Chorus of Disapproval* experience to having "two bites of the cherry": "Working with two extraordinary actors, first Michael Gambon then Colin Blakely on the same part [the Welsh director], was very exciting because Colin came along and gave a totally different reading yet one that was absolutely valid. To have two performances of that calibre on the same play is just a wonderful gift to a writer. . . . When you've got all the added ingredients of an actor's personality, skills and charisma added to a part you've written; that can be really exciting."[2]

Ayckbourn's *Woman in Mind*, produced in the West End in 1986, a year after its first presentation in Scarborough, exists in a single version. There are no alternate scenes, no differing conclusions. Every audience fortunate enough to have attended it during the first months of its London run saw the same play and, until she left the company, the same remarkable performance by Julia McKenzie, several critics calling it her finest portrayal in the best role the actress, usually associated with musicals, had ever had the opportunity to play.[3] Audiences at London's Vaudeville Theatre, despite not having to choose a particular version, were nonetheless seeing yet another Ayckbourn alternate play—of sorts. *Woman in Mind* is presented through the subjective point of view of a woman losing her grasp of reality. Discovered in her garden after stepping on the end of a rake that popped up and hit her in the head, causing a concussion, Susan is attended not only by a doctor and the members of her family, but also by an alternate family of husband, daughter, and brother, in personality and attitude the direct opposites of her actual husband, son, and sister-in-law. The play shifts fluidly between the real and the imagined—the latter in effect a subtext for the former—until the moment of her total mental breakdown when all the characters, the real and the ideal, merge in a surreal nightmare from which there is no awakening, imagined or otherwise. What makes the play effective in its movement from naturalism to expressionism is that the protagonist, until the onset of madness, is a seemingly average human being, ordinary but troubled—a twentieth-century Everywoman.

One age's technical advances in drama are eventually taken for granted and absorbed by the next. The Brechtian devices, for example, in another play that focuses on a disturbed mind, *Equus*, in which the characters narrate their story on a nearly bare stage and move in and out of their scenes while remaining onstage in view of the audience, were as effective in 1973 as they had been when the German dramatist employed them for a different purpose a generation earlier. Brecht wanted to distance his audience, to make them think. Shaffer, on the other hand, wanted to stun his audience, to make them feel, and did so primarily by placing at the center of his play two indelible characters, the psychiatrist and his patient, whose conflict the staging helped to define. So too with Ayckbourn. The A-effect, his unusual focus on the actor as both character and performer, adds a dimension to his plays when they are staged, yet, like all works that are effective in the theater, the plays essentially engage their audiences by offering them a mirror image of themselves, a method shared by the most successful comic playwrights from Shakespeare to Ben Travers. Responsible for some of the most popular plays of the twenties and thirties, Travers acknowledged that his theory of farce depended first of all on recognizable character types in initially credible situations that gradually became more dangerous or outrageous.[4]

Ayckbourn, who dedicated *Taking Steps* to Travers, goes beyond the author of such classic farces as *Rookery Nook*, *Thark*, and *Plunder* in creating not merely character types but characters of depth. As he concocted his Aldwych farces, Travers knew the actors in the company for which he was writing. In play after play he provided parts perfectly tailored to the special talents of his favorite clowns—Tom Walls, the sophisticated bounder, and Ralph Lynn, the inept flounderer—making his characters nearly interchangeable from one work to another. Not so with Ayckbourn. Although he knows the Scarborough company he initially writes for just as intimately as Travers knew the Aldwych regulars, for Ayckbourn character precedes actor, or so he insists.[5] As a result he has fashioned such varied characters as the extroverted, eccentric Dafydd in *A Chorus of Disapproval*; Jack Mc-Cracken, who begins *A Small Family Business* as a down-to-earth businessman unusual only in being honest; and the introverted Doug-las Beechey, out of his element in *Man of the Moment*, that have become memorable, highly-acclaimed performances by a single, first-rate actor—Michael Gambon.

The common denominator for the three roles, what enables one gifted actor to play them all, is the depth of the characterizations, their ring of truth. An audience recognizes their humanity, knows that such persons can and do exist. Despite the extraordinary theatrical fireworks of innovative stagecraft and alternate versions, what makes Ayckbourn one of the foremost dramatists of the latter half of the century is that his plays depend finally not on technical breakthroughs but on the sensitivity with which he handles his subject matter—people going about the everyday process of living. Ayckbourn offers expert actors roles that they can develop under his own guidance as director into full-scale portraits, at once funny and sad, of contempo-rary man and woman.

Behind the plaudits that greeted Julia McKenzie's performance as Susan in *Woman in Mind* was the sad fact that many in the audience, despite the character's disorientation, found the play, more so than any other Ayckbourn comedy, a painfully disturbing experience in-volving intense identification. It was not McKenzie's first essay of an Ayckbourn role; she had played Helen in *Ten Times Table* on stage and Diana in *Absent Friends*, another victim of a breakdown, on television. Nor was it Ayckbourn's first drawing of a woman at the end of her tether; he had been reshaping the character, refining it, ever since his very first play.

Alice Glover in *The Square Cat* is a bored housewife. At one time in love with her husband, she had had a rapturous honeymoon. But neither Alice nor Sidney Glover is young any more. Sidney, no longer romantic, is oblivious to his wife's dissatisfaction, her yearning for mystery and the reawakening of sexual appetite. If there is to be romance in her life, Alice must find it for herself. The comedy ends conventionally with the expected reconciliation of husband and wife, but the ecstacy of love is offered only to the younger couple, the Glovers's daughter Sue and Arthur Brummage, who in the guise of Jerry Wattis had been the object of Alice's frustrated desires.

Sheila in *Relatively Speaking*, aware that her husband Philip is a philanderer, must invent romance for herself. With mysterious letters arriving for her on weekends, the only time Philip is sure to be at home, she hints that she may have to visit Natalie, a cousin her husband has never before heard of, in her country cottage some weekend. But Philip refuses to play her game, to enact the jealous husband: "You're certainly not fooling me and what's more you know you're not. So why bother to keep on with. . . . this fatuous rigmarole. Every damn weekend. I feel I'm humoring a lunatic half the time. Is he coming today? Has he written? Has he phoned? Well, I've played along long enough. I'm sick and tired of it, do you hear? That's it. I seriously think you ought to go and see a doctor. You're . . . (*Gesture of insanity.*)"[6]

That an unhappy, unsatisfied wife might take refuge in madness is first indicated in *Relatively Speaking*, but Ayckbourn himself seems not to take the suggestion seriously—for the moment, for perhaps everyone in the play is just a bit mad. Arriving in the country, Greg, a character who admits to never being sure who he is when he first awakens (13), has a curious cross-purpose conversation with Philip, who begins to believe that perhaps he is in fact his wife's lover whose existence he had doubted, that evokes Greg's assessment of the other's sanity: "You're a bit round the twist, aren't you?" (42). When, later, part of their misunderstanding is cleared up, Greg says, "You must have thought I was rather peculiar too, come to that," to which Philip confesses, "I'm afraid I did, rather" (63). Not yet fully convinced that the other is sane, Greg tells Philip's wife, "He does appear to me to be quite definitely a bit unhinged," which comes as no surprise to Sheila, who admits that she had recently suggested to a doctor that her husband might be a psychopath. Fortunately, the "rather deaf" doctor seems not to have noticed (75–76). But Sheila's conversation with Greg takes such a peculiar turn concerning the question of Ginny's legitimacy, that she is soon forced to transfer her suspicions of insanity to Greg: "You know, you really are completely mad" (78).

If finally no one is actually mad in *Relatively Speaking*, least of all Sheila, who ends the play more aware than all the others despite her seeming at first to be the least stable of the lot, all of them are understandably confused. Accusations of madness merely add to the fun of the delightful game that Ayckbourn is playing with his bewildered characters and his delighted audience. Yet the eventual cause of the breakdowns for several of the playwright's female characters is suggested throughout the play. When Ginny warns Greg that he may not really know her, that "compared to someone else I might be the biggest bitch on earth," and her anxious suitor asks if that is true, she answers, "Be bad luck if we married and then you found out, wouldn't it?" (19). Philip, suggesting to Sheila that she, like himself, surely wants some time to herself, holds up their friends the Coopers as the perfect example of wedded bliss: "Married nearly thirty years. Couldn't have a happier couple. I'm sure it's because he spends nine months of the year in Rio de Janeiro" (26). Sheila, wishing Ginny well, points to marriage's major pitfall: "No matter how much you think you know someone it's always a gamble in the end" (49). And Philip and Sheila, supposedly discussing a hypothetical third party, have a telling exchange:

Sheila: If he was all that remarkable he wouldn't be carrying on behind his wife's back, would he?
Philip: Unless he had a singularly unremarkable wife.
Sheila: Probably his fault if she was. Presumably he was quite happy with her when he married her.
Philip: Perhaps she proved a bit of a disappointment, though. Pretended to be something she wasn't and then turned out to be quite different.
Sheila: He probably did the same to her. (74)

Sheila's final pronouncement on the Ginny-Greg relationship is sadly prophetic for all Ayckbourn's subsequent married couples: "Quite wrong for each other of course. It'll be a disastrous marriage but great fun for them while it lasts" (86).

In a forthright conversation with Ian Watson, Ayckbourn revealed that his own unsatisfactory marriage is at the root of his constant depiction of wedded non-bliss: "I was so rudely hurled into a so-called permanent relationship so early, I became very angry about the fact that nobody told us." But what he sees around him merely confirms his views: "The marriages I do see are either fraught or dull. There are one or two very happy ones, but that's probably because they're new. In general, I don't think people were meant to live with each other for too long. . . . As soon as people feel that they are married, there's a sense of entrapment. That was certainly my reaction."[7]

Although church and society may deny it, the basis of most relationships is sexual. Ayckbourn believes that the expectations young men and women have of one another cannot be fulfilled. Referring to a notorious but popular British tabloid, he told Watson, "There aren't any page three *Sun* women, apart from on page three of the *Sun*." Of "those super blokes that step out of the screen," the male about whom the female fantasizes, Ayckbourn allowed for the intrusion of reality: "They're actually sweaty and spotty."[8]

While some relationships consist of two equal partners in constant shouting matches, even physical battles, what Ayckbourn has often been aware of is that one partner becomes dominant over the other.

While it may be the female who gets the upper hand over the male, forcing the "poor little sod" to have his cigarette out by the garden shed because she "won't have tobacco smoke in the house," the more common occurrence, or so it would seem from the frequency with which it occurs in the Ayckbourn canon, is the wife who "by slow erosion" will "just whittle away" in "a long-term marathon."[9] Ginny in *Relatively Speaking,* a stronger personality than Greg, will obviously never allow that to be her fate, but she suggests to Philip why it has already happened to Sheila. Wanting out of her relationship with Philip, she makes clear to him that she could never be the kind of wife he wants, he needs, he has in Sheila:

> Philip—be honest. Could you really do without her?. . . . Ask yourself, as you're sitting there now, full of the breakfast that she's cooked for you, sitting in the sunshine, waiting for the lunch that's bound to be coming—and the tea and the supper. And you know she'll have made the bed for you, not like me. You'll even get your glass of hot milk, I expect. And your clean shirt in the morning, and your change of socks. They'll be waiting when you get up. And that's all Sheila. I bet she even cleans the bath out after you, doesn't she?

"Now and again," Philip can only mutter reluctantly (55).

Preparing meals, tidying up, accepting the blame for her husband's mistakes, obliging his every whim is the lot of another Ayckbourn wife, Jane in *Absurd Person Singular,* who is kept so busy with her chores at home and in her husband's shop that she has no time to realize how unhappy she is. In one of Ayckbourn's most triumphantly bleak farces, coming surprisingly early in his career, three couples of differing classes are shown to have one aspect of their lives in common, their dreadful marriages. While Jane, like Mary Featherstone in *How the Other Half Loves* a chronic cleaner and duster whether in her own home or another's, will not face her situation as she plays acolyte to her upwardly mobile husband, the play's two other wives no longer pretend to anything other than their misery. This time no young lovers in passionate heat relieve the almost unbearably comic gloom. The three couples entertain each other on three successive Christmas Eves during which the guests along with their hosts spend most of the evening in the kitchen—Jane and Sidney Hopcroft's in a small suburban house in act 1, Eva and Geoffrey Jackson's in a fourth-floor flat in act 2, and Marion and Ronald Brewster-Wright's in an old Victorian house in act 3. With class warfare at the forefront of the play, the dramatist allows at least equal time to another raging battle so evident in his work, the battle of the sexes.

Jane is a constant source of embarrassment to nakedly ambitious Sidney as, single-handed, she turns the first act into a Feydeau-like farce by dashing in and out of doors dressed for the inclement weather in wellington boots, her husband's rain gear too large for her, and an old trilby hat. Both of them hope that the others will neither notice nor recognize the curious-looking apparition that dashes through the house. But the Hopcrofts have run out of tonic, her fault according to Sidney. And Jane, whose credo is, "I don't want to let you down" (19), is off to the off-license. Not wanting to cause Sidney any further embarrassment once she discovers she has been locked out, she spends the rest of the evening in the garden getting soaked in the downpour. Ronald, a banker, has spent the evening reading the instruction book for the stove while his equally bored wife admires the "apartheid" washing machine that separates "whites" from "coloureds" (25). The party, an obvious disaster, is judged to have come off "rather satisfactorily" by Sidney because "these people just weren't anybody." Cautioned by her husband not to get worked up over the situation, Jane solaces herself in what appears to be her customary manner: singing to herself, she picks up a damp cloth and contentedly begins "a full-scale cleaning operation" (43–44).

In the first act Geoffrey and Eva make clear what has undermined their marriage. "As far as he's concerned, my existence ended the day he married me," she says; "I'm just an embarrassing smudge on a marriage license" (32). Geoffrey, an unsuccessful architect but an accomplished womanizer, as his wife knows only too well, tells the men, "She chooses to live with me, she lives by my rules" (40). At the Hopcroft party Eva, taking pills to quiet her nerves, hands the tinfoil that contained them to Sidney and tosses the water glass into a waste bin. Realizing her mistake, she tells her host, "My God, I knew it, I'm going mad. I am finally going mad" (32).

Unlike the characters in *Relatively Speaking*, whose mental states are questioned by one another, Eva is Ayckbourn's first character to have an actual if temporary brush with insanity. By the second act she has been reduced to a zombie existing on a mixture of alcohol and pills. Having been informed by her husband that he is about to move out and live with another woman, Eva, in her dressing gown, unconcerned that guests are about to arrive, spends the evening attempting suicide. Finding her with her head in the oven, Jane assumes that she is trying to clean it and happily takes over. In a series of increasingly frenetic comic failures, more bizarre than a related scene in Beth Henley's later *Crimes of the Heart* (1980), Eva tries jumping to her death, stabbing herself, electrocuting herself, hanging, and overdosing. At every attempt, her guests, oblivious to what is actually occurring, save her by shunting her from one corner of the kitchen to another. Sidney even uses the paper her suicide notes are written on to draw plans for unclogging her sink and repairing an electrical fixture. Before the evening ends, Sidney, under the sink, is drenched when his wife, unaware of the poetic justice of the moment, pours water down the unplugged drain, and, what is worse, Ronald, tinkering with the wiring, suffers a severe electrical shock. Through it all Eva remains unwillingly, unmercifully alive. Not having spoken a single word in the entire act, she ends it by leading the others in a chorus of "On the First Day of Christmas" (69).

In the third act Marion, increasingly bored with her lot in life, has confined herself to her bedroom, where she steadily, secretly drinks. With the heating in the old house on the blink for weeks, she will remain "almost in a state of hibernation" (71) until her ineffectual husband manages to have the system repaired. In the meantime, he stays out of her room and she out of his; despite living together, they see very little of one another. Ronald admits to Eva, now fully recovered, and in a somewhat incredible reversal, taking over the running of her inept husband's business affairs, that he has no understanding whatsoever of women, his two wives included, their unaccountable depressions and unexpected rages. The now seemingly placid Marion, he reveals, once lived on her nerves, "was really one of the jumpiest girls you could ever hope to meet. . . . She's much calmer since she's been with me. If I've done nothing else for her, I've acted as a sort of sedative" (73). What Ronald mistakes for calm is inner desperation. Marion too, admitting to self-loathing, is dangerously near a breakdown. Reminded of her mortality by seeing her once beautiful, now ravished face in a mirror, she bursts into tears (81). Her husband cannot solace her, but another glass of gin helps.

The savage comedy ends with a dance, not a harmonious return to order, mate paired with mate, but a *danse macabre* of individuals jumping, hopping, twirling grotesquely. Calling the tune, Sidney, now a building developer on whom the others depend for their livelihood, forces the rest into a game of forfeits involving apples under the chin, oranges between the knees, pears on spoons in the mouth, as he exhorts them hysterically to "Dance. Dance. Keep dancing. Dance . . ." (93). Three wedded couples, together but alone, must dance or die. Eva may have regained her sanity, but, as Ayckbourn's audience continues to laugh, a world has gone mad.

Three other wedded couples comprise most of the cast of *Absent Friends*, although Marge's husband Gordon, sick in bed at home, never appears. Marge is more nursemaid than wife to the husband she pampers. Everlyn has only contempt for her weak salesman husband John, who subsists on the business his friend Paul throws his way. With her husband's humiliation perhaps a stronger impetus than her own quest for sexual fulfillment, Evelyn has already thrown herself Paul's way, briefly, providing satisfaction for no one, least of all Paul's wife Diana who is aware of her husband's infidelities. Instead of contrasting the unhappiness of established couples with the happiness of young lovers, in *Absent Friends* Ayckbourn suggests that the ideal relationship is one that is imagined rather than actually experienced. Of all the characters in the play only Colin is contented, his situation even more preferable than that of Mr. Cooper, Philip's friend in *Relatively Speaking*, who spends all of nine months each year apart from his wife. Colin has no wife at all, his fiancée, Carol, having drowned before their marriage.

The character least able to cope with her decaying marriage is Diana, who demonstrates that irrational behavior need not be traced to alcohol or pills. She can accept her husband's adultery, she tries to convince herself; it is his deception that she cannot tolerate: "If he takes the trouble, like last Saturday, to tell me he's just going down the road to the football match, he might at least choose a day when they're playing at home" (101). Unlike Eva, who makes a recovery in the third act of *Absurd Person Singular* from her second-act breakdown, unlike Caroline, reeking of gin, who is discovered in a paralyzing depression at the opening of *Suburan Strains* but is soberly reunited—tentatively—with her husband at the conclusion, prim and proper Diana, her outlook bleak, loses total control in the play's waning moments.

What has meant salvation for many women, a dedication to their role as mother, is no solution for Ayckbourn's female characters. Teresa's child is forever in her way in *How the Other Half Loves*. The Brewster-Wrights' sons in *Absurd Person Singular* are yet another nuisance, bringing them less joy than George, her ferocious dog, provides the childless Eva Jackson. Evelyn in *Absent Friends* ignores her baby the others coo over; Diana's children have not enabled her to keep her sanity. The one live Ayckbourn character, as opposed to the maternally programmed robot Nan 300F in *Henceforward . . .*, who exists totally as mother is Lucy in "Mother Figure," a one-act play, part of *Confusions*. With her salesman husband usually away, Lucy is trapped at home as she cares for her three tots, unseen in an adjoining room. When Rosemary, who lives next door, suggests her time with her children is "time well spent," Lucy responds, "I haven't much option."[10] Lucy's husband Harry, unable to get through to his wife on the telephone, has called Rosemary, asking her to check on his family: Lucy as well as the children are fine; she is simply too busy to answer the phone. By the end of the brief but sadly amusing sketch, Lucy has reduced her neighbors, Rosemary and her husband Terry, to two more squabbling children. Only as mother can Lucy relate to another human being.

Seven years before Michael Billington dubbed Ayckbourn "our leading feminist dramatist" in his review of *Woman in Mind*,[11] two years before the first publication of Watson's *Conversations with Ayckbourn* (1981), the playwright revealed to another interviewer, Janet Watts, a thoughtful concern for women contemplating their position at home and in society in a supposedly enlightened age of liberation for the female sex. Ayckbourn agreed that the women in his plays suffered "more than the men—and from the men," but he believed that what was true of the plays was true in life as well. "There's a huge change of role going on at the moment," he said, "and for that reason it's a fascinating period to chronicle, but I don't think it's helped every woman. It has helped a few; it has made others schizophrenic and guilty. Because what do they do now?"[12] One female character who has no answer, who cannot bring herself to ask the question, who is even incapable of speech by the end of the play, is Vera in *Just Between Ourselves*.

Ayckbourn calls the grim comedy "the first of my winter plays" (7). Unlike his earlier work that was "written in late spring for performance during the Scarborough summer season," *Just Between Ourselves* was composed in December of 1975 for performance in January as his company, in preparation for its change from a summer repertory policy and its move from the makeshift Library Theatre to a new year-round home, sought "permanency within the town" by encouraging and developing a "much needed winter audience." Because of the proposed move, Ayckbourn for the first time was relieved of the pressure of producing a play "suited primarily to a holiday audience." He started his new play at night, as was then his custom, as wintry "North Sea storms hurtled round the house . . . and metal chimney cowlings were bounced off parked cars below my window, rebounding hither and thither like demented pinballs." The dramatist contends, however, that he is no "strong believer that the time of year wields some astrological influence over what one writes." The Scarborough theatergoers who had already seen *Absurd Person Singular*, *Absent Friends*, and *Confusions* within a period of four years, despite the more benign tone of *The Norman Conquests* and *Bedroom Farce* in the same period, had to be aware of which way the wind was blowing. They could not have been completely taken by surprise by a play, as Ayckbourn describes it, "with themes concerned with total lack of

understanding, with growing old and with spiritual and mental collapse."

When he began *Just Between Ourselves*, Ayckbourn told an interviewer, he thought he was writing about "a man who hasn't any
friends, who is very, very nice." But out of the corner of his eye he saw
the man's wife. Originally intended as a subsidiary character, she
suddenly became the play's "riveting point of interest."[13] Where
Diana's breakdown in *Absent Friends*, as credible as it is, occurs
unexpectedly, Vera's nervous collapse seems inevitable, complete,
and irreversible. Constantly at odds with her live-in mother-in-law,
she has no one to turn to—no friends, only her embarrassed acquaintances, Neil and Pam, who are themselves at the point of giving up on
a loveless marriage. All the while her husband Dennis spends his
leisure hours puttering about a garage, the play's setting, that is as
hopelessly messy as his life, ineffectually tinkering with faulty ap-
pliances, all of which he only makes worse. Typically, he is trying to
sell a car he cannot get out of the garage because of a malfunctioning
"up and over door."

Dennis's method of coping is to laugh away his problems—the door,
the car, even the wife drifting unnoticed into catatonia—and Vera
cannot penetrate his cheerful oblivion. She had been to a doctor but
had stopped seeing him when he declared her "nearly better" some
months earlier. As her condition worsens, Dennis is convinced she is
progressing, even though Marjorie, his mother, tries to make him see
that "when it's up here, in your head, it's there for good" (30). Amused
by her constantly dropping and breaking things, Dennis teases her
unmercifully, completely unaware how insensitive, even cruel, he is
being. Cautioning others not to laugh at her mishaps, Dennis does so
himself. When Marjorie points out that Vera burst into tears when she
dropped the kettle he is busily repairing, he tells her he is "not
surprised. So did I. Nearly brand new this is." Vera is merely in a rut,
he believes: "She needs cheering up. Taking out of herself. She takes
life too seriously." Making one last, desperate effort to penetrate his
imperturbable calm, Vera pleads with him: "I think I need help,
Dennis. . . . I need help, Dennis." But her husband is still unable,
unwilling to comprehend: "You're not being clear, Vee. You say help
but what sort of help do you mean? . . . . Well, look, tell you what.
When you've got a moment, why don't you sit down, get a bit of paper
and just make a little list of all the things you'd like me to help you
with. Things you'd like me to do, things that need mending or
fixing. . . . (53–54).

Dennis and Vera are not the only husband and wife incapable of communicating. Pam and Neil cannot be forthright with one another either. Unlike an Ayckbourn alternate play where the dramatist himself supplies other possibilities as the subtext of one version gives way to the text of another version, in *Just Between Ourselves,* as in the works of Chekhov that seem to be its model, the audience must hear for themselves the unspoken words of an unfinished teatime conversation:

> *Neil:* I thought you said you wanted to go to night classes.
> *Pam:* There's lots of things I want, Neil. But they're not to be, are they? If you follow me . . .
> *Neil:* How do you mean?
> *Pam:* You know.
> *Neil:* No, what?
> *Pam:* You know perfectly well.
> *Neil:* What?
> *Pam:* I'm not spelling it out, Neil.
> *Neil:* Oh.
> *Pam:* Yes. That.
> *Neil:* Well I . . . *(He picks up a sandwich, embarrassed, and chews it.)* It's not that I . . . well . . .
> *Pam:* You're eating cucumber.
> *Neil:* Oh, God. (35)

Even as Chekhov lightens the mood at the opening of the second act of *The Cherry Orchard* by having Charlotta bite into a cucumber after her sad plaint about not knowing who she is, Ayckbourn has Neil, suffering from chronic indigestion, eat the cucumber sandwich he had been studiously avoiding. Taking his cue from Chekhov, who wrote, "Let the things that happen on the stage be as complex and yet just as simple as they are in life. For instance, people are having a meal at the table, just having a meal, but at the same time their happiness is being created, or their lives are being smashed up,"[14] Ayckbourn frequently draws upon scenes of middle-class rituals involving food—unsuitable food, too little, or too much. More than mere humorous touches, the scenes underscore specific personality traits. In *Table Manners* in *The Norman Conquests* the family shares a meager salad, the only complaints coming from Norman, who cannot refrain from drawing attention to the well-prepared lettuce (69). In *Sisterly Feelings* a none-too-pleased and hardly uncomplaining Uncle Len, continually bypassed as the picnic sandwiches are carefully apportioned, ends up with an empty plate (37–39), as does Austin in *Wildest Dreams* when his sister and her husband themselves eat the sandwiches they had prepared for him—a momentary revenge for his years of bullying. In *Events on a Hotel Terrace* in *Intimate Ecxhanges*, Celia has a decidedly different problem: ingeniously inept Lionel, working as a waiter, forces her to eat countless sandwiches and drink as many cups of tea, the only way he can approach her to profess his love (1:79–89). That each of the four scenes of *Just Between Ourselves* takes place during a birthday observance for each of the characters adds an ironic counterpoint to a Chekhovian play about wasted lives.

Whereas Neil and Pam cannot speak honestly and openly to one another, each one separately voices his troubles to Dennis, who is a bit more sympathetic to them than he is to his wife. Neil speaks more candidly than does his wife about her unfulfilled sexual needs, and it is left to Pam to express to Dennis the affliction of the middle-class, middle-aged, prototypical Ayckbourn female, herself and Vera included: "I feel old, Dennis—old, unfulfilled, frustrated, unattractive, dull, washed out, undesirable—you name it. And I've got absolutely nothing to look forward to" (56).

At least capable of expressing her predicament, if only to a third party, although unable to resolve it, Pam remains discontentedly sane. Vera's situation, as Ayckbourn himself analyzes it in the play's preface, is more serious: "The wife, Vera, hampered by a lack of ability to express herself clearly or maybe too inhibited to do so, suffers from a conventional upbringing that has taught her that the odds on her being wrong and her husband right are high. Slowly, the last vestiges of self-confidence are drained from her" (7–8). As the play ends she sits outdoors enveloped in a large rug on a chilly January morning, totally withdrawn into a world of her own. When the others sing happy birthday to her, her *"lips move silently with them"* (67). Like Chekhov's three sisters she is out-of-doors, dispossessed, her house taken over by another, a mother-in-law rather than a sister-in-law. At the beginning of the play her husband wanted the car out of the garage so that he could get his other car, the one that works, under cover. As the play progresses, the price he is asking for the garaged vehicle keeps falling. By the end of the play he is prepared to give it away. Vera's value too has dropped as drastically. Still, Dennis would "sooner she was in" rather than outside, "exposed to all the elements. I'd be happier. I think we'd all be happier if she was under cover" (63). Vera has become an object, another of Dennis's broken possessions, like the car and the kettle, no longer in working order.

Vera's words fail her; Dennis makes jokes. In *Intimate Exchanges* Celia's past attempts at serious conversations with her husband have deteriorated into their present shouting matches. When Celia insists that they did not shout in the early days, Toby explains why: "We didn't talk to each other in the early days." "If people stopped talking to each other, there wouldn't be any misunderstandings. . . . We sort of half-talk, that's the trouble," Toby tells his wife: "We don't say whole things. We say half things. Because we're frightened the whole thing might be too much for the other one to swallow." He admits that their conversations confuse him: "What on earth did she mean by that? Did she mean what I thought she said? . . . . Only of course, you didn't mean that at all. . . . So you'd have been better off saying nothing in the first place" (*Affairs in a Tent*, 1:17–18). "If I thought you meant half the things you said," Celia tells him, invoking an Ayckbourn wife's favorite form of punishment for her husband, "I'd pour this tea over your head, I really would."

Ayckbourn recognizes, as did Chekhov in *The Cherry Orchard*, Strindberg in *The Ghost Sonata*, and Pirandello in *Six Characters in Search of an Author*, that words can damage as well as mitigate or explain. Empty talk of the weather, polite questions—"How was your day?"—are silences filled with sound. Words can be a screen behind which the speaker hides. They can be misconstrued, inflicting unintended pain. "I've always said a lot of awful things to you," Toby says to Celia, "Let's face it. The mainstay of our whole relationship is based on it. Me saying awful things to you and you accepting them. I can't quite think how it started, but it always has been like that, hasn't it?" (1:29). Discussing Toby with his friend Miles, Celia verifies her husband's observation: "Toby's always called me things. . . . I think originally they were intended to show affection. . . . Only the meaning's been lost over the years. Even in his speech at our wedding day he referred to me as looking like an oven-ready chicken wrapped in butter muslin. Which was only a joke. I think. Mother didn't think so" (*A Cricket Match*, 2:51). Words go awry; marriages go awry.

For a woman to find satisfaction outside marriage is contrary to the rigid social tradition to which many long-suffering Ayckbourn women pay heed, a legacy from an older generation. Trying to convince Sylvie to marry his son Lionel, old Joe Hepplewick tells her that to do otherwise, to attempt to better herself with an education and a career, is like a fish jumping out of water:

Sylvie: You mean, I don't belong?
Joe: No, Sylvie, you don't.
Sylvie: Because I'm a woman.
Joe: Partly. Partly because of your upbringing. Partly because of yourself. Put all those together, Sylvie, and you belong to part of a team looking after a man who works for you and who gives you that precious gift of children. . . . It's your life, Sylvie. You can choose to take the natural

course or you can choose to take the unnatural course. It's a child's duty to kneel before its mother, it's a woman's duty to kneel before a man and it's a man's duty to kneel before God. Those are unfashionable words these days, Sylvie, but you think about it. (*A Garden Fête*, 1:131–32)

In one version, *A One Man Protest*, Sylvie does think about it. Asked what she wants to do with her life, she says: "I don't know. Something exciting. I don't want to do what my mum did, anyway. You know, she's never been more than thirty miles away from here in her life. Except a couple of times. For her brother's funeral in Birmingham and that. Now she's dying. . . . Well, I'm not staying here to wash Lionel Hepplewick's socks, I can tell you" (2:125). Yet in some of *Intimate Exchanges*'s various closing scenes, Sylvie as Mrs. Hepplewick is about to do just that.

Married to dull, conventional Miles, Rowena feels trapped as wife and mother. Raised to take her place in life as helpmate, she had never been encouraged to seek any other option. As a child, Diana in *Absent Friends* had wanted to join the Canadian Royal Mounted Police, but Rowena reveals that she had had a far more unusual ambition, one that her friends believe she has in fact achieved: "What do you want to be when you grow up, Rowena? Please, Miss, a nymphomaniac," a once pejorative term that now designates, to her way of thinking, "a perfectly healthy normal woman" (*A Game of Golf*, 2: 94–95). Like Philip in *Relatively Speaking*, Miles questions his wife's sanity—"I think she's actually going batty but she's very cheerful" (*A Cricket Match*, 2:52)—even suggests to Celia that "you need to be a little mad like Rowena" (2:77), but his wife, sanely unconventional, continues on her merry, promiscuous way, in some versions even offering her favors to her husband.

Celia, rather than Rowena, is like Diana in *Absent Friends*—too genteel for her own good. In one version she goes more than a little mad. Convinced by Lionel that he is an experienced baker, she enters into a catering partnership with him, learning too late that he is as ineffectual in preparing baked goods as he is in tending the school's rutted playing field. In *Events on a Hotel Terrace* Lionel, as a waiter, provides Celia with more food than she can consume, but in *Affairs in a Tent*, as a caterer, he comes up with a peculiarly shaped single loaf of bread with which to feed all the guests at the Bilbury Lodge School Sports Day. Hardly able to cope with her day-to-day chores as wife and mother at home, in the refreshment marquee, where everything goes wrong, Celia flees reality. Where Lucy in "Mother Figure" orders about adults who actually exist, treating them as children, Celia pretends to be in complete control as she prepares to discipline the imaginary creatures she expects will want to be fed: "They will sit where I tell them to sit and they will have proper table manners or they won't be allowed in. . . . Teddy will sit here next to Lucy Ragbags and Dutch Doll here. And I'm going to put Rabbit here and Mr. Fuzzyperks here next to me. And I will pour tea because it is my tea party" (1:52). Before the sun sets on a disastrous Sports Day, Celia, having bitten Miles in the leg—and, in an alternate scene, Lionel as well—is subdued under the serving table bundled in a large tablecloth.

Retaining his major figures' consistent character traits, however they are paired, whatever lies in store for them in the many versions of the play—in itself a staggering feat—Ayckbourn demonstrates once again his startling ability to turn insanity into slapstick fun. The audience that suffers with catatonic Vera in *Just Between Ourselves* has a jolly time laughing at hysterical Celia. The playwright's underlying intention, however, remains serious as, comically but effectively, he probes the possibility throughout *Intimate Exchanges* that the edgy, nervous housewife who spends her days bravely keeping up appearances in a loveless marriage may be dangerously close to the brink of madness. In *Affairs in a Tent* Celia crosses the line.

What mitigates the pain for the audience observing Ayckbourn's characters trying—often failing—to make decisions that will better their lives is the A-effect. With the play in progress, the audience is dazzled by the performance—Celia becoming Rowena becoming Sylvie; Toby becoming Miles becoming Lionel. Afterwards, once the laughter has died, the audience may consider the questions that Ayckbourn has been asking behind the laughter: could Celia realize happiness, at least muster some confidence, by sharing a moment of Sylvie's occasional self-analysis, a touch of Rowena's attitude? Can a casual decision actually change a life? And what of the intrusion of chance? The audience may come to understand not only why Ayckbourn has called for a company of two—one man, one woman— but also that the curious casting that implements the A-effect makes a psychological, and even metaphysical point. The author has himself acknowledged that "it's not accidental that each of the three main characters of each sex is an element of perhaps one bigger character."[15]

In *Me, Myself and I* (1981), one of the lunchtime entertainments devised by Ayckbourn with the composer Paul Todd to make daytime use of the facilities of the Scarborough theater, three women play the three roles of the title. For a time Me is satisfied being a housewife, nothing more, but Myself has qualms about her situation; sophisticated I is the most cynical of the three. Yet all are finally aspects of a single, complex personality. The same is true of Celia, Sylvie, and Rowena. That complex threefold character may be each member of the audience, whose response to an Ayckbourn play is equally varied and ambiguous. The theatergoer who recognized his wife in a character in *Absurd Person Singular*, who sobbed in Richard Briers's dressing-room while others popped round to tell the actor how terribly funny they found him and the play, achieved a catharsis he would not soon forget. Another, a little ashamed of his laughter as he left the theater after a performance of *Just Between Ourselves*, could not leave the play behind him. The woman who loved the radio broadcasts of *Intimate Exchanges* but argued that they should never have been billed as comedies because "they are so sad!" would surely have been swept along by the laughter of an audience in a theater.[16] Laughter comforts, but it does not mask truth.

Saving his most indelible portrait of a woman losing touch with reality for *Woman in Mind*, Ayckbourn, four years before *Intimate Exchanges*, had prepared for his later protagonist, Susan, by sketching a subsidiary character, Louise, in *Joking Apart* (1978). The play was written as the thirty-eight-year-old Ayckbourn, confronted by his "suddenly adult" eighteen-year-old son, had begun, like his characters, to feel his age (9). Unusual in its time span, covering as it does twelve years, *Joking Apart*'s more surprising feature for an Ayckbourn play is its presentation of a perfect male-female relationship. Yet the dramatist is more interested in revealing its disastrous effects on the friends and business associates of the blissfully unmarried charmed couple than he is in exploring the basis of the longstanding relationship of Richard and Anthea. Sven, Richard's partner in Scandinavian Craftware Co. Ltd., is certain he has a better head for business, but it is Richard's instinctive decisions that keep the firm solvent. Once the Finnish Junior Tennis Champion, Sven can only best his partner at the game when Richard, letting him win, plays left-handed. Even worse for Sven than losing would have been, however, is the discovery of his associate's well-meant but nonetheless insulting duplicity on the court. For Brian, who works for the firm, the occasional weekend visits to the ideal couple's country home are particularly painful in light of his unrequited love for Anthea, exacerbated by the fact that his girlfriends find Richard devastatingly attractive. That Brian's three companions, as well as Anthea's daughter Debbie, his last hope for romance, are played by a single actress underscores the futility of Brian's unending search for an Anthea substitute.

Hugh, the local vicar tolerated by his flock, is in love with Anthea too, only to be gently rebuffed when at long last he professes his feelings. Living on the adjoining property, Hugh must suffer Richard's success in his role as father to Anthea's children, a constant reminder of his own failure. His brilliant seventeen-year-old son Christopher, recipient of a University Open Scholarship, refuses to speak to either of his parents, whom he treats "like a couple of deaf-mute retainers" (186). Hugh's shy, birdlike wife Louise, traumatized by the gulf between herself and her husband, herself and her son, drifts toward the inevitable breakdown. At Debbie's eighteenth-birth-day party, Louise, *"bright, like a painted doll, smiling incessantly, but unnaturally, as one under the influence of drugs"* (187), comforts herself by bursting into song—unfortunately a hymn—and must be led away by her mortified husband. If Louise is regressing toward adolescence and childhood, she does not complete the movement as does Hazel in *Wildest Dreams*, who is crawling on all fours by the end of the play.

The woman losing her mind, again a vicar's wife and the mother of a son who has not spoken to his parents for years, moves once more from the periphery to the center of the stage. What makes Susan in *Woman in Mind* Ayckbourn's most devastating study of incipient madness is that the audience views her subjectively, from her own disoriented point of view, a perspective suggested by his reading about a man trying to wrench a woman's head off her shoulders in Oliver Sack's *The Man Who Mistook His Wife for a Hat* (1985).[17] The subjective approach, however, is the inevitable refinement of Ayckbourn's probing of the unbalanced mind, an obsessive theme stemming from his mother's deep but temporary bout of depression. Becoming as fragmented as the character Susan, the audience surrenders to her loss of reason.

Struck in the head by the handle of a rake she has stepped on, Susan, unconscious, is being attended by Bill, the partner of her regular doctor who is away. The audience hears what Susan hears—words not making any sense: "Score grounds appeal cumquat doggy Martha hat sick on the bed."[18] Some repeated phrases, to be heard again as the play ends, have a modicum of meaning: "Choose 'un, choose 'un. . . . December bee" (10). The former echoes her name as it admonishes her to act; the latter, which serves as the play's subtitle, is almost decipherable as the Ghost's injunction to Hamlet—"Remember me." Significantly, Susan's speech at the beginning and throughout most of the play is coherent. Only at the end does the sense of her words border on incoherence.

In Arthur Kopit's *Wings* (1978), a subjectively presented study of a stroke victim's trauma, Emily Stilson speaks to herself almost coherently in the early stages of her illness after working her way through gibberish: "Hapst aporkshop fleetish yes of course it's yes the good ol' times when we would mollis I mean collis all around still what my son's name is cannot for the life of me yet face gleams smiles as he tells them what I did. . . ."[19] But for a time the words of others make little sense to her:

> *First Doctor:* Mrs. Stilson, makey your nameing powers?
> *Mrs. Stilson:* What?
> *Second Doctor:* Canju spokeme?
> *Mrs. Stilson:* Can I what?
> *First Doctor:* Can do peeperear?
> *Mrs. Stilson: Don't believe what's going on!*
> *Second Doctor:* Ahwill.
> *First Doctor:* Pollycadjis.
> *Second Doctor:* Sewyladda?
> *First Doctor (with a nod):* Hm-hm. (30–31)

In the preface to his play, Kopit has revealed that his character is based on a woman, "relatively free of other symptoms," who was suffering from aphasia: her speech "was fluent and possessed normal intonations, cadence, and syntactical structure—in fact, to such an extent that anyone who did not understand English would have sworn she was making sense. Nonetheless, her sentences were laced with a kind of babbled jargon" (ix). For Kopit the word "gibberish" suggests psychosis and dementia; he prefers the term "jargonaphasia." His character, Emily, has suffered a stroke: she is not insane.[20] Susan's blow to the head causes a temporary concussion which can in fact result in aphasia. The brain can heal from such an injury just as a defective word processor spewing out nonsense syllables can be put back into working order. Ayckbourn's Susan does not heal: she is losing her mind, the initial blow a metaphoric rendering of the problematic, sexual cause of her despair.

The dramatist describes the protagonist of *Woman in Mind* as "*an unassuming woman in her forties, used to and happy to play second fiddle to more determinedly motivated personalities than her own. Only now, at this stage of her life, is she beginning to question the role she's played or perhaps been cast in*" (9). The role Susan has chosen for herself, or that has been chosen for her, has brought her no happiness. Her pompous, self-satisfied husband, Reverend Gerald Gannet, pays no attention to her whatsoever, having spent his spare time for some years completing a sixty-page work commissioned by the local Civic Society, a history of his parish covering the six hundred years beginning in 1386.

Susan's sister-in-law Muriel "*is a woman who has known her share of suffering and is anxious others should know about it too"* (22). Having tended an ailing mother for twelve years and an ailing husband for another seven, since their deaths Muriel has lived in her brother's home. Unlike the sister-in-law who is all deadly efficiency as she dispossesses Chekhov's three sisters, Muriel, who might like to take over the household, is incapable of doing so. Expending her energies on calling her inattentive husband Harry back from the dead, she is an extra burden for Susan. Muriel's attempts to help, her cooking and cleaning, result in comic fiascos, her masterpiece—mistaking the tea tin for the spice tin—an Earl Grey omelette.

Susan has not seen her son Rick, once a scholarship student at a school for boys, for the two years he has spent in Hemel Hempstead, a member of a quasi-religious sect that prefers to call itself a philosophical group. The sect's sole teaching seems to be that children must not speak to their parents, caused, or so the Reverend Gerald suspects, by a "somewhat over-emphatic reading" of Matthew, chapter 10, verses 36 and 37 (42). Established religions, quasi religions, and spiritualism have all failed a family in disarray.

The verses from Matthew that Gerald quotes in the King James version along with passages from Mark (chapter 3, verses 31 to 35) that he merely cites—"Who is my mother, or my brethren? . . . For whosoever shall do the will of God, the same is my brother, and my sister, and mother"—might serve, taken out of their biblical context, as epigraphs for *Woman in Mind*. Like Ibsen's Nora, Susan comes to the realization that her husband, in league with his sister and her own son, is her antagonist. Her actual family affording her no comfort as brethren should, she chooses an imaginary one consisting of dashing husband Andy, adoring daughter Lucy, and doting brother Tony. That the alternate family, speaking in loving clichés, make their entrance before their real-life counterparts is what discomfits the audience and keeps them off balance for the rest of the play, arousing in them the emotions of pity for Susan and fear for themselves.

As the doctor's speech at the beginning of the play turns from gibberish to language Susan can understand, she seems to be recovering from her concussion, but she soon lapses into a fugue state. Her tidy little suburban garden is transformed in her imagination into a garden paradise complete with lake, rosebeds, swimming pool, and tennis court—an Edenic estate that stretches ten miles to the main gate. There she is surrounded by an ideal family who refuse to allow her to be carted by ambulance to a hospital for observation, vowing instead to care for her lovingly at home, all the while nourishing her with champagne, salmon, summer pudding, and sorbet. Their words of tenderness are not echoed on his later entry by Susan's husband, more irritated with her than sympathetic. As the action progresses, Susan loses control over the imagined family who at first came to her as she wanted or needed them. Soon the surrogates arrive as they please, interfering and interrupting, no longer waiting to be willed, as wish fulfillment yields to irritation, then to horror.

Susan's conversations with her preoccupied husband reveal more frankly than do the words of any other Ayckbourn woman the cause of her disenchantment with married life. What seemed for other women household drudgery, Susan says, had once been for her an essential component of a relationship which defined her to her own satisfaction: "I used to be a wife. I used to be a mother. And I loved it" (24). All that changed when their sexual union came to an end. Gerald is shocked to learn that the sexual side of their relationship meant so much to her, but Susan tries to make him understand its significance: "Once that's gone . . . . it becomes important. Over-important, really. I mean before, when we—it was just something else we did together. Like gardening. Only now I have to do that on my own as well. It was something we shared. A couple of times a week. Or whatever. . . . The point is that then, everything else, the everyday bits, just ticked along nicely. But take that away, the really joyous part of us—and everything else rather loses its purpose. That's all." But Gerald chooses not to understand: "I rather thought you'd lost interest in all that, you know. . . . I thought that when a woman got to— our age—she more or less . . . switched off" (26–27).

Susan had considered herself a good mother to her son, taking his reluctant father's place in explaining sexual matters to him, becoming chums with his girlfriends. When Rick returns home to visit and, having left the sect, speaks to his mother, he informs her that he has been married for two months and will soon be off to Thailand with the wife he does not want his mother to meet. Susan had always embarrassed Rick and his friends, she now learns, with her openness regarding subjects that they would have preferred not to discuss with an adult, especially a woman. He had not left home because of his father, as she had convinced herself; both his parents, he tells her, were to blame.

Her family having failed her, she having failed her family, Susan begins to be wary as well of the alternate family that is becoming more and more sinister. Reality has insidiously intruded on her inner life, darkening that as well. Tony now carries a twelve-bore shotgun which he is too eager to use—on people as well as animals. Andy drives her further out of kilter as he speaks her words before her, becomes Tony and Lucy too. Susan, feeling herself out of her body, is everywhere and nowhere.

In what may or may not be the real world again Bill, the doctor—like the vicar in *Joking Apart,* like Ibsen's Dr. Rank before him—knowing that he should not do what he is about to do, professes his love for Susan. Aligning her with Celia, Rowena, and Sylvie, he admits to being aware of her ever since first seeing her at a school concert at Bilbury Lodge, the setting of *Intimate Exchanges.* Bill tells Susan about his wife Nora, unlike Ibsen's heroine who saved her husband's life by taking him to Italy, off by herself on a holiday in Portugal or perhaps accompanied there by someone else's husband—Bill's partner Geoff. Just as Bill is substituting for Geoff, Susan's regular doctor who just happens to be off on holiday as well, Geoff may be substituting for Bill in another capacity. Whereas in *A Doll's House* Nora's overly aesthetic husband advised her friend Kristine to choose crocheting over less-pleasing knitting, Bill, at his wife's urging, has taken up macramé, pursuing his new hobby at home at night in the spare room, just as Gerald spends every night in his study making liittle progress on his manuscript. Susan's relationship with Gerald, Bill's with Nora, even Celia and Toby's and Miles and Rowena's—the relationships of all of Ayckbourn's unhappy couples—suffer from the disenchantment brought by time. The effect on Susan, however, is at least as dire as the effect on Vera in *Just Between Ourselves.* For the audience viewing Susan subjectively, not objectively as they had seen Vera, the experience is far more painful. The laughter that accompanies much of the play freezes at its conclusion.

Woman in Mind ends in nightmare. Disappointed that her son has been married in a registry office, Susan anticipates the elegant wedding of her imagined daughter Lucy, only to learn that the groom is her son Rick, dressed in Hollywood fashion as a Thai rickshaw driver. Despite Lucy's bridal gown, the guests have gathered for a horse race instead of a wedding. As Susan's hallucinations have progressed, the inhabitants of the real world have begun to mingle with those of the enchanted garden. At the race meeting the real and the unreal conflate into the surreal. Bill is a bookie, his medical case now emblazoned with the words "HONEST BILL" (84). A very pregnant Muriel, dressed in formal maid's black bombazine with cap and apron, serves champagne (86). Gerald, accoutered in archbishop's garb, embraces Andy, addressing him as "you old devil you," addressing Tony as "you old rascal," calling Bill "Billy Beelzebub himself," the titles affirming Susan's fears that she has been possessed. Andy calls the race with Lucy the winner: "It's Lucy from Macramé Lad and Dead Hubby . . . and they're well clear of Priggish Boy and Smug Vicar . . ." (87–88).

Having failed at keeping the one family from the other, Susan is thrust from her dream until suddenly she is again the center of attention. All the characters encircle her to drink her health. Twice before in the play imaginary characters, foreshadowing the sinister family toast that ends *A Small Family Business*, had raised their glasses to the family (35, 48). As *Woman in Mind* concludes, all toast "the most important person in all our lives. . . . Dearest Susie." Called upon for a speech, Susan begins, "Dearest friends. Family. My happiest moment has been to stand here with you and share this, my most precious of days." But as she continues to speak, her words lose meaning. As an ambulance's flashing blue light illuminates her, Susan's fragmented speech becomes strangely haunting: "December bee? Choose 'un. December choosey. December bee? December bee?" (91–92). Madness has chosen Susan, but the audience will remember her.

To support the characterization of a woman descending into madness and to comment on the metaphysical notion of being, Ayckbourn makes use of archetypes and affective symbolism in a controlled and consistently ironic manner. What in the earlier plays had been presented as comic garnish hinting at deeper preoccupations—the garden as setting, the scenes of eating and drinking, in short the everyday rituals of middle-class life—here become allegorical. Susan's fall in her garden immediately before the play's opening is not a fall from grace but a means of determining her need to challenge a morality which makes no sense to her, the snake in the garden— comically the rake handle—a symbol of her sexual deprivation. Eventually both her imagined paradise and her actual garden confine her, harrowing her soul. The barking dog, at first heard by the doctor but not by Susan, later heard by Susan but not by him—perhaps the contents of her imagined brother's bloodstained hunting bag—charts Susan's mental deterioration, her impending doom. The family circle, broken at the play's outset, reknits at the end in the wedding-race meeting when Susan is ceremoniously toasted by both real and imagined families, but, as the stage direction dictates (90), *"they surround her"* as their prey. Susan has become the scapegoat.

The surrealistic scene dramatizes Ayckbourn's increasingly pessimistic view of man as animal. Susan's imagined daughter, dressed in white for her wedding but without the bridal veil, returns wearing a headdress *"enlivened by the addition of a pair of built-in animal ears and a race winner's rosette"* (88) in a scene that becomes a macabre tableau not unlike an Hieronymous Bosch painting in which humanity yields to bestiality. Susan's anguished plea—"December bee?"— begs for recognition and understanding from both the families, but her contorted words are unanswered, indicating that even within the circle she is alone in the garden. Feigning madness, Hamlet took up his father's cause, as long as memory held a seat in "this distracted globe," to reclaim a garden grown to seed and to restore a time gone out of joint. Susan's madness is as real as Ophelia's; victimized, she has no one to avenge her, to feel for her and with her, unless it be the audience. In *Woman in Mind* Ayckbourn subtly uses the A-effect, not to make character and performer one, but solely to focus on Susan as a character forced to become a performer in her own insane nightmare.

In the madhouse scene in *Peer Gynt*, Begriffenfeldt defines insanity for Peer, the man who claims to have been himself in everything he has done:

> Everyone here is himself to the gills,
> Completely himself and nothing else—
> So far into himself he can't come back,[21]

a definition that calls into question Peer's own state of mind. Inexorably, Susan too has ventured far into the self, the doors of reason closing in on her.

In an earlier scene in the play Susan tells Bill that she is concerned for her sanity and would be relieved if only someone else would see one member of her perfect family. In an attempt to calm her fears, Bill pretends to see Lucy, even talks to the phantom being, directing his words to empty space some distance from where Lucy stands visible to Susan and the audience:

> *Lucy:* How extraordinary. Is he mad?
> *Susan:* Possibly. One of us is anyway. And I'd sooner it were him. (72)

Psychiatrist R. D. Laing, who once treated a patient who referred to herself as "the ghost of the wood garden,"[22] contends that insanity is the rational response to a world gone mad. Invoking Laing in her review of *Woman in Mind*, Joan Smith found Susan "an oasis of sanity in a desert of madness," her schizophrenia "a sign that something's wrong with the whole family, not just one member of it."[23] The family's scapegoat victim is its most sensitive member who is declared insane while the madness of the rest goes unnoticed. In her flight from reason Susan has been no more irrational than Pirandello's Enrico IV in his attempt to live within the frozen moment of history, time in flux the flowing stream that carries one to the grave. As the play ends, with the "jargonaphasia" she imagined hearing from another at the opening now becoming her own gibberish—the concussion giving way to dementia—Susan, like Ophelia, floats to oblivion. In his analysis of Shakespeare's defenseless character, another family victim whom he diagnoses as a schizophrenic, Laing uses language that defines Susan as well: "In her madness, there is no one there. She is not a person. There is no integral selfhood expressed through her actions or utterances. Incomprehensible statements are said by nothing. She has already died. There is now only a vacuum where there was once a person."[24]

What has caused Susan's world to go awry is indirectly the mainspring of Ophelia's madness but the prime mover in Hamlet's melancholy—a wedding that never should have been. When a fire in his study destroys all but page 57 of the manuscript more precious to him than his wife, Gerald blames Susan: "Why? What terrible, nameless, unmentionable thing can I possibly have done to you?" (78). Susan can only answer with a more terrifying question that other Ayckbourn women might well have asked—"Married me?"

5

Men Of and For the Moment

Men too go mad. And women are the cause. In *A One Man Protest*, a version of *Intimate Exchanges*, Miles suffers a severe buffeting from all the women in his life. Celia, for whom he has keener feelings than one ought for the wife of one's best friend, is rude to him when he asks her to stand by her husband Toby whom she is contemplating leaving. His wife Rowena is more than rude when she tries to explain why she is seeing other men, practically the whole of the Squash Club:

> *Rowena:* Imagine you've married a pianist. Now it so happens that my own piano has gone slightly out of tune so I'm having to practice elsewhere.
> *Miles:* My God.
> *Rowena:* I'm not giving concerts. I'm practicing. There is a difference.
> *Miles:* I think this is one of the most distasteful metaphors I have ever heard. (2:120)

Seriously considering Rowena's suggestion that he too needs to have an affair, Miles turns to Sylvie, inviting her to accompany him on a walk right round Britain's entire coastline. In one alternate Sylvie agrees, but in another when she refuses him, something snaps. Having had his fill of women and the world, Miles contemplates suicide in Celia's garden shed—for five weeks. While Miles sorts out his life, Celia, concerned for his appetite, carries trays of food to the shed: "He should be ready for his pudding by now. . . . I hope he likes this. He liked the apple crumble the other day. He had seconds" (2:135). "Hope it bloody chokes him," mutters Toby, who is not altogether pleased at the prospect of his shed earning an Egon Ronay good-food recommendation (2:140).

When Miles finally pulls himself together to emerge from the garden womb, he informs his wife that he will go off somewhere to start again: "We have the choice. We must try. When you see that all the choices you've made so far are getting you nowhere, straight into a wall, you have to break out and start again." Rowena, however, free-spirited though she may be, does not agree: "Nothing changes. We are what we are. You can give up smoking or—wear different clothes or—get your nose altered but victims stay victims and bullies stay bullies" (2: 152). Miles may consider himself the victim in his temporary withdrawal from the world, but the Ayckbourn male is oftentimes the bully, more maddening than mad. Miles's bout with madness is the exception; Vera and Susan's insanity is closer to the rule.

The playwright, who may himself be a bit crazed in his eagerness to dissect sixteen possible ramifications of the male-female relationship in a single multiversion work, had already explored one more possibility in *Bedroom Farce* (1975), a young married couple who alternately victimize and bully one another. Trevor and Susannah are both a little mad and even more maddening, according to the friends whose lives they disrupt. Both of the unstable pair have always been unsure of themselves. Delia, Trevor's mother, admits she and Ernest, her husband, were not good parents, but she suspects the major share of the blame must be laid at the clay feet of the father who "hardly said a word to him all the time he was growing up" (163). For Delia, the surest sign that her son has "lost his sense of proportion" is that he married Susannah, "a very complex sort of girl."

Susanna spends much of her time crying in the bathroom, not necessarily her own. She cries in other people's as well. She admits to a friend her fear of losing her identity. Like Greg in *Relatively Speaking*, she does not always know who she is in the mornings. Alone, she attempts to restore her shattered image with comforting words: "I am confident in myself. I have confidence in myself. I am not unattractive. I am attractive. People still find me attractive. . . . There is nothing to be frightened of" (178). But the mantra has not worked its magic.

Part of Trevor's problem, not unusual for the Ayckbourn male, is his inability to communicate not only with his wife but with anyone else. He tries to explain to his friends Malcolm and Kate what living with Susannah has done to him: "It's a totally draining experience. . . . Once you get yourself committed to a—commitment—like Susannah and I have commited ourselves to, you get a situation of a totally outgoing—non—egotistical—giving—ness . . . a total submerging, you know" (175). More unusual for an Ayckbourn male character is his desperation. Life holds no meaning for Trevor, who ungraciously urges Kate, in whose home he is a guest, to have a close look at innocent children. Should she then take a good look at herself, he suggests, she would surely be as appalled as he: "You try and think of . . . three good reasons why you shouldn't throw yourself out of that window here and now." Kate, taking cover under the bedclothes on being interrupted in her bedroom by Trevor as she is dressing, can only offer one: "I haven't got any clothes on" (176). Once the house-warming party to which they have dutifully been invited gets under-way, Trevor and Susannah, who have arrived separately, confront one another in Kate and Malcolm's bedroom and come to blows. In Ayckbourn's one moment of actual rather than wished-for violence between husband and wife, the two engage in what the stage direc-tion describes as *"mortal combat,"* clawing at one another and pulling hair as they roll on the floor. Before they are effectively separated, Susannah clouts her husband with a bedside lamp (183–84).

Written just before the darker *Just Between Ourselves, Bedroom Farce* finds its author in a relatively sunny mood. Ayckbourn is not seriously probing the psyches of his disturbed couple to find the source of their connubial woe. In *Absent Friends* Colin is oblivious to the pain he is causing the rest with his cheerful smugness about the consummate relationship that never quite was, and in *Joking Apart* all their friends must suffer the ideal relationship of the unwedded Richard and Anthea. In *Bedroom Farce,* too, Ayckbourn examines the effect of one relationship on others, but here the relationship is far from perfect. Delia and Ernest, Nick and Jan, Malcolm and Kate are contented with their own lot, or would be, if only Trevor and Susan-nah would disappear from their lives. Unfortunately for Nick and Jan, and Malcolm and Kate, the impact of the unhappy couple is like that of the Fosters and the Phillips on the Featherstones in *How the Other Half Loves*: they begin a too-close, not-quite-healthy scrutiny of their own relationships. The play ends with Trevor and Susannah in each other's arms in bed—Malcolm and Kate's bed, not their own.

That Susannah begins her mantra again when Trevor falls asleep suggests that the almost-happy ending ought to be regarded like the ending of *Anna Christie.* O'Neill cautioned that the reconciliation of Anna, her father Chris, and her lover Mat was not to be considered a full stop, only a comma. Perhaps the strongest punctuation that can be affixed to the conclusion of *Bedroom Farce* is the semicolon; a look back at the play from the perspective of Ayckbourn's later work suggests that in no time at all either Trevor or Susannah or both, like David Edgar's Mary Barnes, will be in desperate need of one of R. D. Laing's communal treatment centers. *Bedroom Farce's* guarded op-timism is confirmed by its author's statement that none of the charac-ters "finds instant happiness or sudden great self-insight. But at least they retain the dignity of resolving their own destinies" (9).

An immensely amusing comedy of manners about disappointed expectations, *Bedroom Farce* offers neither the titillation nor the frenzy its title suggests, Ayckbourn daringly disappointing that por-tion of his audience that entered the theater anticipating a bed-hopping sex farce. Bed-hopping there is; sex there is not. The discrepancy between the title and the play itself suggests its theme: one must accept life as it is and not as one romantically imagines it ought to be. Its funniest moment, hardly tingling with sexual innuendo, involves the oldest couple settling down in bed for a snack of pilchards on toast. Delia and Ernest may not be ecstatically happy, but like the elderly couple in *Family Circles,* they have made the accommodation that marriage offers only to those who have survived many years of discontent.

Characterization is not *Bedroom Farce's* strongest point, nor was it meant to be. The play may be regarded as one in which its author is perhaps more concerned with solving a puzzle with which he has challenged himself, decidedly worth the effort in that it adds considerably to the audience's delight. Possibly even more effective behind the proscenium arch than it is on an arena stage because of its intricate schema, the comedy is set in three bedrooms, arranged in a row on a conventional stage. With Malcolm and Kate's bedroom in the middle, Ernest and Delia's at stage right and Nick and Jan's at stage left, Ayckbourn manipulates a visual as well as an emotional split and reconciliation for Trevor and Susannah. They battle at Malcolm and Kate's, go their separate ways—Susannah to stage right to her in-laws, Trevor to stage left to his friends. Maintaining the symmetry of the pattern, Ayckbourn even manages to get Susannah into Delia's bed and Trevor into Nick's before the two reaffirm their need for one another at the very center of the stage in Malcolm and Kate's bed. The arrangement allows Ayckbourn a cinematic crosscutting that gives the play, in his words, "an added rhythm over and above what the dialogue normally provides" (8). That Maria Aitken, who played Susannah at the National Theatre, admitted to director Peter Hall that playing Ayckbourn was not necessarily a happy experience for an actor suggests that even when the dramatist is in part preoccupied with a staging pattern, his characters, unsettling the performers, retain more than a mere semblance of truth. Hall considers it a particular problem for any *Bedroom Farce* cast: "The laughs are enormous and continuous, yet if any actor actually plays a laugh, or encourages one by even a lift of the eyebrow, the whole structure collapses. The actor feels like a man addicted to drink who is left in charge of a pub, but mustn't touch a drop."[1]

Unlike dithering Trevor and bumbling Miles, the quintessential Ayckbourn male, something of an opportunist, is perfectly sane. Creating chaos around him, he drives other men mad. On his first appearance he too seems the bumbler. Mint, a piano tuner, the protagonist of *Mr Whatnot* (1963), trips over his cat and falls, bringing down a pile of saucepans.[2] Soon he is manipulating others, arranging matters to suit himself, ending up at the play's conclusion in bed with Amanda, the bride of another, his rival—chinless, lisping Cecil.

Mr Whatnot is basically a mime play with twenty-eight of its sixty-nine typescript pages devoted to elaborate stage directions. Its dialogue consists mainly of speeches of two or three words, the monosyllabic speech of the stereotypically mindless British upper class who have nothing better to do than entertain house quests with afternoon tea, a tour of the duck pond, and a game of tennis. Throughout, Mint, the urban disrupter of serene country life, utters not a single word of dialogue. Out of his element among the landed gentry, he remains silent, but he is neither mute nor stupid. Occasionally he engages in mimed conversations, usually with those of his own class with whom he is comfortable, a pedestrian and a gardener. Called to the Grange to tune the piano, he is soon mistaken by Lord Slingsby-Craddock for a house guest, as all the mistaken-identity ploys that had already served Ayckbourn well in *The Square Cat* and would work again more effectively in *Relatively Speaking* are put into play.

Mint makes a shambles of a game of tennis, even scoring one point from the wrong side of the net; he engages in a game of musical chairs at teatime when the guests outnumber the furniture; and he invents a game of musical glasses. Having too much to drink at dinner—he dutifully downs the wine each time his glass is refilled—he slips under the table, his hand appearing from below to confuse the rest by moving their glasses from one place to another. After dinner when all retire for the night, the lights come up on a scene anticipating the crosscutting between the bedrooms of *Bedroom Farce*. All the household are discovered in their beds, but all of them soon abandon their beds to take to the hallways where some seek out others, some investigate the noise, and all of them strike matches in the dark, a visual treat for the audience.

When Mint finds Amanda and runs off with her, a mimed car chase ensues, ending up at a church. The piano tuner is about to marry the girl of his dreams as the others arrive. In the confusion Lord Slingsby-Craddock's gun goes off, a bullet hitting Mint, who staggers and falls in a mock death, but he immediately arises and, revealing what has saved his life, produces from inside his jacket a large bent spoon. At dinner the previous night, unaccustomed to the elaborate place-setting and unsure which piece to use, Mint had pocketed the silver. The wedding continues, with Cecil in Mint's place at the altar, but Mint is eventually exactly where he wants to be, in Cecil's place in bed with Amanda.

Mr Whatnot, Ayckbourn's first effort as author-director—and conceivably no one else will ever direct it as inventively—is silent-film comedy brought to the stage. There are numerous sight gags, the most delightful the pedestrian revolving on the end of the auto crank, still shaking once Mint has pulled him free. An almost balletic sequence has Mint greeted at the entrance to the Grange by the butler who leads him through a maze of halls and rooms, with the opening and closing of all the doors mimed. When Mint takes a wrong turn, loses his guide and finds himself once again outside the Grange, he pulls the doorbell a second time. As the butler appears once more, Mint apologetically raises his hat—a sublime gesture of Chaplinesque innocence.

Sound too is used effectively. Mint and Cecil engage in a piano duel, the two of them, back to back, crowding one another on a single stool with Cecil at first the one facing the piano. He begins "The Moonlight Sonata," but with a spin of the stool Mint faces the keys and launches into "The Twelfth Street Rag." As the stool continues to spin, the music alternates from classical to jazz. The most imaginative use of sound occurs when Lord Slingsby-Craddock bores the ladies with his war stories, circa World War I, and Cecil, who has only been on maneuvers on Salisbury Plain, tries to top him. When Slingsby-Craddock gets to the point where the Hun attacks as he is in the mess complaining about the quality of the beans, the men make the sounds of bombs and gunfire, which are gradually replaced by the actual noises of war. A veritable Colonel Blimp, Slingsby-Craddock leads the others in a counterattack as tea buns become grenades, but it is Mint who saves the day. Carrying a white flag and pretending to surrender as the others call him coward, like the hero of A. E. W. Mason's *Four Feathers* he proves the bravest of the lot, annihilating the enemy. To the sound of the cheers of a vast multitude and the strains of "Land of Hope and Glory," he is embraced by Amanda. As in "Ernie's Incredible Illucinations" (1969) and *Invisible Friends*, plays for children in which hallucinations materialize, and as in *Woman in Mind* in which Susan cannot distinguish between the unreal and the real, Mint loses himself within a dream. As the dream dissipates, Mint, not quite out from under its spell, kisses Amanda passionately, to the horror of the others who nonetheless maintain their British composure and politesse until Lady Slingsby-Craddock breaks the spell: "Would you care for some more tea, Mr—er . . .?

In his study of the Theatre of the Absurd, Martin Esslin observes that silent-film comedy is the bridge from *commedia dell'arte* to the clowning of music-hall acrobats and comedians to the characters who wander through Samuel Beckett's void. Absurdist theater "has the dreamlike strangeness of a world seen from outside with the uncomprehending eyes of one cut off from reality," he writes. "It has the quality of nightmare and displays a world in constant, and wholly purposeless, movement. . . . The great performers of this cinema, Chaplin and Buster Keaton, are the perfect embodiments of the stoicism of man when faced with a world of mechanical devices that have got out of hand."[3] If the world of *Mr Whatnot* gets out of hand, and it does for the Slingsby-Craddocks but not for Mint, it remains a happy fairy tale of a dream, not the schizophrenic nightmare of *Woman in Mind*. Esslin notes that Eugene Ionesco once told an audience that the three biggest influences on his work were Groucho, Chico, and Harpo. As eloquently silent as Harpo, Mint, never confounded, is like the always-triumphant Marx Brothers, more the anarchist than the stoic as he bests his betters, one of the features of the play so ingratiating to Stephen Joseph, Ayckbourn's mentor. Yet Mint differs from the Marxes—Karl as well as the others—in that he has no master plan. Never devious for a moment, he acts on innocent instinct. And that innocence will become tempered in some of Ayckbourn's refinements of the character. More than a hint of mischief surfaces amid the chaos that Leonard and Norman cause respectively in *Time and Time Again* and *The Norman Conquests*. Innocence in all its purity reappears in Tristram in *Taking Steps* but becomes blurred with folly in Guy in *A Chorus of Disapproval*. In the person of Jack McCracken the innocent becomes the mafioso capo in *A Small Family Business* as silent-film comedy evolves into the way of the world, Mrs. Thatcher's world. At last in *Man of the Moment*, perhaps for Ayckbourn a play of wish-fulfillment, the innocent bests the tyrant.

In *Time and Time Again* (1971), thinking his boss Graham has come between him and his fiancée Joan, Peter, well-built sportsman though he is, voices the task facing the little men of the world: ". . . there comes a time when people like us, the ones that get pushed around, we've got to get together and say—no. No—to little tyrants and petty dictators who take advantage of their class and their money and their so-called position. We've got to stand up and say—to hell with them."[4] Peter, however, will never strike out against his victimizer, for he has not yet realized that his rival is in fact his friend Leonard— one of the "people like us." The enemy must be identified before he can be confronted. But who would ever suspect childlike Leonard of guile?

Time and Time Again is a deceptive play, its seemingly passive, inert protagonist actually its catalyst, a manipulator par excellence. Unemployable Leonard, a former schoolteacher who admits to knowing nothing at all about poetry but who taught it nonetheless, has been locked out of his home by his wife and idles away his days in his sister's garden chatting with his best friend, Bernard, a stone garden gnome. The action begins on the day of Leonard and Anna's mother's funeral, marked by the barking of an unseen dog, a sound that will figure symbolically in *Woman in Mind*, and, curiously enough, Graham, Anna's short-tempered husband, mentions having once hit himself in the knee with a garden rake. An Ayckbourn garden, his favorite setting, is never the safest haven for man or woman, but this time the play reveals the dramatist in what appears to be a gentle vein, Chekhovian in mood and time. *Time and Time Again* is a comedy of quiet desperation that by its conclusion is neither gentle nor quiet; physical injuries abound as the garden's peaceful calm is shattered. By allowing them to be charmed by Leonard and to side with him against Graham, Ayckbourn is slyly leading his audience up the garden path.

Leonard, who played games with his delighted mother, jumping out at her from cupboards right up to a fortnight before her death, is not "off his head" as Graham avers (12) nor is he the innocent the others take him for. Perhaps deluding even himself, his childlike nature may be a pose. Aware that Graham is attracted to his employee's fiancée, can hardly keep his hands off her, Leonard cultivates Peter's friendship by playing cricket for the East Pendon Occasionals, entering a darts contest at Peter's pub, and joining the local football squad, activities aimed at providing him access to Joan. Unlike Peter, who excels at all sports, who once boxed a rival for three rounds for the right to court Joan, Leonard is as inept at manly games as he is in personal relationships. He is bowled out on the first ball at cricket, goes to the wrong pub for darts, and, as the play ends, has wrecked his team's chances by accidentally kicking Peter in the ankle on their way to the football field. By this point in their unlikely friendship Leonard has caused the other even more grievous harm: he is responsible for Peter's jamming his fingers in the lawn mower, has hit him with a cricket ball, and has stolen his fiancée.

That Joan comes to prefer Leonard is as difficult for Graham to swallow as the food he does not like that Anna keeps serving—cod instead of haddock, Dundee cake instead of Battenburg. At teatime, an especially difficult hour for many Ayckbourn characters, he gets a cheese sandwich after specifically requesting that there be no cheese, his wife's quietly efficient way of dealing with her obstreperous spouse. Anna has little to say to her husband, seemingly allowing him his way. The spoken thoughts of the bored wife going through the motions of a sterile, twenty-year marriage in the brief dialogue, "Countdown," written more than a decade earlier (1959), could serve as subtext for Anna. Attributing the change in herself that her brother remarks to "fifteen years of trying to cope" (76), her subtle method of dealing with her husband causes less bodily harm than Leonard's eventual means of giving his hateful brother-in-law his due.

Ayckbourn's unexpected ploy in *Time and Time Again,* one of his most effective theatrical coups, is to direct the audience to anticipate the obligatory scene of a well-made play, then fail to provide it. By the time of the anticlimactic revelation of the secret known to the audience but kept from Peter—Leonard's duplicity in allowing him to think it is Graham whom Joan is seeing on the sly—the obtuse strongman has already vented his frustration on someone else. The expected confrontation between Peter and Leonard, eagerly awaited by Graham and the audience, never materializes. Instead of pummeling Leonard, Peter, the only character still in the dark, amiably seeks his advice over a friendly game of draughts, symbolical of the peculiar stalemate in which they are involved:

> *Leonard:* It's impossible for anyone to win.
> *Peter:* What do you mean? It's possible to win at draughts.
> *Leonard:* Not when you're playing on the white squares and I'm playing on the black. I can't take you and you can't take me! (69–70)

Finally, Joan decides to take neither man. When the deferred scene of physical violence does occur, with Peter surprisingly throttling Graham instead of Leonard, she sees the light: she has been Leonard's pawn. No longer beguiled by his helplessness and self-denigration, Joan is appalled that Leonard has merely stood by, deriving pleasure from the physical assault on his brother-in-law. When he claims that it was not what he wanted, that it "just sort of happened," she is clearsighted enough to observe that "there are a lot of things that just sort of happen when you're around, aren't there?" (83), her words applicable to another disruptive, endearing Ayckbourn male, his best-known character, Norman, yet to make his entrance in an Ayckbourn play.

Leonard escapes unscathed, but everyone around him is subject to wounding. In *Time and Time Again,* even before *The Norman Conquests,* the playwright already reveals his unwillingness to provide an audience with a wholly admirable, totally sympathetic character. Instead, the audience must identify with characters marred by recognizable human weakness. Although Leonard is undeniably appealing as an outsider not bound by convention, he has no sense of responsibility toward friends, family, even self. He lacks a moral center.

In *The Norman Conquests* (1973) the exasperated brother-in-law becomes Sarah, the obsessive sister-in-law; dim Peter becomes the even dimmer local vet, Tom, who also displays his prowess as boxer; while Leonard evolves into the eponymous Norman, irresistably lovable and unredeemably impossible. That the protagonist of *Time and Time Again* had been something of a trial run for the central character of the *Norman* trilogy was underscored in the West End productions of the plays. In 1974, with the A-effect again in play, London audiences watched actor Tom Courtenay play a character who is at heart an actor in search of an audience. Only two years earlier the same audience could have seen the same actor as Leonard, a Norman in embryo.

In *Round and Round the Garden,* in the longest single speech in the three parts of *The Norman Conquests,* Norman tells his disapproving sister-in-law Sarah a tale about a long-ago triumph in another garden. At nine years of age he had been so terrified by a strong-willed little girl who ran ragged over all the boys in their mixed infants primary school that he often played sick and would not attend. One day, when her mother brought her to his home for tea and they were sent out to play together on his own turf, his garden—not hers, the school grounds—he suddenly "picked her up . . . carried her right down . . . by the rubbish tip . . . and found the biggest patch of stinging nettles." "I pulled down her knickers and sat her right in the middle of them," he relates with relish. "I felt marvellous. It was a beautiful moment. Magic. . . . Then she got up, pulled up her knickers, very quietly took hold of my hand, gave me a big kiss and we went in and had our tea" (185–86). Norman knows what little girls, and big girls too, want and need to have. When Sarah rejects the tale as not quite credible, Norman admits "it may have been an allegory." A moment later he is kissing her:

> *Sarah:* That's enough. . . . *(She kisses him)* Quite enough—*(She kisses him)* No more . . .
> *Norman:* Sorry.
> *Sarah:* Enough. *(She kisses him again. This time it develops into a long kiss. Passionately)* Oh my God, what am I doing . . .
> *Norman: (kissing her all over)* I know what you're doing. Don't worry. I'll tell you later. (186)

For the theatergoer who has seen only the other parts of the trilogy, *Table Manners* and *Living Together,* Norman's insinuating himself into Sarah's affections is just another illustration of a consistently unpredictable nature. *Round and Round the Garden,* however, provides the key to his perversity. To seduce Sarah becomes for Norman the ultimate challenge as her husband Reg, Norman's brother-in-law, unwittingly throws down the gauntlet. A few hours before Norman's tale of a precocious Eve's fall in the garden, Reg had told him that a marriage might be invigorated were husband or wife to go off with someone else for a few days. Henpecked Reg, however, would never consider it for himself, and he is certain, he says, uttering the fatal words, that "Sarah would never dream of going off" (178). For Norman, as for Ayckbourn himself, the challenge is all: the more insurmountable it seems, the more imperative his need to accept it.

Norman, an assistant librarian who, having reorganized the Main Index, can never be fired—he alone knows its secret—spends a dizzyingly busy weekend reorganizing the lives of his wife's family, all the while transforming himself into the image of his creator-artist-stage manager-director. Norman, who, according to his wife Ruth, never makes a gesture "unless he has an appreciative audience to applaud him" (129) is also, like the Machiavellian Richard III but fortunately with intent less dire, the consummate actor. At once playing misunderstood husband, supportive friend, and ardent suitor, he makes co-conspirators of the others, casting himself in the role that each requires of him.

For Ruth, Norman is the pet that must be sheltered and fed: "It's a bit like owning an oversized unmanageable dog. . . . He's not very well house-trained, he needs continual exercising . . . . and it's sensible to lock him up if you have visitors. . . . But I'd hate to get rid of him" (195). Five years earlier he had proposed to her in a crowded lift, playing for sympathy to a captive audience that found him so appealing that she could hardly refuse (132). The proposal was the first of numerous occasions, like the present weekend, when Ruth wanted to throttle Norman but ended by cuddling him instead.

On Norman's insisting that he is warm and affectionate, Sarah too likens him to a wayward pet: "So are dogs," she says, "But they don't make particularly good husbands" (97). Yet Norman knows the way to crack her defenses, to offer sympathy and understanding to Sarah in the role in which he encourages her to cast herself—the long-suffering, overly-sensitive spouse who is, he assures her, so like himself: "We feel. We've got nerve-endings sticking out of our heads. We've no cynicism or scepticism to act as shock absorbers" (58). At dinner time he winds her up, setting her in motion by appealing to her at once as homemaker and peacemaker: "For God's sake, this is a family. . . . If we don't care, brothers sisters, husbands wives . . . if we can't finally join hands, what hope is there for anybody? Make it a banquet, Sarah my love, make it a banquet." Grabbing handfuls of cutlery and napkins, he scatters them on the table before her, then makes his escape, for Norman himself never lifts a finger to help: "I've started you off, I'll leave it to you. I'll go and change" (59).

For Annie, Norman is hardly the Greek god he would like her to imagine him, but rather an old English sheepdog, "all woolly and double-ended" (168). Nonetheless, tired of playing Chekhov's Varya to the Lopakhin of Tom who knows he is expected to wed her but cannot bring himself to propose, she needs romance. And only Norman can provide it by rescuing her from her invalid mother, if only for a "dirty weekend" in East Grinstead. Even Annie finds it difficult to envision Norman, "a badly built haystack," as a gallant lover, but she tries, and, miscast though he may be, Norman plays his role to the hilt: "We're not the first lovers who've ever done this—stood up to the whole establishment and said to hell with the status quo, we don't care what's meant to be, we mean this to be. Us" (102).

"I'd like to see you happy. . . . I'd very much like to make you happy" (81) is a refrain that recurs throughout the trilogy with the insistent subtlety of a Wagnerian motif. Norman speaks the words to Sarah, then varies them only slightly for Annie: "I'll make you happy. Don't worry. I'll make you happy" (88). Explaining to his wife that he has discovered his mission in life, he says, "I want you to be happy. I want everyone to be happy. I want to make everyone happy" (152). And he does—momentarily. Each of the three women he plays off against one another has a moment of happiness with Norman when she disengages herself from fighting with the others, denigrating them, calling them names. Norman's real purpose in life, however, is to make only one person completely, eternally happy—himself. The weekend has been a disaster for the rest, but Norman's goal is now in sight. He has spent the night with Ruth, the weekend with Annie is merely postponed, and Sarah is quivering with anticipation. Like Annie's cat up in the tree, Sarah will require only a little more coaxing before she too comes down to earth. His stage managing of the household's comic drama has been so satisfying that Norman prolongs it at the end of *Round and Round the Garden* by deliberately crashing Ruth's car into Reg's, forcing the family to stay together one more day. Like a Priestley play, the end returns to the beginning as those who were about to depart unload their luggage and return to the house. Norman has extended for at least one more performance the run of the play, a masterpiece of his own making, that was about to close. What more could any author-actor-director ask for?

"An artist requires encouragement,"[5] says Bertie Wooster to his man Jeeves in the one large-scale musical, *Jeeves* (1975), with which Ayckbourn, as author of the book and lyrics, has been involved, an unsuccessful collaboration with Andrew Lloyd Webber. Thinking himself the master of every situation, Bertie, muddle-headed upper-class idler, is no Norman. He has the charm of innocence, but not an ounce of ingenuity. Forever getting himself into scrapes, Bertie always has someone at the ready to rescue him in the person of Jeeves, the sublime creation of P. G. Wodehouse, on whose stories the musical is based. Jeeves is the artist, Bertie his own delightful creature. Again Ayckbourn makes use of the A-effect as Bertie, prompted by Jeeves, narrates for the audience how he foiled the foul plot of Sir Roderick Spode. Of course, he did not; Jeeves did, but with the generosity of the true artist who embraces anonymity, Jeeves allows his creature to garner the applause that Bertie, like Norman—they have that in common—feeds on.

The musical's setting is a stage-within-a-stage. The interior stage is a church hall where Bertie is about to perform on the banjo, an occasion important enough that the second string banjo critic of the *News Chronicle* is in attendance, Ayckbourn acknowledging for once that critics do exist. The design enables the audience to see the wings of the interior stage as the playwright once again suggests their need to focus beyond the conventional playing area to the entire theater, Ayckbourn's larger province. With the audience invited to peer into the wings of the stage-within-a-stage, they are made immediately aware of the extent to which Bertie relies on Jeeves. The performer has arrived without his instrument, but Jeeves produces the banjo, enabling the show to go on. But not for long. To the audience's enormous relief, there is a hiatus in Bertie's dreadful performance when all the strings break. While Jeeves goes off in search of replacements, Bertie amuses the audience by recounting his adventures at Totleigh Towers, the heart of the play-within-the-play. Jeeves resolves a double denouement: he reveals the secret that is Sir Roderick's undoing, and he provides Bertie, his puppet, with the latest in totally silent strings. The musical ends with Bertie, would-be artist, pleased with himself and his soundless banjo. He is unaware that all the while Jeeves has been his puppeteer manipulating all the strings, but by then the *News Chronicle* critic has taken his leave.

Bertie Wooster's "art" is an absence of sound, but hardly Keats's unheard sweeter melody. As unkind in their response to *Jeeves* as the *News Chronicle* man's reaction to Bertie's concert, the London theater critics may have been put off by its straightforward objective, no longer acceptable in the age of the concept musical, of providing trifling entertainment. The Wodehouse stories that can so delight the solitary reader are not the stuff from which to fashion a highly anticipated theatrical "event." Ayckbourn returns to the artist-figure in a later play that fills the theater with deafening sound. The rare contemporary comedy that approaches profundity, *Henceforward* . . . (1987) is too disturbing a work despite its oftentimes farcical frenzy to be ignored by either critics or audience.

Jerome, a composer, whose work is his life, sacrifices everything for his art, a cacophony of sound that is ultimately as empty as the blessed silence of Bertie's banjo. Whereas the inspiration behind *The Norman Conquests* is the manipulative drive of the professional man of the theater, the impulse behind *Henceforward* . . . may be the soul-searching of the creative artist pausing to reflect on the worth of his work. Has the artist anything of value to offer to others, or is his art as self-indulgent as Bertie's public display of his amusing but embarrassing vacuity? Norman's undeniable self-indulgence, his search for sexual gratification, does offer pleasure to others; he gives as well as takes. Jerome can only take, the deliberate objective of his sexual act with Zoë to provide fodder for his recording devices to be synthesized into what he believes will be the meaningful expression of a love beyond the physical. In actual practice he is akin to Strindberg's vampire figures who nourish themselves by feeding on others, draining them of their humanity.

Complete in his isolation Jerome leaves his barricaded studio, where he lives with a robot, only to shop at the automated hypermarket. He communicates with others, or rather ignores them, even his best friend's pleas for his attention, through electronic monitors. If the function of art is to mirror life, Jerome's artistry may be a valid reflection of the lifeless world he inhabits where man has become machine. In that world his friend Lupus, a drummer, has been replaced in a tea-dance trio by a drum machine, courtesy of an Arts Council grant. Mervin Bickerdyke of the Department of Child Well-being, a welfare officer whose concerns ought to be human needs, removes his coat to reveal beepers, alarms, and telephone lines on his person; he is as intricately wired as Nan 300F, Jerome's robot. And perhaps Nan is after all more human than Mervyn; Jerome's daughter at least detects a maternal instinct in her, even if it is a programmed emotion, one that her own mother has never displayed.

Rather than to mirror life, if the function of art is to exist for its own sake, then Jerome is the consummate artist. He has chosen a passive role in which he takes no part in preventing the onslaught of the machine. In fulfilling the self by recording the sounds of others, the artist has hastened the process. Not merely the extension of his machines, he has become one: "You're barely human," his wife tells him (82). In the "David," a piece of marble that courses with life, Michelangelo gloriously affirms man's humanity. In his mechanical synthesizing of the word "love," the deepest expression of human emotion, Jerome abandons man. Just as Pirandello in *Six Characters in Search of an Author* denies his own worth as artist by proving the inadequacy of the theater to sustain life in one of the world's dramatic masterpieces, in *Henceforward . . .*, a cautionary parable for the artist and his audience, Ayckbourn too demonstrates the failure of the artist, of himself perhaps. Yet in its denial of a soul for its artist-figure, *Henceforward . . .* is the paradoxical triumph of Ayckbourn the dramatist.

Manipulating others to secure a haven for himself within his claustrophobic refuge, Jerome is nevertheless passive in his acceptance of a world disintegrating beyond his doorstep. Jack McCracken in the earlier *A Small Family Business* (1987) also displays two sides to his nature. He is passive to his immediate family's manipulating of him, active to the point of aggression on discovering his power over his extended "family," an evolution in a single character from good provider to mafioso capo. Before *A Small Family Business,* in Tristram in *Taking Steps* (1979) and Guy in *A Chorus of Disapproval* (1984) Ayckbourn presents the character who is primarily acted upon. As the dramatist once suggested about himself—he never consciously made decisions concerning his career, "things just happened. It's this divine inertia"[6]—Ayckbourn's passive characters too can win out in the end.

The very junior partner in the law firm of Speake, Tacket and Winthrop, Tristram Watson in *Taking Steps* not only beds Elizabeth, wife of Roland, a wealthy, blustering bucket manufacturer—her doing, not his—but also shares another platonic bed with Kitty, the fiancée of Elizabeth's brother Mark, in a play that might more aptly than another be titled *Bedroom Farce*. A most unlikely solicitor, shy, apprehensive Tristram can hardly speak a single sentence that anyone can penetrate. In Roland Crabbe's rented Victorian manor to conclude the bucket king's purchase of the house from Leslie Bainbridge, he "explains" to Mark how he happened to be in bed with Elizabeth:

> Well. It's very simple. Quite simply, I am on a Winthrop. On Mr. Winthrop's, sorry. Behalf of him. For the completion of Mr. Crabbe. And yesterday evening, we were going to be exchanging Mr. Bainbridge. For contracts already drawn. And then, along came Mrs. Crabbe's note. And after it was discovered. The Bull was cancelled, you see. I think, because of the embrocation really. Sounds silly. And so Mr. Crabbe went up and I stayed down instead. And then came all this Scarlet Lucy business and it was a pure mistake. Honestly. In a nutshell (205).

Tristram has been shunted from room to room, from bed to bed, by the others. On learning that Elizabeth may have left him, Roland cannot bring himself to occupy their bedroom nor even stay alone in the large, creaky house—it is of course a dark and stormy night. Thus Tristram spends the night in the master bedroom rather than at the Bull Hotel. With Roland asleep in the attic bedroom and Mark in a third room—there is a delightful Marx Brothers moment with the three men parading through the house in identical Roland-mono-grammed pyjamas—Elizabeth decides to return home and climbs into bed with her husband, she thinks, in the dark. Tristram has already heard the history of the house, complete with ghost, and his apprehension turns to terror. The house, it seems, was once a brothel, and one of the girls was murdered there. She is said to return on occasion to revenge herself on all men by sleeping with anyone she discovers, who will be dead at dawn. By morning, when the solicitor wakes to find himself still among the living, terror gives way to rapture: "Dear God, thank you for a wonderful, wonderful night" (202). He has been manipulated into the most blissful experience of his life.

Before the play ends, the young man with no confidence at all has managed to bolster the ego of a kindred spirit, Kitty, as uncertain of herself as he. Having spent hours imprisoned in the attic closet where she hid when Roland took over the upstairs room for the night, Kitty, like Tristram, is at last fed up with having her life ruled by others, particularly her dull fiancé Mark, a man who puts people to sleep as he talks to them. A new relationship may be dawning with the new day for her and Tristram, whose life is looking up considerably. The author himself has remarked that *Taking Steps* is "a play about inno-cence . . . and freedom" that "proposes the probably naive and cer-tainly unfashionable view that good will triumph" (ix). In an uncharacteristically sunny mood in a farce both bright and brisk, Ayckbourn suggests that meek Tristram may inherit the earth. His later plays, however, demonstrate that not even the dramatist fully credits this proposition.

Guy Jones in *A Chorus of Disapproval* inherits the leading role in the Pendon Amateur Light Opera Society's production of *The Beg-gar's Opera*, but he loses everything else—job, friends, lovers. De-serving of neither his one gain nor his multiple losses, he has been acted upon throughout. Guy makes only a single decision, to audition for the amateur company, a way of starting again following the death of his wife. The company's director Dafydd is pleased to have him in the group, especially since Guy could be the source of useful information in a land deal in which the Welshman and—it so happens—many other Pendonites are involved. His subsequent rise through the ranks from bit player to star comes at the behest of the women who use him for their own particular ends. Neglected Hannah Llewellyn, whom Dafydd refers to as his "Swiss Army Wife" (77), needs someone to love her; she urges her husband to promote Guy from Crook-Fingered Jack to Matt of the Mint. Fay Hubbard requires another sex partner, and her acquiescent husband Ian needs the inside information that may be forthcoming from Guy; she suggests that he take over the role of Filch that Ian withdraws from. Rebecca Huntley-Pike, who finds solace in drink rather than sex, wants to insure Guy's cooperation purely for her husband's business interests; her words to Dafydd turn Guy into the star, the company's Macheath..

The reticent widower, a lowly accountant, has no inside info concerning his corporation's plans for expansion that the others greedily expect will enrich them, nor any means of obtaining it. Nonetheless he becomes everyone's willing but uncomprehending accomplice. When Fay reminds Guy, who has never fathomed the terms of their relationship, that her husband gave up the role of Filch expressly for Guy to fill it, he protests that he did not ask Ian to do so. "No, but you didn't say no, did you?" Fay points out; "But then you haven't actually said no to anything, have you?" (66). None-too-bright Guy has accepted everyone's favors without being aware of those favors as payment for his part in a "deal," Fay calling it that coming to him as a surprise. While the others have awaited a break in the news of the land deal, Guy has done nothing at all. His inviting a seventy-year-old nurse to be the "friend" the Hubbards ask him to bring when they invite him for a night of partner-swapping is typical of his inability to grasp a situation. Playing Gay's cunning highwayman, a character unlike himself in Macheath's ability to do unto others exactly what they plan to do unto him, would be for Guy at best a Pyrrhic victory were he even aware that he has been in a battle. Yet throughout he has been the consummate actor. The audience perceives what Guy cannot, that he is performing two roles at once. He knows he is playing the calculating con artist within the framework of *The Beggar's Opera;* that his fellow players have cast him in the same role within the framework of the community is a concept beyond his ken. For innocent Guy passivity is the only way.

Another innocent, Alistair Wingate, the almost-silent partner in a small firm that manufactures novelty goods in the earlier *Way Upstream* (1981), is as passive as Guy, up to a point. That point is reached not when his own life is in danger, but when his wife Emma is threatened by an unscrupulous ex-convict who takes over the pleasure craft on which Alistair and Emma, along with his dominant partner Keith and his wife June, are by no stretch of the imagination enjoying an ill-fated holiday, planned by Keith, on the River Orb.

Unsure of themselves on terra firma, the Wingates are here all at sea. June, for whom holiday is synonymous with luxury, is miserable in cramped quarters; and Keith, the self-appointed skipper who orders the others about as he navigates and steers with one hand, a boat owner's manual in the other hand, is distracted by threats of a strike at the plant. Taking on Vince as "pilot" once Alistair grounds the craft, the quartet finds itself at the mercy of the seemingly friendly stranger. Getting rid of Keith, his only competitor for command of the vessel, Vince promotes himself from pilot to captain. Although Vince cannot charm him, as he does the women, especially Keith's disgruntled wife, Alistair realizes the interloper is more adept than he at running the craft and acquiesces to the requests that soon become commands. Ordering the three who remain to address him as "Skipper," Vince, having thrown the manual overboard, exercises control through an insidious manipulation of language. Like the tyrant-teacher of Ionesco's "The Lesson," whose at once terrifying and comic air of menace *Way Upstream* achieves in its latter stages, Vince browbeats the group, assigning his own names to the various parts of the boat and its equipment. Under the misconception that he is an experienced river hand, they allow Vince to usurp reason and order as he garbles his terms:

> . . . pay attention, you'll learn something. . . . Now there are the names they print in the brochures for the benefit of the uninitiated and then there are the correct names that any self-respecting boat owner would normally use. So if you don't want to make idiots of yourselves, you'd better learn the proper ones. *(Jumping on to the bow)* This area here is known as your gaff deck. . . . Immediately below, the area beneath that we refer to as the scuppers. . . . Moving along—*(he stands on the saloon roof)*—the weevil deck, all right? And beneath that, what *you* call the saloon and *we* call the mizen. . . . Finally, that narrow corridor running from your snuffle down each side of your dodger, round your kedge, forward again past your weevil and meeting at your gaff are your port and starboard squeezes. They speak for themselves.[7]

After Vince maroons Alistair on an island in the river and forces Emma, who cannot swim, to walk the plank, Alistair at last sheds complacency for action. Taking on the far stronger Vince in a hand-to-hand fight at the water's edge, the weaker man surprisingly emerges the victor. The more expert combatant is caught offguard when Vince's female counterpart Fleur, a birdwatcher, one more passenger picked up along the perilous journey, startles him with her sudden, unexpected sighting of a kingfisher, the one bird that has eluded her. Alistair takes advantage of Vince's momentary lapse of concentration to bring him down with a blow to the head with a tin of baked beans he pulls out of the water at the very instant that Vince is about to plunge him into the river. The serendipitous tin enables Emma, like her husband displaying a newfound courage, to share in the victory: she had tried to get the food to her husband when Vince had ordered that Alistair have no provisions during his exile on the island.

As part of the abundant nature imagery that helps structure the play, the bird that appears to Fleur at the moment of Alistair's victory recalls the myth of Halcyone who threw herself into the sea when her husband, Ceyx, drowned on his way to consult the Oracle of Apollo. The gods turned the two into kingfishers, Zeus quieting the waters for a halcyon seven days on either side of the winter solstice to enable the birds, who, legend has it, hatch their young in a floating nest, to breed undisturbed. The river setting too becomes allegorical as the journey aboard the "Hadforth Bounty" continues up the Orb through Stumble Lock, Slippy Lock, and Pauper's Lock past Armageddon Bridge.

Aware of the new direction he was taking in *Way Upstream*, Ayckbourn has suggested that his departure from the real resulted from his exploration of musical forms in the lunchtime entertainments he devised with his composer, Paul Todd, a collaboration that flowered only a year earlier in the musical play, *Suburban Strains*, in which realistic characters seamlessly but unrealistically express themselves in song.[8] *Way Upstream* moves just as seamlessly from realistic comedy to social allegory. At Armageddon Bridge on the River Orb, resembling a wounded Lord Nelson complete with captain's hat, eyepatch, a blazer over his shoulder giving him the appearance of having one arm—and that in a sling—shy Alistair savors his triumph, his own "radiant orb," in the words of the hero of Trafalgar, to "brave every danger" for king and country. When he insists on hearing English music, Emma plays a cassette of William Byrd's "The Earl of Oxford's March."

Alistair and Emma know that they are not yet free. They are only halfway home and must go back to confront all the Vinces of the world, still a threat to their happiness. But before turning back, just beyond Armageddon, at the conclusion of the play, the contemporary Adam and Eve discover not the gone-to-seed garden of the other plays but a new Eden at the river's source. They shed their clothes to be cleansed in the waters of the Orb, fulfilling at last Alistair's dream of renewal that he could never express to Emma, hardly hope to share with her. No longer fearful of the water, Emma knows that Alistair will keep her afloat, safe from harm. Having earlier rejected Fleur's advances, Alistair, now captain of his destiny, can embrace Emma, liberated from her fears, as his first mate, his only mate.

A new element for Ayckbourn in *Way Upstream*, but part of its allegorical frame, is the motiveless malignity of Vince, who insisted himself upon a playwright credited with the ability to provide a realistic balance for his characters, surprising him and holding him spellbound, as he does the passengers of the "Hadforth Bounty." "He just appears, and one suspects he has no knowledge of the boat, the river, or anything, and what he doesn't know he invents," Ayckbourn has allowed.[9] As he rehearsed the role of Alistair, Robin Herford said to the author-director, "There's a terrible sense of evil in this play, and it's coming from there—Vince."Ayckbourn told Graeme Eton, who first played the role: "Be careful of this man. He never says anything without a reason. There is hardly a single line of his in the play that isn't calculated." Admitting to having made use of subtle class distinctions in the play, Ayckbourn suggests that Vince is like the NCO who exploits the weaknesses of the green officer, in this case Keith, who finds himself relying on him. Ayckbourn himself has likened Vince to the devil in that he works on people through their own weaknesses, June's vanity and conceit, Keith's arrogance and intransigence. The passive Alistair's eventual besting of Vince is consequently a triumph, if only a temporary one, of good over evil, marked by the flight of the kingfisher.

Ayckbourn has created manipulators before, but Leonard and Norman, even the later Jerome, hardly operate, as does Vince, from motives of pure evil. That streak of malignity, however, returns as a pitched battle between good and evil is waged in more realistic terms in *Man of the Moment* (1988). Again the water that will limit future productions of *Way Upstream*, a play that deserves to be remembered for its author's daring rather than its technical difficulties that nearly sank the National Theatre, figures prominently, perhaps more manageably, as a swimming pool, rather than a river, in the later work.

Written nearly three decades after *The Square Cat*, *Man of the Moment* contrasts two men who together are a refinement of a single character in Ayckbourn's first play in which mild-mannered, considerate Arthur Brummage confronted and triumphed over the boorish show-biz personality, Jerry Wattis, his other self. Guy in *A Chorus of Disapproval* might well be Arthur trying on the role of Macheath, an unlikely part for either of them. Those who mistakenly think they have been deliberately conned by him, and they are legion in Pendon, consider Guy as scoundrel perfect casting, adding a challenging dimension to the play. In *Way Upstream* that two-sided single self,

Arthur-Jerry, Guy-Macheath, divides in two, as indecisive Alistair takes on his manhood as he confronts the evil Vince. Two become one again as a complex character, seemingly average Jack McCracken in *A Small Family Business*, allows himself to be engulfed by a corrupt system, resulting in his own perpetration of evil. The one again splits into two in *Man of the Moment* as guileless, acquiescent Douglas Beechey meets up for the second time in his life with Vic Parks, like Vince an ex-convict and ruthless manipulator, who has become, as the result of a meteoric rise on television, an idol of the masses.

The two men had encountered one another seventeen years before the start of the play when Vic, on a bank raid, had taken hostage Nerys Mills, a lovely young employee. Meek, law-abiding Douglas, a bank clerk at the time, had suddenly transformed himself into the hero of the moment by throwing himself at Vic, whose loaded shotgun went off, hitting Nerys in the side of the face, scarring her, changing forever the lives of the three of them. Deserted by her handsome fiancé after the accident, Nerys, who hardly ventures out of her home, had married Douglas, the one man who had remained kind to her. Fired from the bank because gawkers came to stare at the local hero, Douglas, like Guy, a capable if unimaginative accountant good with figures, found a job as a bookkeeper with a double-glazing firm. His "fame," however, was not lasting. One newspaper had begun the Beechey Awards—"We will fight them on the Beecheys"—"given annually to anyone having a go at criminals,"[10] but after the third year they were discontinued. Long before that, Douglas had been either forgotten or remembered only as "the idiot who tackled an armed robber and nearly got someone's head blown off in the process" (74). Jill Rillington, another TV personality, comments on the situation: "Isn't it ironic that the hero is forgotten? And the villain has now become the hero. . . . And isn't that a reflection of our time?" (31). Responsible for bringing the two together for her program, *Their Paths Crossed*, Jill is pinning her hopes for a continuing series on what she expects to prove an intensely dramatic confrontation.

Vic's life has been very different from Douglas's. In prison for eight years—not his first stint there—he had completed an autobiography, *My Life,* "written during Her Majesty's pleasure—and on Her Majesty's stationery" (24). Jill had started him on his sensational career when she interviewed him on his release on her local radio show in Bristol, *Facing Up.* From there he had gone on to read part of his book on *Pick of the Week*, which earned him a spot on *Start of the Week*, which led to *Stop the Week, Any Questions, The Book Programme, Did You See,* then to his own nationwide TV programs, *Ask Vic* for children and *The Vic Parks Show* for adults, giving him a total of nine million viewers, and that on an off-week when some of the faithful have temporarily switched allegiance to the motor show (29). Since his TV career has flowered, Vic has authored, with the help of a ghost-writer, a second book, *Life as a Straight Man,* for five months the nation's number one best-seller.

As much the folk hero as Buster Edwards, Britain's infamous yet oddly beloved "Great Train Robber," Vic Parks, author and media personality, is the true artist of the electronic age, a showman for a time in which television has become the only viable theater. Ayckbourn, always aware that his sometime theater audience is made up of habitual TV watchers comfortable in their passive role, puts them at ease by structuring the play as a talk show that turns into the current favorite television genre, the docudrama. In fact the audience is never sure if what is being presented them are the supposed actual events themselves or, as on such programs as *Unsolved Mysteries* and *A Current Affair,* a reenactment with fictional flourishes with actors as recent newsmakers. The A-effect prominently and inexorably invades primetime viewing hours. At one point with Douglas alone on the patio, Cindy, Vic's young daughter, runs on to present him with a child's bouquet of wild grasses and weeds. Just then Jill comes on, says, "And cut," and thanks him, Douglas inquiring, "Was that all right?" (42) A few minutes later when her crew wants to know if she has finished another shot, Jill, exasperated, shouts, "Idiots. . . . Of course I've finished. . . . Cut!" (50), followed by a sudden blackout signaling the end of the act. The moment recalls a similar one in *Six Characters in Search of an Author* when the manager calls his stage-hand an idiot for mistakenly bringing down the curtain at the end of the second act.

Man of the Moment begins with Jill rehearsing the introduction of her television show, her unintentional sound-reversal bloopers fore-shadowing the more significant reversals the play has in store: "In this edition of *Their Paths Crossed,* we tell a story that started seventeen years ago in the slow and sneet of a Surrey Novem. . . . Keep rolling. We'll go again. Snow and sleet. . . . Here we go . . . Hallo. I'm Rill Jillington . . . My God, I don't believe this" (1). Not quite a Pirandellian exploration of the disparity between illusion and reality, despite its use of the Italian dramatist's trademark techniques, *Man of the Moment* presents an unfortunate reality, what ought not to be but is. Her tongue at last untangled, Jill continues: "But this is no child's fable, it is a true story. This is the real world where nothing is as it seems. This is the real world where heroes are easily forgotten; this is the real world where the villains may, themselves, become heroes" (2).

The play's setting is the paved patio of Vic's villa in a Spanish-speaking area of the Mediterranean. Significantly, unlike other Ayckbourn plays, no garden is in evidence, only *"one or two shrubs in tubs"* (1). Flown there by the TV network, Douglas, already introduced to Vic's wife Trudy and his manager Kenny, notices someone else in the background and asks if it is another family member, only to be informed that Ruy is the gardener. Dressed in pullover and heavy jacket for Purley's foul weather in the glorious heat of the Mediterranean, the new arrival surveys the scene and comments, "Very impressive . . . All you need now is a garden, eh?" (9). Douglas asks Ruy, who, like his wife Marta, ignores everyone but his beloved employer Vic, "Do you get weeds?" and getting no response, adds, "I definitely don't know the Spanish for weed killer" (9–10). Even among paving stones there may be insidious weeds, and, unknowingly, Douglas may be the one to uproot them.

Having already interviewed Douglas in Purley in, as she describes it, his "dingy little house . . . . on the edge of a roaring main trunk road" (18), Jill is certain he will shed his characteristic complacency on seeing how glamorously Vic lives, will reveal at last a human emotion—jealousy—and a desire for revenge. What ought to be Douglas's reaction, is not what is. He is a man with no axe to grind, thus an interviewer's nightmare: "There's absolutely nothing you can say to him that he doesn't agree with. He smothers you with approval" (5). When her frustration causes her to ridicule him, Douglas is impervious, for he is, as his creator states, *"compensated for his apparent lack of aggression by an almost complete invulnerability to attack"* (8):

> Jill: (*With ill-concealed annoyance*) So you have no feelings at all about this place, Mr. Beechey? Like you appear not to have feelings about anything very much?
> Douglas: Oh, I have feelings, Jill. . . . But I sincerely hope that envy is not one of them. Because envy in my book is a deadly sin and as a practising Christian, that is something I try to avoid.
> Jill: Super. I'm glad to hear it. Well, perhaps you ought to tell me something you do feel strongly about and we'll try and include that in the programme. . . . Illegal parking on double yellow lines? Any good? Dogs fouling footpaths? Free double glazing for senior citizens?
> Douglas: (*Thoughtfully*) I suppose evil, really. . . . I feel strongly about that.
> Jill: That's it? Just evil?
> Douglas: Yes. Only, it's often hard to recognize. But there's a lot of it about, you know. (18–19)

At the moment of Douglas's pronouncement on the all-pervasiveness of evil, Vic makes his first entrance, holding his seven-year-old daughter by the hand. His basic concerns seem that of any family man—to provide for his second wife and their two children. As any good father would, he asks Jill to be sure to use the kids in a shot on the show; he has promised them that. The onetime criminal, having paid his debt to society, is now a benefactor of the young and needy. If he once pretended to be visiting sick children in hospital when he was in fact 140 miles away in a London studio, his adoring viewers were never aware of the electronic sleight of hand (4). Crafty and opportune he may be, but evil is not apparent in the much photographed face beloved by millions.

Although boorish in manner, Vic is not the least sensitive person at the villa. Following a brief run-through rehearsal, the audience observes actors playing characters adopting their TV personas, even Douglas making a futile effort to give the interviewer just what she wants. Jill is determined to try to film the meeting of the two men in a single take before lunch, but the shot is nearly wrecked as Ruy enters by the pool with a hosepipe in his hand to watch the proceedings. In attempting to get him out of camera range, someone gives the hose a fierce tug. Caught off balance, Ruy, who cannot swim, falls backward into the pool. In obvious distress, calling for help, he is ignored as Jill insists that the crew and her "actors" carry on: "Don't worry about the gardener, he's not in shot" (48). Despite his concern for the man, Douglas as ever acquiesces; Vic is unperturbed. Only when Jill is pleased with the reenactment of their meeting—"And that's it. Super. Thank you both. . . . George apparently managed to pan off the gardener and still keep the full patio in frame, so we're OK. . . . Lunchtime, is it?" (49)—does Vic pull his exhausted employee out of the water.

In the second act Vic's vicious streak becomes more evident as the gulf between him and his wife Trudy widens. One of their differences concerns the stone seat Ruy is building. The gardener, a Sisyphus, carries rough stone blocks onto the patio throughout much of the act. But Vic cannot decide on the bench's positioning and orders Ruy to erect it, then remove it, over and over again. The actual cause of Trudy's unhappiness is that her husband, all the while abusing her, "has been screwing his way round Television Centre and half of ITV" (76). At his most hateful Vic cruelly baits Sharon, the obese nineteen-year-old hired as the children's nanny, to the point that even Douglas protests until reminded that he is a guest at the villa (66).

Every action in his own life having an ulterior motive, Vic cannot believe that Douglas's reason for being there is the all-expenses-paid trip and the opportunity to appear on television. Vic, like Jill, expects Douglas to make a move, to exact some form of retribution for past events. Not so. The long-ago chance encounter has provided Douglas an ideal existence. The Beecheys live quietly in modest comfort, making no demands on one another. He tells Jill, who is desperate to prick the blissful bubble of a seemingly perfect if incredible relationship, that his sexual union with Nerys came to an end two years after their marriage. As neither one took much pleasure in physical intimacy, neither one misses it. To Trudy, not to Jill, Douglas admits that chance has made him a happy man. Before the bank raid he had worshipped Nerys, who had hardly been aware of him, treating him with the common courtesy one extends to a fellow employee. Douglas analyzes for Trudy his ambivalent feelings about Vic, the husband she can no longer pretend to love. "So what do I say?" he asks, "Yes, I do—I hate Vic because of what he did to the most beautiful woman in the world? Or, thank you very much, Vic, for being instrumental in arranging for me to marry the unattainable girl of my dreams? Difficult to know which to say, isn't it?" (72).

The drama that Jill has been hoping to evoke comes unexpectedly from another source. Miserable in her unrequited love for Vic, who is monstrous to her, Sharon determines to kill herself and jumps into the pool in a wetsuit that in fact marks her resemblance to the whale that Vic has likened her to. Desperately trying to get her husband to dive into the pool to save the girl, Trudy attacks him with her fists, but Vic, who has had too much to drink, is more amused than concerned. Douglas, hearing the commotion, comes onto the patio just in time to see Vic grab Trudy's neck with one hand and pinion her arms with the other. When Vic, without realizing what he is saying, repeats the very words he uttered in the bank seventeen years before—"Don't get excited and nobody'll get hurt, alright?" (78)—Douglas, like Pavlov's dog, reacts with a conditioned response. With a wild, furious yell he rushes at Vic, who releases Trudy, and catches him in the midriff, toppling him into the pool. After much threshing about, Trudy and Douglas looking on helplessly, a great sea creature—Sharon—rises from the water. Relieved that the pathetic girl is still alive, Trudy has a sudden thought:

> *Trudy:* Sharon, where is Mr. Parks?
> *Sharon: (Apologetically)* I'm standing on him, Mrs. Parks. (80)

Vic is pulled from the water, too late, forcing the three survivors to concoct a story for the police and the public.

Suddenly, the key players, all but Jill, are replaced by television actors who reenact the drowning in a manner acceptable to the medium by providing a martyrdom for a public idol. The new Ruy and Marta are more decidedly Spanish, and Sharon, as she must be for television, is downright svelte. In his very first effort to provide a play for the Scarborough company, Ayckbourn had rifled Pirandello, Stephen Joseph sensibly rejecting the script, suggesting it be put away in a drawer. In *Man of the Moment*, three decades later, the playwright again borrows from the Italian's battery of theatrical surprises but puts them to masterful use by effectively casting the theater audience in the role of television-studio audience. Kneeling reverently, the TV actors surround the actor playing Vic as Jill addresses the audience directly. The conclusion of *Man of the Moment* becomes the final minutes of a segment of *Their Paths Crossed,* a program perpetuating a media myth: the criminal-as-hero, the TV star who sacrificed his own life in a gallant attempt to save the life of his hapless employee. Jill reminds her audience to tune in again next week at the same time for "the start of *The Very Best of Vic*—a series of twelve special programmes featuring selected highlights from his recent series" and to attend the first of the Annual Midland Bank Vic Parks Awards for Youth that she will be co-presenting in London next month (87). Having served as midwife to the myth, Jill will continue to feed on it.

As she bids farewell, a TV floor manager appears to give the theater-studio audience their instructions, or rather to coax them into a show of enthusiasm, "as much *warm* applause as you can give us" (89). He himself starts the applause that lasts through the play's curtain call. Not only has Ayckbourn written a play and directed its actors, here he directs the audience's response as well. Despite the play's obvious highlighting of the manipulative, exploitative nature of the medium, despite the openness with which they too have been manipulated and exploited, no audience at a single performance of *Man of the Moment* has withheld the applause demanded of them.

At the conclusion of *As You Like It,* Rosalind requests a show of approval from an audience delighted by a world restored to order; as *Man of the Moment* ends, the audience applauds, not a fairy tale with a happily-ever-after ending, but a reflection of a chaotic world. Once again, as in the killing of Hough in *A Small Family Business,* Ayckbourn demonstrates his uncanny ability to provoke laughter from horror. Yet no audience can resist the irresistible. Early in the play, in his recalling the moment during the bank raid when the gun went off and hit Nerys in the side of the face, Vic says, "It was a miracle, with the gun that close, she didn't lose an eye. A miracle. I thank God for that, at least." After a momentary respectful pause Douglas breaks the silence: "She did lose her ear, though" (34). The eruption of laughter, hardly tinged with an acknowledgment of a human being's pain and suffering, is in fact the audience's response conditioned by the playwright's cunning artistry.

Soon after his arrival Douglas had told Kenny that he and Nerys are physically well, but, he had continued, "Nerys is sometimes . . . But it's mostly in her mind" (15). Later he tells Vic the true reason for his coming to the villa: what happened in the bank has haunted the Beecheys for seventeen years. Both of them still dream about Vic, still wake up frightened in the night, Nerys terrified that Vic is coming to get her—"So, don't take this wrong, but I was hoping this—meeting—might help to exorcise you. If you follow me" (63).

As the play ends, Vic, seemingly the devil, is dead, yet evil cannot die. In *Way Upstream* Alistair has only temporarily vanquished the thoroughly evil Vince, who, very much alive, may be lying in wait for the downstream voyage of the "Hadforth Bounty." In *Othello* the Moor says to Iago, "If that thou be'st a devil, I cannot kill thee." He runs at him with his sword but only wounds him. It is the victim who is dead at the end of Shakespeare's play; the victimizer still lives.

The usual pattern of the Ayckbourn play is to present women as victims of their men, but *Man of the Moment* has yet one more reversal. Vic Parks has victimized Nerys, Trudy, and Sharon, even Kenny, his homosexual manager, but he is himself destroyed by an evil even greater than his own selfish malevolence, the manipulative electronic medium that dictates standards, tastes, and values and creates the hollow heroes who use a pliant public for their own ends. The agent of that evil is Jill Rillington, who, unknowingly, has avenged all of Ayckbourn's put-upon women. Having started Vic on the road to fame and fortune, she, not Douglas, has demanded he pay a price, to appear on *Their Paths Crossed* because, as she puts it, "He owes me one" (6). That appearance has brought Vic face to face with another of Jill's puppets, Douglas, a good man living a Christian life but the catalyst for Vic's destruction, with chance too taking a hand. Vic and Douglas, refinements of Ayckbourn's recurring male characters, have been poles apart in their treatment of women, the one marring Nerys's beauty and causing Sharon's attempted suicide, the other coming to the rescue of damsels in distress, first Nerys, later Trudy. But a woman, Jill, manipulates them both and engineers their fatal reunion. Chance encounters may upend men's lives, but their reenactments make for good television and, in a deceptively disturbing play, better theater.

6
Upstream and Off Course, the World

The subtext that Stephen Joseph uncovered in *Mr Whatnot*—that anarchy is preferable to the status quo—reveals more about the older director's social attitudes than it does about its young author's political leanings. There is no formulated political program hidden in the depths of the whimsical piece, for in 1963 Alan Ayckbourn was more concerned with forging his place in the theater than in changing the face of the world. Whereas his own personality as well as that of his mentor, Joseph, does color the characterization of Mint, Ayckbourn's silent protagonist, something else lies at the heart of the work—the film comedy of an earlier era. "I suppose a lot that influenced me has nothing to do with the theatre at all," Ayckbourn confessed to Watson; "*Whatnot* is the outstanding example, which was totally to do with films—people like René Clair and Renoir, and going back to Buster Keaton and Laurel and Hardy, who still remain, I suppose, my major comic influence. . . . A lot of my stuff is actually closer to that . . . than I suspect it is to my contemporary comic dramatists."[1]

The technique of film, as well as its content, plays an important part in much of Ayckbourn's work: "A lot of my stuff is obviously filched from film. The thing about film is that it's developed its own tense flexibility."[2] A stage direction in a late Ayckbourn play, *The Revengers' Comedies*, introducing a scene in which mourners silently react to the situation as well as to one another in a churchyard, reads: "*It is as though we are watching the scene in long shot.*"[3] The playwright-director is viewing his characters through the camera's lens.

The film-editing technique that Ayckbourn most uses in his work for the stage is the presentation of simultaneous action by means of crosscutting. Tennessee Williams, a self-admitted movie addict, also experimented with the device in the multiple locales of *Summer and Smoke* and more intricately in the last scene of *Period of Adjustment*, which alternates between living room and bedroom. Ralph and Dorothea prepare for bed in the one room while Isabel and George do the same in the other. The opening and closing of the bathroom door directs the focus of attention as light enters the bedroom and is shut off again, making the alternating action in the two rooms a simultaneous occurrence.[4] Ayckbourn acknowledges that crosscutting provided the essential fluidity for the three-locale setting of *Bedroom Farce*. Fourteen years later he relied even more on the technique in *The Revengers' Comedies* (1989), a two-part, four-act play, presented on two nights or on a single day at a matinee and evening performance. Here the focus alternates between the personal life of Henry Bell in the country and the public life of Karen Knightly in the city, dictating the tempo of the work. A stage direction late in the first half reads: *"From now on the action accelerates and the scenes begin to cross cut faster and faster."*

In *The Revengers' Comedies* Ayckbourn consciously refines for the stage those devices perfected for the screen by American pioneer director D. W. Griffith as early as 1914. Griffith shot thousands of feet of film, then edited them into exhilarating sequences of nail-biting suspense at the climax of his films. Admitting to a fascination with film techniques, Ayckbourn considers that what he does is to "pre-edit." He is aware of the increasing gravity of the themes he continues to explore, but he remains equally conscious of his need to provide his audience with a fulfilling theatrical experience: "If I tell my stories terribly solemnly and seriously . . . nobody wants to see them. I've really got to make them entertaining. I've really got to make them eye-catching."[5] By design, his plays are ineffective on the radio, a medium for which he does not write, unless the text is adapted to make allowance for the essential visual element. The same film devices that enable the ride of the Klan in Griffith's *The Birth of a Nation* to grip even a contemporary audience unsympathetic to its message Ayckbourn adapts to the stage in *The Revengers' Comedies*, a black comic saga that charts the decline of another nation, while mirroring the predicament of a wider world. In 1981, as his comedies were unmistakably darkening nearly a decade before *The Revengers' Comedies*, Ayckbourn told Watson, "It's up to me to employ whatever technical resources I have; but I always try to be extremely careful that the technical resources do not deny the characters their true destinies."[6] Technique never overwhelmed *The Revengers' Comedies* in its Scarborough premiere, but an over-elaborate subsequent London production may have blurred the painful truths already evident in his earlier work, diminishing the effect of an extraordinary play.

In an early scene in *Intimate Exchanges*, incorporated in both *Affairs in a Tent* and *Events on a Hotel Terrace*, Celia gets more than she bargained for when she asks her husband Toby, an alcoholic, why he drinks. She and her mother have had several arguments about whether the women in the family "all marry men who are drawn to drink or whether it's we that drive them to it." Toby considers it his duty to disabuse her of the notion that she and her mother are the sole cause; there are more important reasons why a man should take to drink:

> Number one: I think the whole of life has become one long losing battle, all right? That's the first reason I'm drinking. Number two: I find myself hemmed in by an increasing number of quite appalling people all flying under the flags of various breeds of socialism, all of whom so far as I can gather are hell bent on courses of self-reward and self-remuneration that make the biggest capitalist look like Trotsky's Aunt Mildred. Number three: On the other hand, we have the rest of the country who don't even have the decency to pretend that they're doing it for the benefit of their fellow men. Ha ha. They're just grabbing hand over fist the most they can get for the minimum of effort by whatever grubby underhand means they can muster. Number four: We have half the men going around looking like women and half the women looking like men and the rest of us in the middle no longer knowing what the bloody hell we are. Number five: And the few remaining women who don't look like men are busy ripping their clothes off and prancing around on video cassettes and soft porn discs trying to persuade us that sex can be fun. . . . So can World War Three. Number six:—are you still with me?—We now have a police force that . . . . is more dishonest than the people we're paying them to arrest. Don't, for God's sake, ask them the time, just hang on to your watch. Number seven: They've started this filthy floodlit cricket with cricketers wearing tin hats and advertisements for contraceptives on their boots. Number eight: You can no longer walk through the centre of any town anywhere in this country without being set upon by thousands of bald tattooed Neanderthals. Number nine: You can't get a hotel room in London for love nor money because they're all booked up by hordes of bloody foreigners in black berets busy wiring up suitcases full of bloody explosives to blow the rest of us up. And Number ten: whisky very, very shortly is going to be ten quid a bottle. Have I made my point, Celia? (1: 18–19)

Whereas Toby's listing of modern civilization's horrors moves from the universal to the personal, the direction of Ayckbourn's work has taken the opposite course, from the imaginary yet very real village of Pendon, the setting of many of the plays, to a nation and a world involved in corruption at every level. Evil has crossed national boundaries as multinational corporations dictate events that shape the lives of villagers going about their daily rituals at home, at work, at play.

Ayckbourn's early work is inspired by events from his own life and his observations of his neighbors. At first the world at large is not the concern of characters attempting, oftentimes failing, to find satisfaction in dull routine with equally dull mates. But local government intrudes in *Ten Times Table* when the very committee meetings Ayckbourn was forced to attend begin to affect the life of the town. A boat trip on the Norfolk Broads with his family inspires an allegory about the ship of state journeying *Way Upstream*. In *A Chorus of Disapproval* an amateur light opera group in Pendon sings its way through big-business intrigues. *A Small Family Business* charts the inroads of a worldwide evil on an ideal family. The futuristic *Henceforward* . . . becomes a cautionary fable for a contemporary world. *Man of the Moment* demonstrates the corruption of civilized values by the home-invading media. The movement crystallizes in *The Revengers' Comedies*, a play demonstrating the dramatist's increasingly pessimistic vision of a world too far off course, completing a movement from little Pendon through larger Britain to farther horizons. The film comedy clowns Ayckbourn once named as contributors to the essence of *Mr Whatnot*—Keaton, Laurel and Hardy—have, significantly, influenced absurdist dramatists Beckett and Ionesco, too, as they have acknowledged. Ayckbourn's major theme, like theirs, has become mankind's bewilderment in a universe out of control.

When Tennessee Williams's characters in *Battle of Angels*, *The Eccentricities of a Nightingale*, *Kingdom of Earth*, and "This Property Is Condemned" blot out sordid reality with comforting illusion by seeing a movie, they go to the same picture palace, the Delta Brilliant. A not-so-safe haven for young lovers in *Summer and Smoke*, *A Streetcar Named Desire*, and *Orpheus Descending* is the Moon Lake Casino. Again and again Williams employs as setting a small town in the Mississippi Delta that represents America's southland, a festering world that mirrors the souls of his walking wounded. Seemingly more placid than the overheated Williams landscape, Ayckbourn country centers on fictitious Pendon, a pretty village in the Home Counties of southern England, the land of Ayckbourn's youth which he still considers home ground despite his having transplanted himself to the unlikely theatrical mecca of Scarborough in northern England.

Ayckbourn himself locates Pendon in Berkshire, on the outskirts of Reading, a "non-town," as he calls it, about a forty-five-minute train journey west of London.[7] Comfortable and prosperous, its population civic-minded, Pendon is an ideal place to live, if not to love, for no relationship there is as serene as the surrounding lush green countryside. In *Sisterly Feelings* the action takes place on Pendon Common, a marshland as unstable as the marriage of Abigail and Patrick, from which "*the distant rumble of traffic on the main Pendon to Reading road*" may be heard (1). Yet Pendon, always placed in the

Home Counties, is not firmly anchored; like the relationships of its inhabitants, its location is subject to change. In *Relatively Speaking* Sheila, who is having a problem with a husband with a roving eye, lives at the Willows, Lower Pendon, Buckinghamshire. Leonard in *Time and Time Again*, who undercuts his sister's marriage and wrecks his friend's engagement, plays cricket—badly—for the East Pendon Occasionals. In "Gosforth's Fête," one of five interlinked one-act plays that comprise *Confusions* (1974), the Little Pendon Wolf Cubs help turn the Grand Fête into as much a shambles as the relationship of Stewart and Milly; Stewart is understandably distressed to learn, as does the entire community over a public address system inadvertently left on, that his fiancée is pregnant by another. Pendon has shifted to the south and east, to the county of Kent in the one-act play, yet it is still the recognizable Ayckbourn world where the Conservatives—right-wing fascists, according to Stewart who is drowning his sorrows (53)—comfortably maintain the upper hand over the Labour Party. Local politics heat up in *Ten Times Table* as the townspeople of Pendon stage a pageant as foredoomed as the Grand Fête. In *Way Upstream*, a play charting the social and political climate of the Thatcher era, Alistair and Emma must journey past Armageddon Bridge, well beyond Pendon Lock, before reaching a utopia where Alistair can fulfill his dream. *A Chorus of Disapproval* reveals what is happening in Pendon, perhaps even as *Way Upstream*'s boat, the "Hadforth Bounty," goes by: a once tranquil community has grown corrupt. The Pendon Amateur Light Opera Society blithely rehearses *The Beggar's Opera*, itself concerned with the very intrigues of sex and "business" that are occurring backstage. In fact Pendon affairs mirror those of Gay's London, without the charms of historical distance softening the irony of an eighteenth-century ballad opera for a twentieth-century audience. The residents of a once-idyllic village might well be advised not to depend on the kindness of good neighbors, for Pendon has become in the Thatcher decade a microcosm for an imperfect world.

Alcoholic Toby of *Intimate Exchanges* is painfully aware of both his own decline and that of the world about him. Even the playing fields of the school of which he is headmaster, the Bilbury Lodge Preparatory School for Boys and Girls, are no longer properly tended, for Lionel, the groundskeeper, is as ineffectual as he. Doctor Bill Windsor first met Susan of *Woman in Mind* at student concerts at Bilbury Lodge, their children's school. Although the town itself in *Intimate Exchanges* and *Woman in Mind* is unnamed, it has the unmistakable Pendon ambience, Ayckbourn himself revealing that his own preparatory Home Counties school suggested the gentle chaos of Bilbury

Lodge. The interrelationship of his plays, oftentimes intentional, has on occasion even surprised the precognitive author. Directing a revival of *Relatively Speaking*, Ayckbourn was startled by a line of dialogue indicating that Greg and Ginny had met at Malcolm's party, the setting ten years later of *Bedroom Farce*—a small world indeed.[8]

As early as 1978 *Sunday Times* critic John Peter noted a widening focus in Ayckbourn's work. In *Ten Times Table*, a pretty little town becomes "England writ small by a cool and caustic chronicler of large frustrations in small places."[9] The rift between Lawrence Adamson, a minor character, and his wife Charlotte, who never appears, is an embellishment, not the center, of a Pendon play in which the major concern transcends domestic arrangements. *Observer* critic Robert Cushman, reviewing the London production of *Ten Times Table* in a piece that also included his assessment of a revival of a play by Arnold Wesker, concurred: "There is actually a clearer political polarization visible in [the Ayckbourn play]. . . . The opposition in 'Chicken Soup with Barley' is kept off-stage; Mr Ayckbourn offers a Tory lady, a young Marxist schoolteacher and several indeterminates between . . . literally a departure. Having explored kitchen, bedroom, livingroom and garden shed, Mr Ayckbourn has finally left home."[10]

To experience the event that inspired *Ten Times Table*, the dramatist did not have to travel far—merely to the center of the town of Scarborough. Ayckbourn is successful as a company man as long as, in his own quiet way, he calls the tune. A gentle, politic—if not political—man, he can transform a theater company into an effective working body. Bonds are formed, but all the participants recognize the leader among them. As a creative artist, he has learned from experience that he is uncomfortable, not at his best, in the role of collaborator. As a committee person he is out of his element totally, yet his administrative position with the Scarborough theater on occasion forces him to take up that role. An exasperating but artistically profitable experience occurred in 1976 when Ayckbourn of necessity attended frequent, time-consuming but not always productive meetings when the Scarborough company needed to finance and facilitate a move from the first floor of the Public Library to the more commodious ground floor of the Boys' Grammar School. As tedious as the meetings were, Ayckbourn became intrigued by them, observing curious personality transformations as boredom and frustrations mounted. A committee of well-intentioned Scarborough citizens was surely no different from any disparate group of people forced to convene to solve a common problem. A small civic-minded group probably acted no differently from a corporate board, perhaps even a government cabinet: "Apparent strong men weaken. Nonentities in-

herit the floor. Silent men gabble on inarticulately and to no point.
Talkative men grow silent and merely emit low indecipherable moans
of dissent and agreement. *Ten Times Table* is a study of the committee
person."[11] The play is actually something more—Ayckbourn's first
dramatic confrontation of the political extremes which terrify him—
the far left and the far right.

In the decaying ballroom of the dreary Swan Hotel—no longer up
to its offical three-star rating—a committee draws plans for the First
Pendon Folk Festival. The centerpiece of the occasion is to be a
modest pageant based on a historic event that supposedly took place
two hundred years earlier, the Massacre of the Pendon Twelve. According to E. Arnott Hutchings's account in the now out-of-print
Through Haunts of Coot and Hern, it seems a local farmer, Jonathan
Cockle, had so vigorously protested against unfair taxation that the
militia summoned to quell the disturbance mortally wounded the
agitator and several of his followers. That the doors of the ballroom the
committee uses as its meeting place open onto the Market Square,
scene of the massacre, is a fortuitous sign, and the committee goes
about its work with enthusiasm.

Trouble begins brewing with a clash of temperaments between
Helen Dixon, an arch-Conservative, who sees the pageant as an
opportunity for her to wear an elaborate period costume, and Eric
Collins, a self-proclaimed Marxist who teaches modern history at the
Catherine Stoker Comprehensive School, who plans to turn the event
into a populist rally. Insisting that "this is not a political meeting. And
I won't have any politics," Helen's husband Ray, the committee
chairman, attempts to keep peace (82), but to no avail. The local
councillor Donald Evans and his eighty-year-old mother Audrey, the
nearly deaf committee secretary, merely add to the meetings' tedium
and confusion. Evans, a member of every existing Pendon organization, civic or otherwise, is nonetheless ineffectual in obtaining per-
mits from the local police or grants from the Leisure and Amenities
Committee, but he is a nonpareil at pinpointing misspellings in any
written report. Mrs. Evans, never quite sure what is going on, is
understandably remiss in submitting her minutes. The never-visible
Bernard Lorne-Messiter, local property owner and entrepreneur,
regrets his inability to attend a single meeting, eventually offering his
resignation along with a £5 contribution to the worthy cause. Lawrence Adamson, never to be seen without a whisky glass in hand, does
attend the occasional meeting but is even more oblivious to the
proceedings than old Mrs. Evans.

Battle lines are drawn when Eric suggests that the committee
appoint leaders for the pageant's two opposing factions, Cockle's

followers and the Earl of Dorset's militia. Anticipating the most stirring speech of his political life, Eric will himself take on the role of chief insurgent who, according to author Hutchings, "spoke with much fire and feelings," while his friend, a giant of a man, Max Kirkov—from Slough, not Russia—will be Cockle's henchman William Brunt, who was capable of inflaming a crowd "with his fierce appearance and wild gestures . . . and would often for wagers toss his fellows high in the air to the amusement and recreation of all" (81). Helen, who refers to the opposition as "those Trotskys" (82), quickly counters by enlisting the aid of an ex-army man Captain Tim Barton with an impassioned plea: "Your country needs you" (110). A dog breeder rumored to sleep with a revolver under his pillow, Barton, dubbed by Eric with some justification "a stupid fascist loony" (125), is eager for the fray once his sister Sophie, with a long record of abandonment by her lovers to her discredit, takes up with the Marxist. Eric is perfectly willing to exploit Sophie for a cause despite the presence of his live-in girlfriend Philippa. With his map at the ready, Barton plots strategy for his military campaign with the urgency of Napoleon at Austerlitz. "Drunken scum," he calls the opposing faction, who, lured by Cockle T-shirts and free beer, well outnumber his puny militia of four. "They may want to destroy our country but they don't mind drinking our beer. . . . This is war" (118–19).

By the day of the pageant, Ray Dixon's cautionary words, "We seem to be losing a lot of the fun of this thing" (109), have long since been forgotten. It is indeed war. Locked into the ballroom to forestall his attack, Barton shoots open the door with the revolver he had agreed not to carry and wounds Eric in the leg. As the Earl of Dorset, Lawrence drunkenly falls from the stylized horse on wheels he insists has thrown him. Looking positively splendid in her costume, Helen rallies her pathetic force with a cry of "Come on, you cowards, come on . . . Kill, kill" (124), only to be the one tossed high in the air by Kirkov-Brunt as her husband Ray is bloodied in the battle. Her disheveled reappearance suggests that the tossing is not the extent of the humiliation she has suffered—or perhaps enjoyed. Nearly blind without his glasses, Councillor Evans, whirling his wooden musket, hits Barton on the back of his head, rendering him unconscious. All the while at the ballroom piano, where she adds to the din by practicing her repertoire of unsuitable light operetta selections and 1920s popular numbers for the eighteenth-century banquet to follow, Evan's mother is the only unscathed participant once the left and the right have a go at one another. Surprised to learn that the pageant is over, that she has missed the fun, Audrey reveals to Ray that her research into the authenticity of the Massacre of the Pendon Twelve has turned up nothing: "I've a feeling Elizabeth Arnott Hutchings made the whole thing up. Isn't that naughty?" But she has discovered that "when the Romans first arrived in Britain, they met a very strong pocket of resistance round here. From the Britons. Just on the edge of Pendon" (129). Perhaps next year. . . .

The opposing factions of *Ten Times Table* have no particular political programs to support other than their contrasting ideas about the pageant's point and purpose. Pendon is at peace before the pageant is proposed, and presumably Pendonites of all classes will resume normal behavior, at least until they take sides as Romans or Britons. The politics of the piece do not extend beyond Ayckbourn's use of class stereotypes in drawing his characters, who are less well observed here than in his domestic comedies. Even a member of his company has suggested that the author was not himself familiar enough with a character like Eric to provide him with a convincing depth.[12] The importance of *Ten Times Table*, a modestly successful play, lies in the dramatist's consciousness of a need to expand, to grapple with larger themes.

Only a year before he was himself forced to become a "committee person" as he dealt with the future of the Scarborough theater, Ayckbourn told an interviewer that his "commitments are rather more general than to do with politics," which he found boring. "I don't know much about . . . Marxist rallies," he said, adding that he did not believe that the theatergoing public knew or cared about them either: "They worry about their leaking roof, their central heating."[13] Of the political dimension of *Ten Times Table* he has said, "The play could be described . . . as a predominantly sedentary farce with faintly allegorical overtones" (8). Perhaps the more pronounced allegorical overtones, the increasingly political nature of a later play like *Way Upstream* (1981), can be explained by a comment about his own work once made by Graham Greene, ill at ease with the label "political author": "Politics are in the air we breathe, like the presence or absence of a God."[14] Having "left home" with *Ten Times Table*, Ayckbourn inevitably found himself in the world, breathing its less-than-pure air.

Unlike the political stances arbitrarily imposed on *Ten Times Table*'s stereotypes, those taken up by the characters of *Way Upstream* are inevitable responses to the developing situation within the play. Just as J. B. Priestley's *Good Night Children: A Comedy of Broadcasting* (1942) seems a forerunner of *Man of the Moment* in its condemnation of the trivial, even dangerous waste of a valuable medium, *Way Upstream* may have been influenced by Priestley's *Bees on the Boat Deck*, an unsuccessful combination of political allegory and comedy, subtitled *A Farcical Tragedy in Two Acts*. Ayckbourn, however, handles what might appear an unmanageable mix more adroitly than his north country compatriot. Priestley's play is set on the "S.S. Gloriana," owned by the White Albion Line, out of service in a backwater of Trim Estuary. Demonstrating solid English virtues as well as brains and brawn, Gridley and Patch, her chief engineer and second officer, guard the disabled ship until she can be taken out to sea again, fending off communists, fascists, and corrupt capitalists who would blow her up for their own political motives and profit. But Priestley's characters are little more than caricatures, not unlike Helen Dixon, Eric Collins, and Captain Barton of *Ten Times Table*. The farce inherent in the Priestley piece is denied a logic of its own, giving way instead to bald pleas for democratic action on the part of right-minded men. The solution to the problem that Britain shares with the world at large is simplistically proclaimed by the author himself through his mouthpiece, Gridley: "I don't want a party, yours or anybody else's. I don't care about capitalists and proletarians, masses and bosses, red shirts, black shirts, brown shirts, green shirts. I want to see some men about, real men who know what sense is, and duty is, and order is. . . . I'm tired of living among millions of howling monkeys. For God's sake, show me some men."[15]

Ayckbourn, as fed up with political parties as Gridley, does not repeat Priestley's mistake. The words of the "Gloriana"'s chief engineer could be spoken by Alistair, a reluctant passenger aboard the "Hadforth Bounty" in *Way Upstream*, but for the fact that Ayckbourn's character delineation and his characters' pronouncements are more subtle. At first tentative and hesitant, Alistair learns the necessity of taking a stand. His heroic response to the evil Vince is not a sudden reversal but the action of a man who gradually awakens to the absolute necessity of taking matters into his own hands if he and those he loves are to survive. And that realization is a long time in coming. Alistair complacently allows his partner Keith, more neo-fascist than mere capitalist, to abuse their workers.[16] Displaying only token resistance, he follows orders when Vince initially takes over the command of the boat through a manipulation of language as mesmerizing as Hitler's. As Marxist Eric makes clear to Sophie in *Ten Times Table*, rhetoric is a powerful political tool (116). Alistair is not galvanized into action until his wife's very life is endangered.

In a backstage discussion of *Way Upstream*, Ayckbourn admitted his own growing political awareness but related the play to personal experience and private concerns.[17] His own "boat play" could have been written by someone who had neither seen nor read *Bees on a Boat Deck*. All it took was the inspired sensibility of a writer who had himself taken a trip on the Norfolk Broads to be aware of, to make use of that curious phenomenon that takes place on boats: "People start issuing orders to each other"—something political pollutes even the air of East Anglia. Ayckbourn recalls with amusement his own disastrous boat trip:

> I did the maddest thing, that no one in his right mind should do, shortly after I was married. I went up a river with my in-laws, my wife and my mother. On the first day my mother fell off the side of the boat and cracked her ribs and had to lie in the front cabin for the whole trip just moaning quietly and looking out the porthole on one elbow, saying, "No, no, I'll just enjoy the scenery." And my father-in-law and I decided we weren't going to get on very well and just screamed at each other. A lot of what happens in the play happened to us, including running aground three times. I'm like Alistair. I kept getting jammed under bridges. An extraordinary microcosm exists on boats.[18]

Like Alistair, Ayckbourn suspects that he would be slow to take action in a threatening situation, but he cannot be sure: "Every ordinary non-violent liberal-minded person such as myself always wonders what he would do if. . . . People have asked me that and I've always said facetiously, 'I'd run away,' but I don't know. If a man with a machine gun came in the door, I hope I'd be very brave, but I hope it never happens. Maybe we can talk him out of it for a bit, but eventually. . . ."[19]

In *Taking Steps* Ayckbourn suggests that meek Tristram may inherit the earth, but Alistair and Emma, he says, may not. What they must first do is recognize the moral evil that Vince embodies and act: "They don't stand a chance unless they go back and face it. The tendency for the bulk of the people I know, the English, is to duck—and hope that eventually these lunatics, the left and the right, will eventually shoot each other, which they never do. They always manage to hit the people in the middle."[20]

With Ayckbourn obviously on the side of those in the middle, critics, theatergoers, even Robin Herford who created the role of Alistair, understandably considered *Way Upstream* to be its author's favorable response to the unexpected emergence of a new political party suddenly challenging with reason and moderation the power of the two firmly entrenched parties, Margaret Thatcher's Conservatives running the show and Anthony Wedgwood Benn's vociferous leftwing faction among the Labourites attempting to block their every move to the right, resulting in a country at a bitter standstill. In 1981, exasperated by Labour's sharp turn away from Europe, NATO, and the realities of a market economy, David Owen, William Rodgers, Shirley

Williams, and Roy Jenkins broke away to form the Social Democratic Party that would take position on middle ground. Forming an alliance with David Steel's Liberal Party, the SDP seemed to be heralding a new day. Their triumph, offering a glimmer of hope to disenchanted Britons was, however, shortlived. The popular victory in the Falklands War strengthened Mrs. Thatcher's position as unquestioned leader of her party, and SDP supporters, never a large band, began to fall away. By 1990 only three Members of Parliament were Social Democrats and party membership had dwindled to a mere six thousand.[21]

"It just so happened that the SDP appeared about the same time as my play. *Way Upstream* is not my SDP play," Ayckbourn insisted in 1982; "that would just narrow things down again to another political party. Until the SDP is proven, they are no more likely to be the rational party than the other two." Ayckbourn discussed the political scene as he then saw it:

> There remains an acute polarization between Mrs. Thatcher on one side and Wedgwood Benn on the other, neither of which a lot of us particularly fancy because they both exclude a lot of good things. There are good things about private enterprise and good things about a national health service. Why the hell should we lay down rules about either of them to the exclusion of the other? I think that's genuinely the feeling of a lot of people. But I do think you may eventually wake up one morning and find you've nailed up your privileges.[22]

In the early 1980s Ayckbourn already understood that politics finally cannot be avoided, that his plays too, not as obviously as those of Edward Bond and David Hare, contained statements that might in the future become even more overtly political. "What I hope that I would avoid doing," he said, "is to write an unbalanced political play. What irritates me in the theater is when the play fails to present any decent conflict—because that's just bad drama. I think it is fair enough for a play to come down and say that the left is right or the right is right, but some plays which are political make such boring statements that they have no place in the theater. Their place is on platforms."[23] Ayckbourn pointed to Trevor Griffiths, author of *Comedians* (1975), as a contemporary who can write effective political drama while maintaining balance. "It is possible to do so, and it is likely that that element will continue to creep into my work."

The war in the Falklands, coming between the Scarborough premier of *Way Upstream* in 1981 and its London presentation at the

National Theatre the following year, might have been expected to reinforce the view of the play as a political statement, if not an outright endorsement of SDP. Britain had successfully engaged Argentina in an armed conflict that necessitated the unlikely occurrence of a naval fleet sailing across the Atlantic under the command of Rear-Admiral John "Sandy" Woodward, as astonished as Alistair to find himself a hero: "I am . . . an ordinary person who lives in South West London in suburbia. . . . I have been a virtual civil servant for the past three years, commuting into London every day."[24] Woodward might well be an Ayckbourn protagonist, but Mrs. Thatcher's popular but by no means unavoidable war represents just the sort of unnecessary aggression expending human life that the dramatist would prefer a nation to avoid at all cost. The international action together with such crises on the domestic front as rampant inflation, rising unemployment, the disenfranchisement of the lower classes, labor disputes, the privatization of industry, and the debate over the extent of Britain's participation in the European Community might well have provoked Ayckbourn some years later to say, "Recently I have wanted to show how power—political and private—often resides with the wrong person. There used to be a Christian consensus in this country about how people should behave. Now there is none. There is no moral leadership. My worry is we have so burned our boats with politicians from both sides that if we got a real nut, some 'idealist', he could take the whole country with him."[25]

That "real nut," a woman increasingly revealed to be mad, appears in *The Revengers' Comedies*. Karen Knightly takes with her an entire multinational corporation that operates on the same principles, or lack thereof, as national governments. If her rise to power, as phenomenal as that of Margaret Thatcher, the grocer's daughter, parallels Guy's achievement of stardom in *A Chorus of Disapproval*, what separates Karen and Guy is their level of awareness: Karen acts, whereas Guy is acted upon. Ayckbourn had already sketched in the effect of the multinationals, whose actual product other than great profits remains a mystery, on a community in *A Chorus of Disapproval* and even on the smaller social group, the family, in *A Small Family Business*. BLM, Guy's employer in the former—"We're a multi-national company that's become extremely diversified. . . . And so it's a bit difficult to pin down" (38)—may or may not wish to expand its local operation; thus the acquisition of property owned by Jarvis Huntley-Pike motivates the on stage and backstage maneuverings of the members of the Pendon Amateur Light Opera Society. Jack McCracken, at first passive then active in his accelerating career in the latter play, enters into a profitable but not quite straightforward relationship with Italians whose business may exist primarily as a front for illegal drug trafficking.

Ayckbourn may have chosen an Italian connection for the firm of Ayres and Graces in *A Small Family Business* for reasons other than the obvious Mafia link. That governments too play multinational corporate games was evidenced by the maneuverings of Mrs. Thatcher's own Tory cabinet in 1986, one year before the Scarborough production of the Ayckbourn play, when the Prime Minister forced the resignation of her Defense Secretary, Michael Heseltine, for attempting to rescue Westland PLC, a British helicopter manufacturer, from bankruptcy with the infusion of funds from a European consortium, one of whose members was an Italian aerospace firm, Augusta. Declaring herself neutral, Mrs. Thatcher, stating publicly that she was in favor of the corporate world solving its own problems without government intervention, actually appeared to be throwing her own considerable weight behind the scenes toward what was misleadingly called an "American" consortium, that in fact comprised United Technologies and yet another Italian company—Fiat. On the disclosure that the contents of a letter embarrassing to Heseltine had been leaked by Thatcher's own office, another Cabinet Minister, Leon Brittan, Secretary for Trade and Industries, had to go the way of all those who became a threat to the "Iron Lady's" absolute rule of the Conservative Party. During a Parliamentary debate stemming from the political issue that divided the government—would Great Britain profit more from an economic alliance with Europe or the technological advances being made in the United States?—Thatcher, seated beside Brittan, distanced herself from him, disavowing the disclosure of the letter in question, saying, "I did not like the way it was done."[26]

Governments do involve themselves in corporate dealings, some of which, like the stock manipulation of Guinness and Polly Peck—the latter a curious conglomerate with such diverse holdings as Del Monte fruit, a consumer electronics business, and hotels—become national scandals. To survive, heads of state as well as corporate heads often play a power game by rules of their own making. As those for her and against her conceded, one who played the political power game brilliantly for eleven and a half years was Prime Minister Thatcher. One who plays the game with dizzying expertise within the corporate world is *The Revengers' Comedies'* Karen Knightly. But as both the actual woman and the fictional one must learn, stubborn convictions and an iron will do not always win out in the end.

That ousted politicians do not necessarily fade away, as did once-powerful Labour MP Wedgwood Benn, became evident between the

Scarborough and London presentations of *The Revengers' Comedies*, a seemingly prophetic play, when Heseltine, abetted by the defection of Sir Geoffrey Howe, Thatcher's Deputy Minister, reappeared to confront Britain's first woman Prime Minister with the final challenge of her political career, just as she had once wrested control of the Tories away from Edward Heath. In a ballot for party leadership Thatcher received 204 votes from Conservative MPs to Heseltine's 152 with 16 abstentions. According to party rules, she needed not just a majority but a victory margin of 15 per cent—56 votes. She had fallen short by four.[27] The next day a still determined Thatcher announced that she would take part in a runoff ballot requiring a simple majority for the winner. Yet one day later, convinced by high-ranking Conservatives that the poll tax that had caused riots earlier in the year together with her continuing stand against a European federation could cost her the runoff, Thatcher faced a difficult choice—humiliating defeat or dignified acceptance of her place in history. On 22 November 1990, she resigned as Prime Minister, ending the Thatcher era. Heseltine had forced the Iron Lady's ouster, but the mantle of the Prime Minister fell to John Major. In the cabinet shuffle that followed, Heseltine, as the new Environment Secretary, found himself forced to cope with the sticky question of the unpopular poll tax—a Pyrrhic victory indeed.

In *The Revengers' Comedies*, Karen Knightly meets her match in Henry Bell and offers him choices he cannot accept. Instead, he defeats her at her own game. The rules by which she had played the game, she learns, may be taken up by others like her and used against her. Henry Bell's victory, like Alistair's over Vince, like Heseltine's over Thatcher, is not necessarily a lasting one. Only time will tell if an era has actually come to an end.

Ayckbourn does not encourage his audience to view Karen Knightly as a surrogate Margaret Thatcher. In fact for the London production of *The Revengers' Comedies* he cast the willowy, attractive Lia Williams, who played Karen as a strong-willed but shallow Sloane Ranger, a self-indulgent, spoiled young socialite, a kindred spirit to Lady Di and her circle of well-born, beautiful friends. Karen's un-scrupulous methods, however, Ayckbourn seems to suggest, unfor-tunately parallel those of the leaders of the corporate world, even of government itself, in whom ordinary citizens, having no recourse, place their trust. Yet to view Ayckbourn's play merely as political satire is to limit its author's concerns. A rich work about leaders in high places and their fall from high places, *The Revengers' Comedies* at the same time examines the domestic arrangements at the root of many Ayckbourn plays. Karen not only controls the destiny of

Lembridge Tennit, a multinational corporation, she is responsible for the disintegration of the relationship of her neighbors, Anthony and Imogen Staxton-Billings as she encourages the relationship of Henry Bell and Imogen. Casting Henry in the role of pawn and sometime lover, she mistakenly believes him to be acting solely in her interest as she seeks revenge on Imogen for taking back her husband Anthony after Karen's brief sexual liaison with him. If Karen's motive for disrupting the world around her seems petty, it is no more trivial than those given by the Marquis de Sade in Peter Weiss's *Marat/Sade* (1964) as the underlying reasons for the masses embracing an action as cataclysmic as the French Revolution:

> Their soup's burnt
> They shout for better soup
> A woman finds her husband too short
> she wants a taller one
> A man finds his wife too skinny
> he wants a plumper one
> A man's shoes pinch
> but his neighbour's shoes fit comfortably. . . .[28]

Karen's petty jealousy dictates choices which result in the chance occurrences that shape the lives of those around her, one of Ayckbourn's abiding preoccupations. That the others allow a madwoman to manipulate them, that sane men and women permit others to encroach on their personal affairs and daily lives, that a nation's citizens complacently sit by while a chosen few—the self-chosen few—dictate actions of earthshaking proportions is at the core of a work in which Ayckbourn's themes at once coalesce and expand. To support a work of such scope, the playwright calls upon what are for him new techniques of structure and chracterization as he enters the realm of the mock epic.

Ayckbourn's two-part play, his longest single work as opposed to such a play as *Intimate Exchanges* with its alternate versions, *The Revengers' Comedies* is closer in its reliance on brief scenes held together by crosscutting to the structure of a film than on a work for the stage. Even as he edits cinematically, the playwright makes use of frequent glancing allusions to film to underscore the impact of image and iconography on contemporary life that he had already indicated in *Henceforward . . .* and *Man of the Moment.* The composer Jerome, like Vince in *Way Upstream,* manipulates language but deceives himself, believing he can turn sounds devoid of meaning into a work of art. Television personality Jill Rillington seeks high ratings, not art, as she singlemindedly manipulates image. In *The Revengers' Comedies* Ayckbourn makes use of cinematic images old and new, from both sides of the Atlantic, just as Karen, the instigator of the play's action, herself manipulates image. Like the immigrant movie moguls who, enriching themselves, instilled acceptable if anesthetizing values on the primarily white, Anglo-Saxon sensibilities of Britain and America by means of comforting, sanitized images; like the political leaders who mouth platitudes about a nation becoming kinder and gentler while using aggression as a means to peace in the Middle East, Karen knows that image is all. She herself is chameleon-like. Adopting any image that furthers her ends, Karen operates as does the craftsman who arranges bits and pieces, the tesserae, into a complete mosaic. Ayckbourn too, artist and artisan, masterfully shapes disparate strands, a myriad of images, into a unified whole. He too understands the power of the image and would once again have his audience recognize how they too are manipulated—in the theater and in the world.

Hollywood images inform *The Revengers' Comedies*, which its author has called "my Saturday morning picture show for adults,"[29] Vivien Leigh and Robert Taylor meet on a bridge in London in *Waterloo Bridge* (1940), better known than the Robert E. Sherwood play on which it is based, and there she ends her life—nobly and beautifully. In *The Lonely Guy* (1983), adapted by Neil Simon from a book by Bruce Jay Friedman, the notion of the noble suicide is undercut: Steve Martin persuades Charles Grodin not to jump from the Manhattan Bridge—"A sort of 'in' spot for suicidal lonely guys"— as four others, one of them named Henry, do jump. The film ends with Martin on the bridge rail ready to end it all when Judith Ivey, jumping from a higher level, falls into his outstretched arms. The scenes are reminiscent of Murray Schisgal's play, *Luv*, a comedy about three desperate people resolving their relationships on a bridge, itself adapted as a film in 1967.

Other Hollywood moments are echoed in *The Revengers' Comedies*. Perennial hero Robert Taylor wounds perennial villain Henry Daniell in a duel with pistols in *Camille* (1937), adapted from the younger Dumas's novel and play. Rita Hayworth in a Jerome Kern musical, *Cover Girl* (1944), adopts the wrong image for an interview at the urging of a devious competitor for the same job. Jane Fonda, Dolly Parton, and Lily Tomlin are secretaries taking revenge on their boss in *Nine to Five* (1990). Melanie Griffith, dressing more and more stylishly in each scene of Mike Nichols's *Working Girl* (1988), is a secretary who becomes a key player in a corporate merger. Snow White and her dwarfs await Prince Charming in Walt Disney's animated film (1938). Snobbish women fall from horses with some regularity in Hollywood movies of the thirties and are rescued by the men with whom they will fall in love. Madcap heiresses in screwball comedies, like Katharine Hepburn in Howard Hawks's *Bringing Up Baby* (1938), take in hand reluctant introverts—Cary Grant—and complicate their lives.

Films from countries other than the United States come into play as well: Alec Guinness in various guises dying many "accidental" deaths in the British film, *Kind Hearts and Coronets*; Death riding a motorcycle in Jean Cocteau's *Orphée* (1950), an adaptation of his 1925 play; the marquis upholding a decaying society's good form in Jean Renoir's *La Règle du Jeu* (1939)—its English title, *The Rules of the Game*, echoed in Ayckbourn's dialogue—by proclaiming a death the regrettable accident that it is not. The work of British director Alfred Hitchcock in his Hollywood period receives special homage: Judith Anderson as Mrs. Danvers burning down Manderley in an adaptation of Daphne du Maurier's *Rebecca* (1940); Cary Grant in *North by Northwest* (1959) dodging a threatening airplane which becomes in the Ayckbourn play the motorcycle with its fearsome rider; *North by Northwest*'s plane metamorphosing into the swooping creatures of *The Birds* (1936), based on a du Maurier short story. And, most emphatically, the film echo that initiates the action of *The Revengers' Comedies*, Robert Walker planning the perfect crime by swapping motives with Farley Granger in an adaptation of Patricia Highsmith's *Strangers on a Train* (1951).

References to the drama of all eras also abound: Karen insisting, like the Ghost in *Hamlet*, the ultimate revenge play, like Susan in *Woman in Mind*, that the world "remember me"; Karen and her brother Oliver refusing, like Peter Pan, like the adult children of Giles Cooper's *Happy Family* (1966), to grow up; Karen gulling a pathetic secretary, like Malvolio in *Twelfth Night*, into believing an adored employer is in love with an underling; Oliver referring to their home as a "Wendy house"; Karen renewing the life of Henry Bell, whom she always calls "HenryBell," as Peter Pan urges the audience to restore health to the fading Tinker Bell; Colonel Lipscott, like Claudius in *Hamlet* the most powerful man in the community if not its most honest, deviously making certain the outcome of a duel. Images from films and echoes from plays are used in *The Revengers' Comedies* as T. S. Eliot's objective correlatives, "a set of objects, a situation, a chain of events,"[30] not as a formula to express emotion, but to give meaning to the whole.

The A-effect, having diverged early in Ayckbourn's works from the *Verfremdungseffekt*, or V-effect, of the epic theater, is realigned in

The Revengers' Comedies with the Brechtian distancing device. Like the German, the British playwright insists that what matters this time is not the psychological development of the characters as in *Just Between Ourselves* and *Woman in Mind*, but, as in *The Good Woman of Setzuan* and *The Caucasian Chalk Circle*, the parable itself. The medium is the message that is transmitted by cartoon-like characters similar to those sketched effectively but economically by Brecht and by Frank Wedekind before him in such a play as *The Marquis of Keith*. Like the sketches in another medium by George Grosz in his "Ecce Homo," a portfolio of drawings and watercolors depicting the people of Germany in the years immediately following World War I that conveys the horror of a world gone mad, Ayckbourn confidently uses caricature that stops just short of expressionism to populate a play about a nation too far off course ever to recover its sanity, humanity, and morality. Utilizing audacious structuring and characterization, Ayckbourn in *The Revengers' Comedies* integrates diverse elements into his own dazzling mosaic—a frequently hilarious, sometimes sobering, but always riveting saga of revenge.

Karen and Henry meet on London's Albert Bridge where both have come to commit suicide, although she may never have planned to go through with hers. Her belt, intentionally or not, has caught on a railing, stopping her fall. About to jump himself, Henry hears her cries for help and rescues her. She takes him to a transport cafe near Salisbury, a long distance to travel for tea and sympathy, but, the audience soon realizes, Karen acts impulsively. Once her mind is made up, however, she cannot be deterred. She is angry that Anthony Staxton-Billing has not obeyed her command to meet her on the bridge. Anthony, with whom her affair had ended some months earlier, has gone to Chelsea Bridge as she ordered, not to stop her, he later admits, but to watch her jump. Karen has mistakenly staged her suicide on the wrong bridge.

His wife having divorced him a year earlier out of sheer boredom, Henry has an additional reason to be depressed. He has just lost his job, been "made redundant," as the firm prefers to put it, part of a policy of "Redefining the job profile. Rationalizing the department. Restructuring the management team" (11–12). Jargon is preferable to unadorned truth at Lembridge Tennit, a multinational involved in everything "from biscuits to bicycles," that may be guilty of "polluting the rivers, poisoning the atmosphere and secretly financing right-wing revolutionaries." Henry, an innocent, certain that he was doing a good job, was fully expecting a promotion, but, as Karen remarks, "being good is never enough in itself." He has been replaced by Bruce Tick, who knows how to work the system: "Chatting up the right people. Buying the drinks that matter. . . . Losing the right game of squash. Missing the right putt. . . . Wearing the right bloody underwear. Screwing the right secretary" (12–13). Karen, no innocent, understands: "It's just a game, that's all," to which Henry responds: "And you either play by the rules and win, like he did. Or you ignore them and lose, like me." When he admits he "came very close to murdering" Tick, and Karen tells him he should have, naive Henry assumes she is joking.

Karen does not joke. She presents Henry with a plan: she will take care of Tick, and he will take revenge for her on Anthony's wife Imogen, not, as one might expect, on Anthony himself. That Imogen has taken him back is to the singleminded if somewhat illogical Karen an unforgiveable action. "How could he do that to *me?*" she wails as she tells Henry about Anthony's failure on another occasion to meet her at a designated train station, then adds, "I'll kill her!" (15).

Karen takes the reluctant Henry to her fifty-eight room house in Dorset, Furtherfield House, which is further afield from Pendon and the Home Counties than any Ayckbourn character has yet strayed, where she beds her exhausted would-be accomplice despite his Tristram-like protestations. According to Karen's plan, to which Henry has not yet agreed, to swap revenges they must exchange milieux: Karen will go to London to seek employment at Lembridge Tennit to have access to Bruce Tick; Henry will remain at Furtherfield to be near Imogen. Their manner of dress too must conform to their images. Her strapless evening dress of the first scene is replaced with an unflattering suit and flat shoes, the illusion completed by her combing back her hair, wearing minimal make-up, and carrying a hefty handbag on the day she applies for a secretarial position. For Henry, accustomed to a conservative business suit, she provides a costume more suitable to the horsey set. Whereas Karen creates for herself exactly the image she has in mind, she is not quite on target with Henry's. Introduced to Karen's neighbors as her accountant, Henry is taken for a turf accountant or a brewer, but he soon finds clothing more suitable for a country squire.

When Imogen, assured that Karen will not be at home, attends a charity fête committee-meeting at Furtherfield and unexpectedly encounters her former rival, she is so upset that she is uncharacteristically rude to Henry. Convinced by her uncalled-for behavior that Imogen is as unpleasant as Karen has pictured her, Henry is goaded into agreeing to the double revenge.

From this point the play follows two actions simultaneously: Karen, like Vince in *Way Upstream*, brilliantly cutting a swath through Lembridge Tennit, decimating its ranks by playing on the weaknesses of those who are—briefly—her superiors; Henry gradually learning that his first impression of Imogen was by no means accurate. When Imogen falls from a horse and he comes to her rescue, they are attracted to one another, secretly meeting wherever they can—in a pig pen, a hen house, a cow shed. All his dull life ill at ease in an urban environment, Henry suddenly thrives, finding himself, as is Imogen, at one with nature. Imogen loves animals; her husband loves to shoot them.

Hired by Lembridge Tennit—her new image perfectly suiting Mrs. Bulley, Head of Personnel (Secretarial)—Karen disrupts Tick's life by arousing his wife's jealousy with strange telephone calls and strategically placed undergarments. As a result of the tension at home, the gluttonous, overweight executive begins to suffer severe indigestion. No longer can he devour what had been his customary business lunch: "mulligatawny soup to start with. Then fresh lobster. Then. . . . whole roast guinea fowl, all the trimmings, of course, game chips, lovely home-made stuffing, breadcrumbs, beautiful firm brussel sprouts, roast potatoes and fresh crispy *mange-tout*" followed by "steamed treacle sponge. Moist. Plenty of treacle. Coffee. *Petits-fours,*" all washed down with "a bottle of Chablis, a bottle of Nuits-Saint-Georges, and a glass of magnificent vintage port" (72), all of which he had burned up as fast as he ate it, he was wont to boast, because of a perfect metabolism that since Karen's advent has failed him.

In a wine bar, while he is trying to placate an angry wife who has not yet met Karen but is convinced her husband is carrying on with her, the Ticks are suddenly confronted not by the mousey, unattractive, nondescript secretary he had been eager to introduce to his wife, but by a sensationally beautiful woman, exuding sensuality. Apoplectic at the discovery that Karen, in league with Henry Bell, is his betrayer, Tick drops dead, as she later explains to Henry, of a combination of "Cholesterol. And over-excitement." Karen has not actually killed Tick, "just nudged him in the general direction of—death, that's all" (100).

Her part of the bargain now complete, Karen, aware how easy it is to play the corporate game and curious to see just how far she can go, stays on at Lembridge Tennit, where she nudges her next boss in the wrong direction as well. Working for Graham Seeds, a brilliant but nervous executive prone to panic, she is responsible for his thinking a fire drill the real thing. Believing, no doubt at Karen's suggestion, that the fire is rising from below, he rushes to the roof of the 32-story building and falls to his death. The rest is child's play, and Karen, climbing the corporate ladder, plays the game with the zest of the spoiled child she still is at heart, a child determined to have her way at any price.

Devious behavior takes place in the country too. Winnie, the family retainer, will retire from her duties at Furtherfield once young Norma is properly trained to replace her as housekeeper. Not eager to abandon her post, Winnie sees to it that perpetually flustered Norma will never be capable of serving a meal properly, let alone running the household. And Winnie can never be fired. She knows the truth about the family's dark secret: the death of Karen's parents in a fire in the summer house when the willful child was only thirteen.

Deceit and hypocrisy thrive among the upper class as well. The landed gentry of the county live by traditional rules assuring that their authority is unquestioned and their values unchallenged. When Henry, misled by Winnie, informs Daphne Teale, Anthony's current mistress, that Anthony is carrying on with Norma, Daphne's niece, a terrible row ensues at the Fox and Hounds. Anthony demands satisfaction, his real reason being a refusal to tolerate Henry paying court to his wife. That Anthony no longer loves Imogen is beside the point. To his amazement, Henry learns that duelling is still the preferred method for settling disputes in the county. He halfheartedly agrees to take part once Colonel Marcus Lipscott, Imogen's uncle, convinces him he has no choice. And the advantages should he survive could be considerable: Anthony's death would not only afford Henry the opportunity to marry Imogen but would also create a vacancy on the board of Marcus's firm. That the firm, which manufactures sewage pipes, appears to be failing prompts Henry to suggest to Imogen, who has invested in it, that she may be literally throwing her money "down the drain" (65), but the prospect of being united with the one woman with whom he has truly experienced love is too strong to be denied. Never having handled a gun, Henry asks Oliver, Karen's brother, to be his second and to help him prepare for the fateful encounter.

In the duel itself, with the customary ten paces having been stepped off, Henry suddenly lowers his gun: "I'm sorry, just a minute. This is totally mad" (158). Appalled to find himself playing yet another game by someone else's rules, Henry, becoming perhaps the raisonneur for an author questioning the traditions and values of a world in moral chaos, explodes with pent-up fury: "This is stupid and foolish and crass and—insane . . . And this is the twentieth century and not the Dark Ages and we are grown up and we should know a damn sight better and I'm having nothing to do with it, so there!" He throws the gun to the ground, inadvertently setting off the trigger mechanism that Oliver had fiddled with, mortally wounding Anthony. Henry tries to explain that it was an accident, but Anthony will have none of it:

"Some . . . bloody . . . accident . . ." The stage direction reads: *"He dies laughing"* (159).

Like Renoir's Marquis de la Chesnaye, Marcus, the purveyor of good form, has all the while been prepared to inform the authorities of an accident occurring during a shooting party. He sends someone to deal with Chief Inspector Rogers: "He tends to deal with these sorts of things rather tactfully." Marcus reveals that he had made certain beforehand that Henry would emerge the victor. He removes two cartridges from Anthony's gun and replaces them. Without a glimmer of surprise he says to a bystander, "Good Lord, Percy, what do you think are the chances of that? Two dud cartridges at once. What are the odds on that happening?" Percy, smiling, replies, "Almost astronomic, I should imagine" (160). The pillar of the community knows how to rid the environment of an undesirable element. Philandering Anthony, his niece's husband, had become an embarrassment to the family. Corruption under the guise of civility is sanctioned in a bogus Eden.

The play's strands come together when Lembridge Tennit takes over Marcus's firm. Karen, at this point *"the very essence of a top executive"* (197), with her last superior now one of her assistants, is now dictating terms. An assistant tells Marcus, "Just a warning. . . . I think she's going to insist on a great deal of strengthening at board level" (198). The one who has got to go is Anthony's replacement—Henry. By then Karen has learned that her "accomplice" plans to marry Imogen once a suitable time has elapsed—Henry too abiding by tradition and appearances. She had imagined that Henry, "a true artist" like herself (176), had been toying with Imogen and would break her heart by betraying her. Learning that his love is sincere, Karen refuses to allow him "to break the rules" of their pact. Henry states his philosophy culled from experience: "Life is not a game. . . . There's a much bigger board, for one thing. People keep stealing your counters and changing the rules. Life's a lot more complicated and a good deal harder to play"—words that might well serve as epigraph for a later play, *Wildest Dreams* (1991). But he is wrong, insists Karen: "It's easy. Easy-peasy" (177–78). All one must do is play by the rules of one's own making. Life is only difficult when those rules are broken.

The play ends as it began. At her insistence, Karen and Henry meet again on Albert Bridge where she announces his options: "I bring you a choice" (206). They can continue to play the game; or Henry must jump from the bridge, breaking Imogen's heart; or Henry can change sides and join Karen, who declares her love for him. Detecting a loophole in her logic, Henry refuses the offered choices and, remaining strictly within her rules, brings the game to an end. He chooses Imogen, who has arrived on the scene, and goes off with her. Karen has no recourse but to begin a new game: "Go home to your cosy little country cottage with your pigs and your cows and your hideous children. You'll never be free of me. You'll remember me with guilt in your hearts for ever. For ever . . . Ever . . . HenryBell!" (210). With a triumphant cry of "Reve-e-e-e-n-n-g-e!" she jumps from the bridge.

The central concern of *The Revengers' Comedies* is not revenge, as some of Ayckbourn's critics have claimed,[31] no more than is *Hamlet's*. Karen sees herself and Henry, like the Ghost of Hamlet's father, as "unquiet spirits. . . . The wrongs that have been done to us have got to be put right. We're never going to rest. . . . until we've done that" (20). The revenge motif in both plays frames a dramatic action that charts the incursion of evil on a once healthy land gone to rot. Even the green world of the Ayckbourn play is not the paradise it seems; it reflects the urban world that is encroaching on it. Lembridge Tennit is expanding. When Karen—not Winnie, the play's enigmatic, faithful servant—burns down Furtherfield House in a moment of madness as undisguised as that of Mrs. Danvers or Ophelia, the multinational— with Karen still at its helm—devours the land to build a plastics factory. Karen herself is ravaging the countryside, dispossessing Henry and Imogen of their "cosy little country cottage," her ultimate revenge on them both. And her demise cannot stop the inevitable. Even Karen can be replaced atop the Lembridge Tennit corporate ladder. The game goes on.

The Revengers' Comedies has been cited as one of Ayckbourn's most optimistic plays.[32] Seemingly, good has triumphed; evil has perished. But Ayckbourn has made the point early on that goodness is never enough, and he underscores it later in the play. When Marcus protests that Henry should not be removed from the board, that he is a good man, Karen's assistant says, "Ah yes, no doubt. Would that goodness were enough in itself, Colonel. But sadly not" (198). In any community, even a democratic society, those in high places dictate to the rest. The system—no more than a game with arbitrary rules— only works for those in charge, the privileged few.

Throughout the play, whenever Henry is in Furtherfield House, birds, like the Furies, dive at him from above. They are variously described by Oliver as wrens or blue tits, by Marcus as green woodpeckers. None of them are creatures threatening to humans, but Henry, accustomed to being victimized, remains wary. Perhaps now, incredibly, "The world is grown so bad / That wrens make prey. . . ." as Shakespeare's Duke of Gloucester, like Karen a Machiavel at the root of the chaos, knowingly muses as he plots to snatch the crown.

There is trouble in paradise, upheaval in Pendon, in Britain, in the world. Alan Ayckbourn is indeed traveling further afield.

The dramatist's widening horizon does not necessarily guarantee him a wider audience. The London production of *The Revengers' Comedies,* despite the representative review in which a critic called it a "ripping yarn" that would have the theatergoer "on the edge of your seat waiting to find out what happens next,"[33] lasted a mere twelve weeks. Perhaps the dramatist's own self-indulgence—his two-part play requires an audience to come to the theater twice, purchasing separate tickets for each half—contributed to its early demise. Allowing that he had conceived it on a grand scale as a fiftieth birthday present to himself,[34] Ayckbourn ignored those who advised him that it could be shortened into a single complete performance. Two separate visits to a theater for the resolution of an involved plot seemed one too many for those who viewed *The Revengers' Comedies* as no more than a tale of revenge. The brief run may have been due to the failure of the critics, caught up in the intricate plotting as well as the technical brilliance of a complex production framed in its opening and closing scenes by a spectacular setting of a bridge, to recognize the significance of Ayckbourn's thematic concerns. His judgment perhaps clouded as well by the audience's laughter, one critic advised his readers that "those looking for the depth and social vision that have informed much of Ayckbourn's recent work are likely to be disappointed."[35] Only two critics noted that the dramatist may have attempted something more than the inversion of a Jacobean epic tragedy in the manner of Tourneur, Middleton, Webster, or Ford into a modern day epic comedy. Ian Shuttleworth commented on the play's "vague implication that big business corrupts and/or corruption tends toward big business."[36] Sheridan Morley detected that *The Revengers' Comedies* was in essence, "as many of Ayckbourn's best plays have been over the last decade," concerned "with the moral collapse of the way Britain now lives and works," but he found the references and starting points "rather more widespread than in his usual suburban norm."[37]

The close of the Thatcher era may have blinded an audience, eager to forget those years, to the depths of Britain's—and the world's— moral decay. The theater company that dares to revive the challenging *The Revengers' Comedies,* a multiple-set play with a cast of twenty-three that requires but rewards an audience's concentration and dedication, may some day demonstrate with a less elaborate production, one closer to Ayckbourn's original Scarborough one, how clear-eyed the dramatist's vision remained in the chaotic waning years of the twentieth century.

7

The Wilder Dreams of Children at Play

The question of ethical behavior on the domestic scene in Ayckbourn's early works gave way later, in *A Chorus of Disapproval* and *A Small Family Business*, to a probing of ethics in the broader context of the business community. By extension the world of high finance in *The Revengers' Comedies* paralleled the political realm that Ayckbourn had explored in the allegorical setting of *Way Upstream*. Do husbands have the ethical license to dictate the behavior of their wives? Do corporate executives have the right to manipulate the lives of their underlings? Do world leaders have the power of life and death over their subjects? In *The Revengers' Comedies*, Karen Knightly is hoist with her own petard. Having toyed with others, she sees the loss of her own life as the winning move in a deadly game of revenge. In her progress from spurned lover to unscrupulous corporate head, her methods reveal an ethical obliquity, but they have become, Ayckbourn suggests, the accepted way of the world.

In *Body Language* (1990) the ethical questions move to yet another plane. Are there no bounds to man's grasp for control of his universe? Can man ultimately play God? Since gods themselves may nod, what havoc may occur as the result of fallible man assuming omnipotent power? Ayckbourn had already raised these issues in *Henceforward . . .* when Jerome endowed robot Nan with the borrowed, very human traits of Zoë. Man and machine had become interchangeable. In *Body Language* human parts become interchangeable when a crazed doctor, the ancient but still sexually driven Professor Hravic Zyergefoovc, mistakenly switches the heads of two thirty-year-old women decapitated by a helicopter's rotary blade. In an age in which organ transplants have become commonplace and biogenetic corporations proliferate, the device that generates the plot of the heartless, hilarious comedy seems even less unlikely than the multi-year traffic jam of *Standing Room Only*, the playwright's earlier venture into a futuristic absurd universe. As in *Henceforward . . .* the future may already have arrived. In fact the author dictates in his stage direction that the play takes place in "June–October, recently."[1]

Having already explored the image-making of television in *Man of the Moment*, Ayckbourn in *Body Language* appropriately sets his deeper probing of a world in which image is constantly reshaped and reaffirmed in a clinic for cosmetic surgery. At the Othman Clinic in an isolated section of rural England, Angie Dell, a much-in-demand if none-too-bright model with a perfectly proportioned body, is recuperating after the removal of a nonmalignant growth on her shapely backside. Visited by her fifty-year-old estranged husband, pop musician Mal Bennet—in leather jacket and designer jeans "a living triumph of image over age"—she rejects his plea for a reconciliation. Angie is, however, touched by the unusual present he brings her. In the past he had showered her with gifts, like see-through nightdresses, aimed at increasing his pleasure. For Mal, as for all men, Angie exists as sex object. But this time the present is a book, *Crime and Punishment*. Actually, Mal had intended another book entirely, a fully illustrated volume recommended by a friend, *Punishment without Crime: A Short History of Erotic Bondage from Roman Times to the Present*, but there had been some confusion over titles at the bookshop. Believing he may now be seeing her in a new light, as a person rather than a bimbo, Angie runs toward the helicopter whose motor Mal, more adept on the bass than at the controls of a flying machine, is revving in preparation for his departure. Also at the clinic to interview visiting Professor Zyergefoovc, renowned for his unusual transplants, is Jo Knapton, an obsese radio reporter. Seeing the model move dangerously close to the unsteady machine, Jo sprints after Angie to get her out of the way. Too late, she, as well as Angie, literally loses her head.

The swapping of the books is paralleled by the switching of the heads at the hands of Zyergefoovc, an eighty-four-year-old still eager for any contact, surgical or otherwise, with a woman's body, serendipitously on the scene but somewhat careless in his execution. Jo, onetime fat woman, regains consciousness some weeks after the operation to discover that her head is on Angie's svelte, silicone-enhanced body that is nauseated by food and insistent on constant attention and rigorous exercise. She is not happy at contemplating life looking like a pipe cleaner, or being what she had called Angie before the accident, "the chest with legs." Angie is equally distressed at discovering herself attached to Jo's oversized, flabby, uncared-for body: "It's like living in a disused elephant." Once again the A-effect is called into play. Even as it enjoyed two performers taking their turn as a single robot in *Henceforward . . .*, here the audience revels in the visual joke of two performers having switched bodies, even conjectures about their actual size. Despite the fact that a second operation may be even more dangerous than the extraordinary first one, Jo and Angie insist that Zyergefoovc mend the error of his ways and reattach the heads to the appropriate bodies.

Until his words are translated, with the fouler language edited out, by Freya Roope, Zyergefoovc's nurse, the audience can only comprehend the Professor's pseudo-Slavic gibberish by means of his body language. Freya both distrusts and detests her celebrated employer who, constantly abusing her, calls her "Memmer Hrootpucker"—Madam Dyke. Zyergefoovc may think of himself as a god—"Keet gool dent it dent gool keet, eek klingt? (God is man or man is God, who knows?)" Knowing him all too well, however, his assistant sees him in another guise, as, at one and the same time, a dirty old man and a mischievous little boy. Freya is worried about what the brilliant doctor, who has "pioneered some of the most extraordinary surgical techniques. . . . in the entire history of surgery" will do next. Having already performed "ethically dubious" procedures, such as sewing dogs' heads on pigs, some of them even involving humans in strange transplants, he will surely not be satisfied with merely replacing the women's heads once again. "He will do another operation instead, I know him," she tells Benjamin Cooper, the bland surgeon who runs the clinic, who stands "humbled and in total awe" of Zyergefoovc's skill, who considers that through the beauty of the older surgeon's hands, he has himself momentarily "glimpsed divinity itself." But for Freya men are not gods. Zyergefoovc is merely the wanton boy who torments flies, like a god only in his indifference to man: "Hravic is a small boy still. . . . And like all nosey boys he takes things to pieces. The toaster, his grandfather's clock. . . ." Her words recall Dennis in *Just Between Ourselves*, always tinkering with gadgets that ultimately defeat him, all the while oblivious to the suffering of his wife, yet another mechanism beyond repair. But the professor is more dangerous still: "Hravic does not play with toasters or clocks now, he plays with people. Always he loves to take people to pieces. . . . Always he wants to see how they work. Only like all small boys, many times he cannot put them together again. Or worse still, he tries to improve them. I tell you, Benjamin, the man is mad."

Freya's method of preventing the second operation points to the play's major theme. Man will play God as long as passive woman accepts his view of her and fashions herself in the image he demands—as his plaything, as sexual object. Until she rejects that image, she cannot release the self trapped within the body he covets. When Angie tells Freya that her father abused her and her four sisters, calling them, as Zyergefoovc calls her, by insulting names,

Freya asks, "He hates women? He is a homosexual, your father?" to which Angie responds with a surprising negative insight, "Oh, no. You don't have to be homosexual to hate women. Just a man, really." Until she understands the implication of Angie's statement, no woman, the action demonstrates, can embrace her identity, satisfy her sexuality, realize her potential for independence, even for power—for good or for ill. Twice Freya exercises her power, once by pole-axing Derek Short, a trespassing paparazzo, and more effectively by making her prediction about Zyergefoovc's eventual fate come to pass: "He will learn the power of woman's anger. Someone one day, I promise, will do him to death. Maybe me, who knows?" By extending to him her Amazonian sexual favors, Freya ironically but purposefully kills the lecherous old doctor with kindness, proving to him at the same time her unquestionable heterosexuality.

Zyergefoovc's death ends Angie and Jo's hope of ever having their heads switched back, allowing them to be again the selves they were. Their initial distress, however, eventually turns into the joyous acceptance of a symbiotic relationship. No longer will the two women be subservient to the men in their lives. Once Freya takes the first steps in freeing them from bondage by demonstrating the dominance of the female over the male, Angie and Jo begin to dictate terms: To Ronnie, Angie's agent who now wants his suddenly enormous client to model foundation garments and other "fashions for the fuller figure;" to Derek, the insensitive photographer, Jo's former lover who may have left her or whom she may have thrown out—for memory is, after all, in both Pinter and Ayckbourn's terms, merely creative imagination— who now feeds on the anguish of both women; to Mal, the husband who lusts for his wife's body even when it is that of another woman. None of the men will again have his way with either. Even Benjamin, the clinic's administrator, seems to be losing his authority to the strong-willed Freya, to whom he finds himself irresistibly drawn.

Angie and Jo will neither sell the rights to their own story to another, nor reject the newfound identities which for a time they had resisted. Soon after the bungled emergency operation, they were barely able to look at one another, had even refused to speak. Yet as each begins to realize how the other's body dictates her appetites— sexual, gastronomic, and intellectual—each gradually becomes aware of a need for the other's sympathy and understanding. Even while they think of themselves as merely temporary guardians of the body of the other, they begin to forge a bond, with Angie feeding the gross body to which she is now attached and Jo exercising and starving the lean body that is nauseated by food and, unlike Jo before the accident, unresponsive to sex. Gradually, they become friends, even to the point of thinking themselves "sisters under the skin." They mark their bond by embracing:

> Funny hugging yourself, isn't it?
> You for me and me for you.

By the end of the play Angie and Jo plan to work together on writing and marketing their story, "My Life in Another Woman's Body." They *"seem happier than we've ever seen them."* The stage direction reads: *"They stand facing each other and hold up one hand apiece and press the palms together"* as each vows to hand over her body to the other "that she may hereon treat it according to her personal wishes and whims . . . . without fear of recrimination from its previous owner." The vow ends with "So help me God," as the women acknowledge a power beyond man himself. The play's final image is the two of them experiencing a moment of silent joy as they exercise together while sharing a chocolate bar. Angie and Jo will not only dictate to the men, they will no longer be dictated to by their bodies. Mind has taken control. The language their bodies must learn to understand has become at last their own.

Body Language completes the movement begun in Ayckbourn's first play, *The Square Cat,* in which one man led a fragmented life as two distinct personalities. At last two separate, incomplete women fulfill themselves by becoming a single integrated whole. Yet what may seem to be the rare happy ending to an Ayckbourn play is finally hardly that. One sex still dominates the other, but now the female rather than the male may be on the verge of a tyrannical reign. The sisterhood formed in *Body Language* might well be the germ of the Daughters of Darkness of the earlier, futuristic *Henceforward* . . .. Together Angie and Jo, aided by Freya, have achieved happiness at the expense of the men in their lives. The healthy, integrated relationship of a man and a woman is yet again an impossibility in Ayckbourn's still clouded universe.

That a dramatist with such a dark view of human nature should consider writing plays for children a vital part of his work may seem paradoxical. Yet the seeds for some of his adult plays may be discerned in the children's plays to which Ayckbourn returned in 1989 after a nearly twenty-year hiatus. The device that germinates the plot of *Body Language* is similar to that of a delightful piece with disturbing overtones that Ayckbourn devised as an entertainment for the Christmas season in Scarborough in 1988. *Mr A's Amazing Maze Plays* presents a precursor of the character of Zyergefoovc, himself an adult child who plays with people as well as animals as his toys, taking parts from one being and grafting them onto another. The villain of the children's play, the attractive yet sinister Mr Accousticus, objects to loud noises and other unpleasant sounds, even poor singing voices. He takes action by stealing voices and animal sounds, sometimes even interchanging them. When Suzy and her dog Neville search his scary mansion for Neville's missing bark, they encounter a bat that makes the sound of a car horn, a music box that baas like a sheep, and a doll that strikes like a clock. A whistle makes the sound of crashing glass, a piano produces a trumpet fanfare, and a harp makes a drumming rat-a-tat-tat. The floor the girl and her faithful dog walk on snorts like a pig. When they discover the Cabinet of Sounds where Accousticus stores what offends him, they open drawers that emit a cacophonic miscellany of animal cries, road drills, church bells, and the like. Before Neville recovers his own bark, he tries out the barks of other dogs, larger and smaller than himself, even a human voice smartly saying, "Hallo, hallo, hallo, old boy."[2]

Other works by Ayckbourn stem from and give rise to his children's plays. Characters, situations, themes all flow from the adult works to the children's plays and back again. Whereas Accousticus foreshadows Zyergefoovc, he in turn had been foreshadowed by the composer, Jerome, in *Henceforward . . .* (1987) who in a sense stole voices as he recorded spoken language to be synthesized as the basis for his sterile avant-garde music. In *My Very Own Story* (1991), a children's play, Peter, Paul, and Percy all steal each other's stories and hi-jack their leading roles from one another, with Paul popping up in Percy's Victorian yarn and Peter suddenly appearing in Paul's gothic tale. And yet another play for children, *Callisto 5* (1990), about a boy isolated on a planet with only a robot and a computer for company, owes its inspiration to the relationship of *Henceforward . . .*'s gadget-obsessed Jerome and Nan 300F.

Ayckbourn's serious consideration of children's plays, or, as he prefers to call them, "family plays" or "adult plays for children,"[3] grew from an increasing awareness that his Scarborough audience "was getting older," that he too "was getting older and there was a severe danger that one day we'd all drop dead and there would be no one left in the theatre." Where would the audience of the future come from, or would an audience even exist—for his plays as well as for the plays of anyone else? "I think children's drama needs to be respectableized a bit, done by a few of our top dramatists," he has stated.[4] Several successful American playwrights seem to agree with Ayckbourn in both word and deed: Marsha Norman's adaptation of Frances Hodgson Burnett's *The Secret Garden* as a Broadway musical opened in 1991, the same year a consortium of children's theater companies across the United States, with the aid of a federal grant, commissioned plays from Mark Medoff, Tina Howe, and David Henry Hwang.[5] British writers, with the notable exception of Alan Bennett, who adapted Kenneth Grahame's *The Wind in the Willows* for the Royal National Theatre in 1990, have not taken up the cause.

In his early years at the theater in Scarborough, Stephen Joseph cultivated an audience of the young and encouraged his budding playwrights, Ayckbourn and David Campton, to write for children. Ayckbourn dismisses two of his own early efforts in this vein as deserving of oblivion, one of them, *Dad's Tale* (1960), actually begun as a collaboration between Joseph's two proteges. The other, *Xmas v. Mastermind*, was performed in Stoke-on-Trent at Christmas, 1962, but, perhaps with an assist on the part of the author, it has since "disappeared without trace."[6] About a conflict involving Father Christmas and the Crimson Golliwog, Ayckbourn calls the piece, "the most disastrous play I've ever done."[7]

Ayckbourn's third play for children, "Ernie's Incredible Illucinations" (1969), has enjoyed a longer life. That it stems from the Ayckbourn persona and relates to its author's ideas about the theater, that it is a cunning metaphor for theater itself, may be the contributing factors to its success. In the brief but thoroughly engaging one-act, a young boy is taken to a doctor because his "illucinations" have gotten out of hand. "He imagines things and they happen,"[8] his father tells the doctor; and what happens encompasses innocent bystanders as well as Ernie. Whoever happens to be in the vicinity when he hallucinates becomes an active participant in the occurrence. Mum and dad, Auntie May, even the skeptical doctor, all become performers in a soldiers' raid on the home of a resistance spy, a boxing match, a mountain rescue, and a parade featuring a brass band. Ernie, perhaps inspired by Ayckbourn himself, becomes the author-director who imagines a situation, then actually supervises its embodiment in a theatrical performance that so envelopes and engrosses its audience that the line between illusion and reality is ultimately blurred.

At times in Ayckbourn's plays, those written for adults as well as those for children, the A-effect enmeshes the audience as well as the performers. At the conclusion of *Man of the Moment*, for example, the audience willingly and collectively enacts the role of the studio audience of a television show. The spectator becomes the performer. In its initial in-the-round production at Scarborough, spectators could view those seated across from them as fellow audience members and, at the same time, participants in the play. In *Mr A's Amazing Maze Plays*, the Cabinet of Sounds can be placed in any one of the imagined rooms of Mr Accousticus's mansion so that not even the performers can be certain as the play begins at which point they will find it. Nor do they know the direction the search will take in yet another Ayckbourn play composed of many alternate scenes, for here the audience participates by dictating a number of Suzy and Neville's moves. The intricate play might be considered an animated board game for children by an author himself obsessed, like Reg in *The Norman Conquests*, with inventing new games.

Unlike Bernard in *Season's Greetings,* who bores his family with an inept puppet show every Christmas, Ayckbourn has discovered the key to the successful play for children—respect for the audience. According to Ayckbourn, a mistake others have made is to assume that "the only things that will attract children are the very very loud and the very very crude, mostly in terms of wide slapstick. Children can take fear, they can take excitement, they can take tension, they can take sorrow. They can take Bambi's mother dying. One hopes that the spectrum of emotion isn't filtered out and you don't just get custard being poured over people, although I think a bit of custard, even in adult plays, is fine."[9] And how well a bit of custard works in an adult play is demonstrated by the climactic scene of *Absent Friends*.

Ayckbourn has pointed to one essential difference in writing for children: "You have to be responsible and try to say something positive, whereas in adult plays you can be a bit more despairing and finish up on a negative."[10] Two related Ayckbourn plays, one for adults and one for children, illustrate his point. *Woman in Mind*, in which an unhappy wife imagines an alternate family, is heartbreaking; *Invisible Friends*, in which an unhappy thirteen-year-old girl imagines an alternate family, is, on the other hand, a joyous experience for children as well as for the adults who Ayckbourn hopes will accompany them to the theater.

The protagonists of both plays conjure up an imaginary family after suffering a blow to the head, Susan being struck by a rake handle in *Woman in Mind*, Lucy by falling on the stairs in *Invisible Friends*. For both of them the imagined family is for a time an idealized one; both fantasy-families, however, turn sinister. Early in the former play, Susan's doctor wants her taken to the hospital for observation, but the imaginary family will not hear of it: they will care for her at home. As the play ends, Susan, no longer in touch with reality, is lit by the reflection of the blue flashing light of the ambulance in which she is to be taken away. The latter play moves in a counter direction. Early in *Invisible Friends* Joy, Lucy's mother, despairing of her daughter's dependence on Zara, the "friend" no one else can see or hear, tells her daughter, "I think you're going barmy, girl. They'll lock you up for good one of these days. . . . We're going to have to call the van out for you, I can see that."[11] At the end of the play young Doctor Ziegler, who, not surprisingly, might well pass for Zara's twin, at first wants Lucy to spend the night in hospital after her fall, "just so they can keep a proper eye on you" (67). When she becomes aware of Lucy's fear of being separated from the real family with whom she thinks she has just been reunited, Doctor Ziegler changes her mind. Lucy is obviously in good hands at home, secure in the love of flesh-and-blood mother, father, and brother.

Once again Ayckbourn's art is drawn from the author's own experience, this time one shared by many children. Ayckbourn too had an imaginary friend: "He was my minder really. . . . I was quite thin and fragile and Tim had a deep voice and was rather tough," as well as being invisible; "it's an extraordinarily common phenomenon. I laid an extra place at the table for him and kept demanding two sets of pillows. I was an only kid in a single-parent family. Then my mother remarried and I inherited a step-brother and Tim went away."[12]

Invisible Friend's teenage Lucy first called upon her "friend" Zara at age seven or eight when she was too ill to go out and play. Now she relies on her for comforting reassurance following the too-frequent occasions when she is ignored by her conventionally unimaginative and undemonstrative lower-middle-class family consisting of Mum— Joy, and *"seldom can anyone have been more unsuitably named"* (1); Dad—Walter, "who's the current *Guinness Book of Records* twenty-four-hour sleeping champion," (6), generally in front of the telly; and brother Gary—Grisly Gary, as Lucy calls him, constantly hooked up to his Walkman when he is not on his "building course at the technical college, training to be a bucket" (7).

Whereas Ernie's "illucinations" began in boredom during "one of those exciting afternoon rave-ups we usually have in our house" (2), illustrated with Mum knitting in silence, Dad gazing ahead of him, and Ernie reading a book, Lucy's problems begin when no one reacts, will even listen, to the "exciting news" that she has "been chosen for the school swimming team" (1–2). Only Zara appreciates Lucy's extraordinary accomplishment. Soon Zara is quietly disrupting the household. The frequent tea-time mix-ups in Ayckbourn's plays which recall Gwendolyn's complaint to Cecily in *The Importance of Being Earnest*—"You have filled my tea with lumps of sugar, and though I asked distinctly for bread and butter, you have given me cake" (583)—reach a hilarious peak at breakfast in Lucy's home when the mischievous friend switches Walt's Cornflakes and Gary's Krispies. Walt is convinced that the cereal firm has filled the packets incorrectly, but when he attempts to prove his point by pouring more Krispies out of the Cornflakes packet only to find a topping of Cornflakes in his dish, he is at first bewildered and then so annoyed that he threatens "to write and complain about this" (31).

Once Lucy, goaded by Zara, makes her family disappear so that she can spend her time happily with the friend who has mysteriously materialized, an imaginary father and brother, the elegant Felix and Chuck, appear as well, "*a pristine unreality about them*" as there is about Zara (36). For a brief time, as they let her win all their card games, Lucy is content. But soon the new family that has insinuated itself into her home, like that in Edward Chodorov's *Kind Lady* (1935), begins to take over to the point that Lucy, like Chekhov's three sisters, finds herself displaced and out of the house. At the end of *Invisible Friends* turncoat Zara becomes the kindly Doctor Ziegler who attends Lucy after she again falls on the stairs and hits her head, "*mirroring the fall she had earlier in the play*" (66); Felix and Chuck, friends as false as Rosencrantz and Guildenstern, become the helpful ambulance men whom, fortunately, the doctor can dismiss. What appears a decidedly happy ending for children may hold for adults an ominous, ambiguous note. Anyone familiar with Ayckbourn's plays for a mature audience might well ask, "Will the adult Lucy have the identical problems with an uncommunicative future husband and child that she has had with an unresponsive father, mother, and brother? Will Lucy one day become *Woman in Mind*'s Susan?" Even in an Ayckbourn play for children, the intruding dark shadows cannot be fully dispelled.

Invisible Friends contains brief counterpoint alternate scenes that are part of each performance—Lucy's indifferent parents suddenly bill and coo their way through an extract from *The Beggar's Opera* ("I would love thee ev'ry day . . .") in a what-might-have-been scene (7), as well as moments of magic—a room tidies itself up as "*objects shoot under the bed and back into cupboards*" (40)—like those in the earlier children's plays, *Dad's Tale* and "Ernie's Incredible Illucinations." With the exceptions of *Standing Room Only* and *Henceforward . . .*, however, in which bizarre occurrences become commonplace once the vaguely futuristic settings are established, Ayckbourn's plays for adults were bounded, despite the tricks of time and place in a play like *How the Other Half Loves*, by an unvarying naturalistic style. Of necessity that style gave way to a freer form, a world populated in part by cartoonlike figures in *The Revengers' Comedies*. Grotesque events impossible in the world today, if not totally improbable in the near future, like the head transplants of *Body Language*, were the next step in widening the horizons of the author of adult plays who had already embraced the always possible fantasies of the world of imaginative children.

As *Invisible Friends*, first performed at the Stephen Joseph Theatre in 1989, was about to be presented at London's Royal National Theatre in 1991 only seven weeks before the Scarborough premiere of a new play for adults, *Wildest Dreams*, Ayckbourn considered his changing style: "I think my plays are getting more free. . . . I'm sure it's just hang-ups in me, but a lot of freedoms have occurred since writing children's plays. When I came back to writing for adults this summer, I felt liberated from the hold of naturalism. You don't feel such a fool."[13] The author in fact acknowledged the impact that his writing for a younger audience had made on his work for adults: "I've been slowly moving towards a much more graphic narrative style and the plays have got much bigger in their field, much darker, and more fantastic. And for fantastic, read childlike."[14]

An adult play promised for the future in which there are "three different time scales, each one reflecting the relationships of the others,"[15] is anticipated in *Invisible Friends* as Lucy's two falls become one fall which obliterates her imaginings in between. If double or triple time scales call to mind once again the plays of J. B. Priestley, the world of the Yorkshireman-by-adoption is far more complex than that of the native northerner. More immediately, even more directly, a line from *Invisible Friends* illuminates the theme of one of the most challenging of all Ayckbourn's plays for adults. Of the whereabouts of the real family that she has wished away in the children's play, Lucy says, "They were just in another plane, like in another universe, practically the same as the one we're in, only running alongside it. But quite separate. It's difficult to explain" (37). In *Wildest Dreams* four unhappy people take refuge from a world with which they cannot cope by moving to another plane by means of a board game similar to "Dungeons and Dragons," a children's game that can transport even troubled adults to an imaginary world where for a while earthly wounds and unquiet souls may be solaced.

The players of the game in *Wildest Dreams* all have need of another plane of existence. Stanley and Hazel Inchbridge go through the motions of a childless marriage. A teacher of English at Whinnythrop Lane, Stanley has reached the occasional rare student in the classroom, but out of school he is out of touch even with his wife. Hazel's job at a building society does not afford her even the temporary satisfaction his allows him. They share a home, or, what is closer to the actual arrangement, keep house for Hazel's brother Austen Skate, a bullying VAT inspector for Her Majesty's Customs and Excise.

Austen's "punctilious" use of obscure words, like "idiolect" and "exigent," is just one more means of taunting his noncombative brother-in-law who regards Austen's irritating habit as a form of "nit picking."[16] Austen may be overbearing, but he is no fool. He understands better than do the Inchbridges their need for the game he does not participate in. At the beginning of *Wildest Dreams* Austen asks Stanley the meaning of the word "fugue." Stanley defines it as "a piece of music that repeats on itself," but later in the play Austen reveals its other, apt meaning: "Fugue can also mean a form of amnesia which is a flight from reality. Isn't that interesting?" The unhappy Stanley and Hazel have as much need to take refuge in a fugue state as does Susan in *Woman in Mind*, and even more reason than Lucy in *Invisible Friends*.

The Inchbridges's flight from reality takes the form of the game they have played each week for five years with two others younger than themselves. Rick Toller, a twenty-one-year-old woman of indeterminate sexuality, lives alone in squalor in the basement of the house in which her mother abandoned her some years earlier. Seventeen-year-old computer-whiz Warren Wrigley, a loner, lives with his mother, whom he does not permit to enter his private lair, an attic-den filled with computer-driven equipment. He is the inventor of the game that has become central to his life and that of his equally maladjusted weekly companions. The diversion that has become an all-consuming obsession is based, Warren explains, "on a standard role playing game which I update and upprogramme every week, thus allowing the computer to select and print out variable parameters and random options as and when we require them." The computer, in fact, has become for all of them a god.

The game is played on a board subdivided into squares on which stand four model figures, the counters that are moved by the players they symbolize in a mystical world:

> *The first of them is the figure of a wise 'ancient', Alric, stooped and elderly with a stick and flowing robes. The second, Idonia, the mystic and magical one, childlike, beautiful in a dress and a mane of flowing hair. Next, a strange, green-faced creature, half-man, half-beast—Xenos, the stranger or alien, possessor of special powers of sight and hearing. Finally, the compact, powerful figure of Herwin, the masculine-named female battle warrior, armoured, carrying a broad-sword drawn, shield held ready in case of sudden attack.*

What becomes apparent to the audience as the play and the game progress is that the players grow to resemble ever more closely the counters that represent them, although they never quite make their own, as they might wish, their figures' dominant traits. Paradoxically, gentle, ineffectual Stanley assumes the role of Alric, the confident leader. Hazel is impetuous Idonia; Warren, convinced that he is actually an alien in a world of humans, is Xenos; and Rick, who will not allow her given name Alice to be spoken by anyone, is the cross-gendered Herwin.

Into the lives of the players comes Marcie Banks, an attractive, seemingly well-adjusted young woman about the same age as Rick, a waitress in the restaurant where Rick does the washing up. She first appears at Rick's home in a disheveled state as she seeks sanctuary from the husband who abuses her, but once she tidies herself up, she appears "almost pristine." She is the Zara of *Invisible Friends* for whom Lucy pines, the friend in need of protection whom Rick could never have dared to dream into being, the damsel in distress whom every man might wish to rescue and claim as his own. Like Colin in *Absent Friends,* like Richard and Anthea in *Joking Apart,* who offer unthinking indiscriminate friendship to all around them, unaware of their oftentimes disastrous effect on others, Marcie offers a sympathetic ear to anyone and everyone as well as an inviting smile that suggests more than she in fact intends. When Marcie is invited by the smitten Stanley and Warren to join the game, to the discomfiture of Rick who has qualms about sharing her friend, and Hazel who fears the younger woman means to share her husband, she becomes Novia the Newcomer. Novia soon breaks protocol, disrupting the proceedings by offering advice to Alric, the wise one, which, to the amazement of the rest, he willingly accepts.

The object of the game is to seek out and destroy Balaak, the personification of the evil that is present in the make-believe world but pervasive as well in the lives of the players. For Stanley the representation of true evil is his brother-in-law Austen, who, he claims, "can never be right. Even when he's right, he's wrong." For Warren evil resides in those who do not share his belief in himself as a powerful alien creature with other-worldly intelligence. He has focused all the disbelievers into a single adversary, his godfearing mother who relies on the power of prayer, together with a cup of tea or cocoa, to solve all the world's problems. According to her son, Mrs. Wrigley is an Orgue, a species only fit to be the slaves of the Laks. For Rick, the evil is Larry, Marcie's husband, whom she sees as all the men in the world, like her mother's lover, who would use and abuse her. For Hazel, Marcie is herself the evil, the always-to-be-feared other woman.

The intensity of the players' emotions as well as the level of energy that they redirect from living their lives to playing their game is revealed in the alarming scene that ends the first act when, with cries of "Onward!" they move their pieces toward a confrontation with Balaak: "The danger increases still more, Wise One. Clouds are gathering. There is impenetrable darkness ahead." Despite the fact that they are in the Inchbridges's "*unexceptional front room in an ordinary, modern semi-detached house in an unremarkable street in an undistinguished town,*" as a thunderous roaring wind builds to a wail, "*there is a sudden, final thunderous explosion as if the devil's hoofbeats had ridden over them.*" It is a moment of terror as well as orgiastic ecstacy that leaves Marcie, uttering a cry of "Fantastic!" breathlessly radiant from the experience. Stanley later attempts to explain away the phenomenon as "a sort of freak gathering of psychic energy," but he cannot convince even himself. The five of them have experienced an intense if momentary merging of illusion and reality. They will never again be certain where the dream ends and life begins.

For the others, Marcie, the play's catalyst, becomes the cause of eventual disenchantment with the game. Her entry into their lives forces them to see a remedy beyond the game for the emptiness within themselves, unaware that their quest, their attempt to make the renewal she seems to offer an integral part of their lives, is as much a dream as is the game. For Hazel, fearful of losing her husband, the new dream is to become someone whom Stanley cannot abandon, must continually care for. The barren Martha of Edward Albee's *Who's Afraid of Virginia Woolf* (1962) imagines she has a child, but Hazel becomes herself the child. Having looked into a mirror, and, like Marion in *Absurd Person Singular,* despairing of what she sees, she wills herself to grow young, like Idonia in the game, and ends the play an incontinent baby crawling on all fours, barking like a dog as she plays with a toy animal. Stanley makes a declaration of love for Marcie, but she rejects him: "By the time I'm at an age where I could really do with someone, someone to look after me, you'd be dead." Warren, who immerses himself in a science fiction world when he is not playing the game, is certain that he is becoming a Lak, a superior being. He sees Marcie as a Trilla, with whom the Laks, like Angie and Jo of *Body Language,* enter into a perfect symbiotic relationship. Yet at the end of the play when he removes the ski mask he has been wearing to hide from the others the metamorphosis he is sure he is undergoing, she can see no change, only the face of a bad-complexioned adolescent. For Rick, seeking to become the masculine protector, the lesbian relationship into which she enters with Marcie becomes something other than she had anticipated: it is Marcie, issuing orders that Rick meekly carries out, who becomes the dominant figure.

During the three-day Christmas holiday that concludes the play's action, evil appears vanquished, or so the players wish to believe. Stanley corrects Austen's substitution of the word "cumulus" for "tumulus" but goes beyond semantic niceties. He forces his brother-in-law into the realization that Austen's incestuous desire for his sister has been the stumbling block preventing the fulfillment of the Inchbridges's relationship, a painful truth that causes Austen to suffer a stroke. Warren imprisons his mother in her room by switching "force fields to prevent unauthorised movement around the house," so that she receives an electrical shock when she touches the door handle, frustrating even her attempts to go to the toilet. And Rick breaks Larry's nose. But the rebirth the season promises comes only to Hazel in her regression to a grotesque infancy. With Marcie no longer their hope for salvation, the others vow to end the game. When the time comes to do so, however, they realize that they cannot. They have grown too dependent upon it. The final image of the play is a repetition of its opening moment. Stanley, Warren, Rick, and baby Hazel are grouped around the board. Another game is about to begin. The play's last word is a repeated "Onwards." The players of the game, with nowhere to go, are like Didi and Gogo at the end of *Waiting for Godot*, motionless at the moment of departure. Like Pirandello's Enrico IV who gathers his mock courtiers around him at the end of the play, they are trapped within the game.

Ayckbourn's plays continue to sound echoes of other significant dramatic works, achieving thereby an added resonance. The horror of *Wildest Dreams*'s closure is intensified as the alienated foursome, immobile in the void, mirror Beckett's tramps, their pathetic cry of "Onwards!" recalling the devastating plaint of Pirandello's supposed madman: "Here we are . . . together . . . for ever!"[17] Isolated moments in *Wildest Dreams* bring to mind still other plays. A young woman's recounting of her abandonment by her mother and the mother's lover who abused her—"If she believed me, what would that make him? And if he was that, what would that do to her who couldn't live without him?"—define *Streetcar*'s Stella and Stanley as it sheds light on Rick's stunted emotional growth. But the déjà vu the audience experiences here is primarily a revisiting of the works of a single author. In *Wildest Dreams* Ayckbourn echoes Ayckbourn. Hazel is yet another desperate wife who loses her sanity; her realization that her husband no longer loves her, is attracted to another, parallels the dilemma that finally defeats poor Louise in *Joking Apart*. Rick is akin to *Henceforward . . .*'s crossdressing Geain; she is also like Freya in *Body Language* as she easily fells a man, like Lucy in *Invisible Friends* as she attempts to impress a newfound friend by cooking for her—and failing. Austen is as spiteful a brother-in-law as Graham in *Time and Time Again,* his stroke a fuller retribution for past offences than the throttling Graham suffers at Peter's hands. A further development of the boy with a computer in *Callisto 5,* Warren redirects sounds as does Jerome in *Henceforward . . .* and Mr. Accousticus in *Mr A's Amazing Maze Plays.* The violent indoor wind storm that occurs as Lucy's family vanishes in *Invisible Friends* recurs with intensified furor during the game's most telling moment. *Wildest Dreams,* however, is more than the mere sum of the parts of other Ayckbourn plays. As the pieces coalesce into a stunning mosaic, the unified work reveals a design of its own that is related to but transcends the more tentative symbolic substructure of an earlier work such as *Way Upstream. Wildest Dreams* demonstrates a writer at the peak of his powers, using his seasoned craft to lift his artistry to a metaphysical plane he had never before attained.

In *Invisible Friends* Lucy wonders why her father has tuned the telly to a gardening show as their house has no garden. The three-part setting of *Wildest Dreams* also depicts only interiors. But beyond those interiors are signs of a stark and threatening natural world that can no longer be tamed into the serenity of a manicured English garden. Ayckbourn goes beyond the Edenic imagery that illuminated Susan's descent into madness in *Woman in Mind* to suggest ancient archetypes as counterpoint to the sterility of a modern wasteland. With the mystique derived from J. R. R. Tolkien's popular "Hobbit" tales, Frank Herbert's "Dune" stories, the *Star Wars* movies and *Star Trek* television shows, together with the intellectual challenges of the Dungeons and Dragons game as a starting point, he constructs parallel texts in which reality merges with fugue. The common metaphor is the barrenness of both the imagined setting of the game and the mundane reality in which the characters are immersed. The hierophantic elements are employed comically through the pretentious language of the game that reflects Austen's smug semantic one-upmanship; and magically, through the life that the game's token figures assume in the mystically charged moment when Hazel attempts to join them by playing with them. The language of the game together with the method of its play underscore the notion of a society searching for meaning in a spiritually devastated landscape. The rituals of the game devised by the players extend even to their taking of food and drink. The ritual afternoon tea mimics the game's pseudo-ancient rites as the players seek but fail to find spiritual connection in the here-and-now.

The direction the players travel within the game finally makes no difference to them nor to its outcome, for wherever they go, they must confront the truth of the self, the void within, that all of them fear. As in Greek myth there is a curse on the land as well as its inhabitants. The world of the game reifies the barren landscapes of Sir James Frazer's *The Golden Bough*, but a queen, significantly a Virgin Queen, has replaced the Fisher King: "To the North are hills, the Mountains of Ag. Beyond that lies the Kingdom of Endocia, the Virgin Queen, Ruler of the Fish People. To the West, the Kingdom of Orrich, Lord of all oak trees and the Forest of Emptiness. To the East, the Grey River which winds into the Valley of Disappointment and Despair. And to the South? There lie-eth the Dead Place." Whatever compass point the players choose, they cannot evade the private demons of the self in a god-bereft world where the devil is rampant. Stanley, Hazel, Warren, and Rick, with Marcie the catalyst, never make a conscious choice for good or for evil, a choice preferable to moral stagnation for it at least implies the adventure of living. The players never actually enter heraldry's sacred, hierophantic precincts. With the subtext of the ritual beyond their comprehension, they abandon their search for meaning. The return to the board at the conclusion of *Wildest Dreams* signifies no more than the playing of a game.

Despite his perilous voyage into the wasteland, Ayckbourn has not forgotten a dramatist's responsibility to his audience: they expect to be and must be entertained. *Wildest Dreams* is a bleak play that still fills a theater with laughter. It is not the laughter evoked by such early plays as *Mr Whatnot* and *Relatively Speaking*. It is the crueler laughter of the later plays, of *Man of the Moment, The Revengers' Comedies*, and *Body Language*—apoplectic Austen on the verge of a stroke, a mother imprisoned by her son, a grown woman crawling on the floor in nappies. A human being reduced to an object is, according to Henri Bergson, the stuff of comedy. In all his plays Ayckbourn turns humankind into the objectified counters of the sadly hilarious game of life. The irresistible laughter may seem heartless, but *Wildest Dreams*, in the words of John Peter, "is the kind of brilliant comedy of cruelty . . . which can only be written by someone deeply compassionate."[18]

A one-time farceur, Ayckbourn now writes plays that explore humankind's ethical and moral behavior in both real and imaginary worlds, his comedies, like Shaw's, as thought-provoking as they are entertaining. Shaw never offered his audience a choice. The theatergoer was encouraged to laugh but could not overlook the didacticism of the dramatic debates; and Shaw's readers had his "Prefaces"

to drive the lesson home. Ayckbourn offers choice without didacticism. Even as his drama presents ever darker scenes, his audience
may leave the theater merely laughing, or that laughter may be
tempered with thought, at times even thoughtful despair. Director
Mike Nichols once described his ambiguous response to a performance of Beckett's *Rockaby*: "The Beckett experience is that when the
play is over, you sit there and you're utterly depressed because there
seems to be no hope at all. And then you walk 15 blocks, and you feel
good, and finally you feel great, because somebody has told the truth,
and the truth . . . can uplift you and make you feel actually joyous."[19]
Perhaps the reverse is true of the audience's response to Ayckbourn's
later plays, even to some of the earlier ones. The man who laughed at
a performance of *Just Between Ourselves* wondered what he had been
laughing at by the time he reached the pub. What follows the laughter
is the profounder joy that comes with the truth that is the hallmark
not only of the dark comedies of Beckett, but of Ayckbourn too.

Truth may be harsh, but it is not—as it may at first seem—the
province of the pessimist, or so yet another dramatist understands.
Arthur Miller once said, "If you're looking at truth you're an optimist,
and if you're fleeing from it, even laughing all the way, it's really
pessimism. The art that offers us an escape from reality is the art that
fails."[20] In that light or any other, the art of Alan Ayckbourn succeeds.
His characters may flee reality; he confronts it.

Notes

Chapter 1. A Chorus of Approval

1. Peter Hall, *Peter Hall's Diaries*, ed. John Goodwin (London: Hamish Hamilton Paperback, 1984), 361.
2. Anthony Masters, "The essentially ambiguous response," *Times*, 4 February 1981, 8.
3. Mel Gussow, "Bard of the British Bourgeoisie," *New York Times Magazine*, 28 January 1990, 23.
4. Ibid., 84.
5. Ibid.
6. Ian Watson, *Conversations with Ayckbourn* (London: Faber & Faber, 1988), 4. Unless otherwise noted, cited passages from this work are the words of Ayckbourn. This is the consistent practice throughout for citations from all published interviews with Ayckbourn.
7. Russell Miller, "The Hit-Man from Scarborough," *Sunday Times Magazine*, 20 February 1977, 24.
8. Watson, *Conversations*, 131.
9. Ibid., 8.
10. Ibid., 11, 13.
11. Jack Tinker, *Daily Mail*, 28 February 1978, 7.
12. Stephen Joseph, *New Theatre Forms* (London: Sir Isaac Pitman & Sons, 1968), 64.
13. Miller, "Hit-Man," 26.
14. Joseph, *New Theatre Forms*, 64–65.
15. Watson, *Conversations*, 20.
16. In conversation with Kalson at the Alley Theatre, Houston, Texas, 4 March 1982, Robin Herford, a former member of the Scarborough company, mentioned Ayckbourn's shyness in dealing with his actors until he gets to know them well and works with them more than once. In the program for *Ten Times Table*, Theatre Royal, Windsor, 13 June to 1 July 1989, Herford, who directed the production, writes: "To the outside world he's very shy. In fact during rehearsals he's very relaxed, always stories and jokes, but he doesn't let you get too close to him. . . . One respects his space and he respects yours." Gussow reports that Ayckbourn "warmed to the conversation" when he interviewed him, "but, later, when speaking to a class in stagecraft at the Westborough Methodist Church, he became less informal, answering questions but avoiding eye contact with his questioners," (24). In his *Diaries* Peter Hall writes perceptively: "Alan is a strange, shy creature: jovial, eyes darting all over the place or palely looking at his boots, never glancing at you if he can avoid it; a warm, careful man. He is very vulnerable, and always afraid of saying something serious and so being thought ridiculous. He preempts this by making himself ridiculous before we have the chance. He's always laughing at himself" (406). Ayckbourn has spoken of Joseph's shyness to Watson: "He was such a shy man when

you first met him, he always stared at his blotter" (21). Joseph apparently once conducted an entire interview with an applicant to his company without looking directly at the person. At the end of the interview he was amazed on looking up to learn he had just hired a woman as the theater's touring manager. Ayckbourn, who worked side-by-side with Joseph for nearly a decade, does not himself recognize his mentor as the inspiration for some of his characters, yet the amusing stories he has recounted about him to interviewers, Watson among them, point to Joseph as well as to the dramatist himself as an Ayckbourn creation.

17. Stephen Joseph, *Theatre in the Round* (London: Barrie & Rockcliff, 1967), 57.
18. Watson, *Conversations*, 22.
19. Ibid., 17.
20. Ibid., 16.
21. Ibid., 25.
22. Janet Watts, "Absurd persons, plural and suburban," *Observer*, 4 March 1979, 39. (The first part of the quoted passages is Watts's description of Ayckbourn, the last part Ayckbourn's own words.)
23. David Campton, "Personal Progress," in *Laughter and Fear: Nine One-Act Plays*, ed. Michael Marland (London and Glasgow: Blackie & Son, 1969), 230.
24. Michael Coveney, "Scarborough Fare," *Plays and Players*, September 1975, 18.
25. Miller, "Hit-Man," 26.
26. Domenico Vittorini, *The Drama of Luigi Pirandello* (Philadelphia: University of Pennsylvania Press, 1935), 24.
27. John Heilpern, "Striking sparks off suburbia," *Observer*, 13 February 1977, 14.
28. Alan Ayckbourn, *Relatively Speaking* (London: Evans Plays, 1968), introduction. All subsequent citations are to this edition.
29. Joseph, *Theatre in the Round*, 57.
30. Philip Hope-Wallace, *Guardian*, 7 August 1964.
31. Heilpern, 4 (the interviewer's words).
32. Eugène Scribe, quoted and translated by Stephen S. Stanton, *Camille and Other Plays*, ed. Stanton (New York: Hill & Wang, 1957), introduction, vii.
33. Miller, "Hit-Man," 26.
34. Watson, *Conversations*, 71.
35. Scribe, viii.
36. Alan Ayckbourn, *Three Plays: Absurd Person Singular, Absent Friends, Bedroom Farce* (New York: Grove Press, 1979), preface, 8. All subsequent citations to *Absurd Person Singular*, *Absent Friends*, and *Bedroom Farce* are to this edition.

Chapter 2. Other Dramatists, Absent Friends

1. Watson, *Conversations*, 36.
2. John Harvey, *Anouilh: A Study in Theatrics* (New Haven and London: Yale University Press, 1964), 173.
3. Watson, *Conversations*, p. 35.
4. Harvey, *Anouilh*, 130, n.11.
5. Jean Anouilh, *Dinner with the Family*, trans. Edward Owen Marsh (London: Methuen, 1958), 82. A subsequent citation to *Dinner with the Family* is to this edition. Marsh changes some of the characters' names. Robert becomes Jacques; Henriette becomes Christine.

6. Alan Ayckbourn, *The Square Cat*, unpublished manuscript.

7. In conversation with Kalson in London, 28 February 1991, Ayckbourn revealed that "Countdown" was written in 1959 for Oscar Quitak as a contribution to an evening of one-act plays. The author no longer can remember where it was first performed. Subsequently, in 1969, when Quitak was assembling an entertainment called *We Who Are About To . . .* for the Hampstead Theatre Club, he asked to use the piece again. Later that year the collection of playlets was performed at London's Comedy Theatre under the title *Mixed Doubles*. Ian Watson, Michael Billington, and Sidney Howard White all mistakenly assume that the Hampstead and London productions were the piece's earliest stagings. When asked about the impetus for so dark a mood in 1959, surprisingly early on in his career, Ayckbourn responded, "Well, by then I'd been married a year."

8. Watson, *Conversations*, 145.

9. Thomas Bishop, *Pirandello and the French Theater* (New York: New York University Press, 1960), 118.

10. Miller, "Hit-Man," 26.

11. Noël Coward, *Play Parade* (London: Heinemann, 1950), 2, introduction, ix–xx.

12. John Lahr, *Coward: The Playwright* (New York: Avon Discus Book, 1983), 41.

13. Ayckbourn, *Relatively Speaking*, introduction. The play was first performed in Scarborough in 1965 as *Meet My Father*.

14. Publisher's blurb, back cover of *Relatively Speaking*.

15. Oscar Wilde, *The Importance of Being Earnest*, in *Nineteenth-Century British Drama*, ed. Leonard R. N. Ashley (Glenview, Illinois: Scott, Foresman & Co., 1967), 591. All subsequent citations to *The Importance of Being Earnest* are to this edition.

16. Cole Lesley, *The Life of Noël Coward* (London: Jonathan Cape, 1976), 434.

17. Alan Ayckbourn, letter to Kalson, 28 February 1989. Ayckbourn told an audience at a "Platform Performance," a public interview at the Royal National Theatre, 12 March 1991, that on the one occasion that he met Neil Simon in that very building, he jokingly informed his so-called American counterpart that the major difference between them was that Simon's name is always spelled correctly. This occurred shortly after the British playwright, walking across Waterloo Bridge, saw his own name misspelled on the National's electric signboard.

18. Lahr, *Coward*, 8.

19. Alan Ayckbourn, *The Norman Conquests* (New York: Grove Press, 1979), 223. All subsequent citations to *The Norman Conquests* are to this edition.

20. Alan Ayckbourn, *Season's Greetings* (London: Samuel French, 1982), 79.

21. Brian Connell, "Playing for laughs to a lady typist: A *Times* Profile," 5 January 1976, 5.

22. Lahr, *Coward*, 8.

23. Connell, "Playing for laughs," 5.

24. Ayckbourn, conversation with Kalson, Alley Theatre, Houston, Texas, 12 October 1987.

25. Connell, "Playing for laughs," 5.

26. Ayckbourn, conversation with Kalson; Alan Ayckbourn, *Just Between Ourselves*, in *Joking Apart and Other Plays* (Harmondsworth, Middlesex, England: Penguin Books, 1982), 36. All subsequent citations to *Just Between Ourselves, Ten Times Table,* and *Joking Apart* are to this edition.

27. Ayckbourn, *Absent Friends*, in *Three Plays*, 156.

28. Connell, "Playing for laughs," 5.

29. Harold Pinter, quoted by John Russell Taylor, *Anger and After: A Guide to the New British Drama* London: Methuen, 1962), 231.

30. Michael Billington, *Alan Ayckbourn*, 2d ed. (Houndmills, Basingstoke, Hampshire and London: Macmillan Education Ltd., 1990), 24.

31. Coveney, "Scarborough Fare," 18.

32. Harold Pinter, *Old Times* (New York: Grove Press, 1971), 8. Because Ayckbourn, Pinter, Frayn, and other dramatists frequently punctuate with three periods (. . .), four periods (. . . .) are used to indicate ellipses in the cited dialogue of all plays under discussion in this study.

33. Alan Ayckbourn, *A Trip to Scarborough*, unpublished manuscript.

34. Yet another play about a group of amateurs, this time convicts in Australia in 1789, rehearsing an actual play—George Farquhar's *The Recruiting Officer* (1706)—that comments on society then and now, as well as the worth of theater and drama, is Timberlake Wertenbaker's *Our Country's Good*, based on Thomas Keneally's 1987 novel, *The Playmaker*, and first performed in 1988, four years after the first production of *A Chorus of Disapproval*. Like Ayckbourn, Wertenbaker is well versed in the plays of Anouilh, having translated his *Leocadia* as well as Marivaux's *False Admissions* and *Successful Strategies*.

35. Michael Frayn, *Benefactors* (London: Faber & Faber, 1987), 30.

36. Ayckbourn, conversation with Kalson.

37. Alan Ayckbourn, *A Small Family Business* (London: Faber & Faber, 1987), 31. All subsequent citations to *A Small Family Business* are to this edition.

38. Lillian Hellman, *Pentimento: A Book of Portraits* (Boston: Little, Brown & Co., 1973), 3.

39. J. B. Priestley, *An Inspector Calls* (London: Heinemann, 1947), vii.

40. *An Inspector Calls*, in *The Plays of J. B. Priestley* (London: Heinemann, 1950), 3: 269; subsequent citations to *An Inspector Calls* are to this edition.

41. Watson, *Conversations*, 145.

42. John Peter, *Sunday Times*, 27 May 1990, E5.

43. Gussow, "Bard of the British Bourgeoisie," 24.

Chapter 3. Exchanges, Intimate or Otherwise

1. Herford, conversation with Kalson, 4 March 1982.

2. Alan Ayckbourn, *How the Other Half Loves* (London: Evans Plays, 1972), 69.

3. Alan Ayckbourn, *Suburban Strains* (London: Samuel French, 1982), 49.

4. Alan Ayckbourn, *Intimate Exchanges* (London: Samuel French, 1985, 2 vol.), 2:154, 156, 162–63. All subsequent citations to *Intimate Exchanges* are to this edition.

5. Watson, *Conversations*, 70.

6. Herford, conversation with Kalson. In 1991 New York's Circle in the Square Theatre staged the play in the round.

7. Alan Ayckbourn, *Henceforward . . .* (London: Faber & Faber, 1988), 30. All subsequent citations to *Henceforward . . .* are to this edition.

8. Guido Almansi, "Victims of Circumstance," *Encounter*, April 1978, 62.

9. Mary James, to interviewer Miller, "Hit-Man," 26.

10. Almansi, "Victims," 60.

11. Ayckbourn, *Three Plays*, preface, 8.

12. Watson, *Conversations*, 61.

13. Alan Ayckbourn, *Sisterly Feelings and Taking Steps* (London: Chatto & Windus, 1981), 4. All subsequent citations to *Sisterly Feelings* and *Taking Steps* are to this edition.

14. Ayckbourn, conversation with Kalson, London, 28 February 1991.

15. In the National Theatre production, two actors—Stephen Moore (Simon) and Michael Gambon (Patrick)—preferred not to be stimulated at the early performances that were actually to be left to chance. In his workshop at home Gambon devised a two-headed coin that appeared to be, unless one examined it closely, perfectly normal. Taking the matter of chance or choice into their own hands, the two knew where their performances were headed whenever they preferred to know. At the end of the run they presented the coin to the unsuspecting author, according to Mel Gussow, in "Profiles: The Complete Actor," *The New Yorker*, 28 January 1991, 76.

16. Watson, *Conversations*, 161.

17. Ibid., 184.

18. Alan Ayckbourn, *Family Circles*, unpublished manuscript.

19. Alan Ayckbourn, *It Could Be Any One of Us*, unpublished manuscript.

20. *Times*, 9 June 1984, 20.

21. Herford, conversation with Kalson, Scarborough, 20 January 1984.

22. John Gay, *The Beggar's Opera*, in Ayckbourn, *A Chorus of Disapproval* (London: Faber & Faber, 1986), 9, 95. All subsequent citations to *A Chorus of Disapproval* are to this edition.

Chapter 4. Women In and Out of Mind

1. Michael Leech, "National Ayckbourn," *Drama: The Quarterly Theatre Review* (1986): IV, 10.

2. Ibid.

3. Michael Billington, *Guardian*, 5 September 1986; Clive Hirschorn, *Sunday Express* and Kenneth Hurren, *Mail on Sunday*, 7 September 1986; all reprinted in *London Theatre Record*, 27 August–9 September 1986, 953–54.

4. Barbara J. Small, "Ben Travers," *Dictionary of Literary Biography*," vol. 10: *Modern British Dramatists, 1900–1945* (Detroit, Michigan: A Bruccoli Clark Book, Gale Research Company, 1982), pt. 2, p. 186.

5. Ayckbourn, conversation with Kalson, Houston, Texas, 4 March 1982); also Leech, "National Ayckbourn," 10.

6. Ayckbourn, *Relatively Speaking*, 29.

7. Watson, *Conversations*, 94, 96.

8. Ibid., 94.

9. Ibid., 96.

10. Alan Ayckbourn, *Confusions* (London: Samuel French, 1977), 2. A subsequent citation to *Confusions* is to this edition.

11. Billington, *Guardian*, 5 September 1986.

12. Watts, "Absurd persons," 39.

13. Ibid.

14. Anton Chekhov, *Plays*, trans. Elisaveta Fen (Harmondsworth, Middlesex, England: Penguin Books, 1959), introduction, 19.

15. Watson, *Conversations*, 135.

16. Masters, "The essentially ambiguous response," 8; Gordon House, *London Calling*, the program journal of the BBC World Service in English, September 1990, 9.

17. Watson, *Conversations*, 141.

18. Alan Ayckbourn, *Woman in Mind* (London: Faber & Faber, 1986), 9; all subsequent citations to *Woman in Mind* are to this edition; Bernard Dukore, in "Craft, Character, Comedy: Ayckbourn's *Woman in Mind*," *Twentieth Century Liter-*

ature (Spring 1986), 25–26, "translates" some of the lines of the opening scene into English.

19. Arthur Kopit, *Wings* (New York: Hill & Wang, 1978), 25.

20. See ibid., xiv.

21. Henrik Ibsen, *Peer Gynt*, trans. Rolf Fjelde (New York: Signet Classics, New American Library, 1964), 173.

22. R. D. Laing, *The Divided Self* (New York: Pantheon Books, 1960), 222.

23. Joan Smith, *Sunday Today*, 21 September 1986, reprinted in *London Theatre Record*, 29 August–9 September 1986, 962.

24. Laing, *The Divided Self*, 212, n.1.

Chapter 5. Men Of and For the Moment

1. *Peter Hall's Diaries*, 285–86.

2. Alan Ayckbourn, *Mr Whatnot*, unpublished manuscript.

3. Martin Esslin, *The Theatre of the Absurd*, rev. ed. (Woodstock, New York: The Overlook Press, 1973), 289.

4. Alan Ayckbourn, *Time and Time Again* (London: Samuel French, 1973), 80. All subsequent citations to *Time and Time Again* are to this edition.

5. Alan Ayckbourn, *Jeeves*, unpublished manuscript.

6. Watson, *Conversations*, 16.

7. Alan Ayckbourn, *Way Upstream* (London: Samuel French, 1983), 43–44. Billington, in *Alan Ayckbourn*, 162, calls the speech "the theatrical equivalent" of a poem by Henry Reed, "Naming of Parts."

8. Ayckbourn, conversastion with Kalson, Houston, Texas, 4 March 1982.

9. Ibid.

10. Ayckbourn, *Man of the Moment* (London: Faber & Faber, 1990), 29. Subsequent citations to *Man of the Moment* are to be this edition.

Chapter 6: Upstream and Off Course, The World

1. Watson, *Conversations*, 85.

2. Ibid., 71.

3. Alan Ayckbourn, *The Revengers' Comedies* (London: Faber & Faber, 1991), 160–61. All subsequent citations to *The Revengers' Comedies* are to this edition.

4. Albert E. Kalson, "Tennessee Williams at the Delta Brilliant," in *Tennessee Williams: 13 Essays*, ed. Jac Tharpe (Jackson: University Press of Mississippi, 1980), 222–23.

5. Watson, *Conversations*, 11.

6. Ibid.

7. Ayckbourn, conversation with Kalson, 4 March 1982.

8. Ibid.

9. *Sunday Times*, 16 April 1978, 37.

10. *Observer*, 9 April 1978, 33.

11. Ayckbourn, *Joking Apart and Other Plays*, preface, 8. Billington, in *Alan Ayckbourn*, 122, likens *Ten Times Table* to Ron Hutchinson's *The Irish Play*, in which a committee plans a pageant that turns chaotic, but J. B. Priestley's panoramic novel, *Festival at Farbridge* (1951) has a similar structure with Tory pitted against Labour while the communist vacillates between the two: the first section of the long three-

part novel ends with a debate over whether the festival should or should not be held, which turns into a farcical near riot.

12. Robin Herford, conversation with Kalson, 4 March 1982.

13. Shiva Naipaul, "Scarborough—Where to Succeed in Show Business," *Radio Times*, 22 August 1975.

14. Graham Greene, quoted by Marie-Francoise Allain, *The Other Man: Conversations with Graham Greene* (New York: Simon & Schuster, 1983), 84.

15. J. B. Priestley, *Bees on the Boat Deck*, in *The Plays of J. B. Priestley* (London: Heinemann, 1949), 2:137.

16. Billington, in *Alan Ayckbourn,* sees Vince representing "fascism" and Keith "capitalist arrogance," p. 159, but Ayckbourn's own comments on Vince suggest that his evil transcends any political label. Richard Allen Cave, in *New British Drama in Performance on the London Stage: 1970–1985* (New York: St. Martin's Press, 1988), suggests that Ayckbourn "tried to make his social criticism covertly political" as early as *Absurd Person Singular;* he writes: "There is a power-hungry Hitler inside little Sydney [*sic*] Hopcroft," 69.

17. Ayckbourn, conversation with Kalson.

18. Ibid.

19. Ibid.

20. Ibid.

21. *New York Times,* 11 July 1990, A6.

22. Ayckbourn, conversation with Kalson.

23. Ibid.

24. John Woodward, quoted by Alan Sked and Chris Cook, *Post-War Britain: A Political History,* 2d ed. (Harmondsworth, Middlesex, England: Penguin Books, 1984), 403.

25. "Profile: Alan Ayckbourn," *Sunday Times,* 18 June 1989, A15.

26. *New York Times,* 24 January 1986, 1:6; for a complete account of Heseltine's resignation and the controversy that followed, see *Times* (London), 3, 4, 9, 10, 11, 17, 20, 22, 23, 24 January 1986; and *Daily Telegraph,* 25 January 1986.

27. *New York Times,* 22 November 1990, A3.

28. Peter Weiss, *The Persecution and Assassination of Jean-Paul Marat as Performed by the Inmates of the Asylum of Charenton under the Direction of the Marquis de Sade,* English version by Geoffrey Skelton (New York: Atheneum, 1966), 61.

29. Ayckbourn, quoted by Charles Spencer, *Daily Telegraph,* 18 October 1991, reprinted in *Theatre Record,* XI 21, 1991, 1293–94.

30. T. S. Eliot, *Selected Essays: 1917–1932* (New York: Harcourt, Brace & Co., 1932), 124–25.

31. Billington, *Alan Ayckbourn,* 209.

32. Ibid., 210.

33. Jane Edwardes, *Time Out,* 23 October 1991, reprinted in *Theatre Record,* XI 21, 1991, 1293–94.

34. Spencer, *Daily Telegraph.*

35. Ibid.

36. *City Limits,* 24 October 1991, reprinted in *Theatre Record,* 1292.

37. *Herald Tribune,* 23 October 1991, reprinted in *Theatre Record,* 1296.

Chapter 7. The Wilder Dreams of Children at Play

1. Alan Ayckbourn, *Body Language,* unpublished manuscript.

2. Alan Ayckbourn, *Mr A's Amazing Maze Plays* (London: Faber & Faber, 1988), 67.

3. Annalena McAfee, "Alan's invisible asset," *Evening Standard,* 8 March 1991, 24.

4. Sarah Hemming, "Children in mind," *Independent,* 6 March 1991, 19.

5. Andrew Adler, "Stage One: The Louisville Children's Theatre, the 1991–92 Season," 21 April 1991, I:1.

6. Ian Watson, *Alan Ayckbourn: Bibliography, Biography, Playography; Theatre Checklist, No. 21* (London: TQ Publications, 1980), 4.

7. Watson, *Conversations with Ayckbourn,* 180.

8. Alan Ayckbourn, "Ernie's Incredible Illucinations" (London: Samuel French, 1969), 17. A subsequent citation to "Ernie's Incredible Illucinations" is to this edition.

9. McAfee, "Alan's invisible asset," 24.

10. Ibid.

11. Alan Ayckbourn, *Invisible Friends* (London: Faber & Faber, 1991), 25–26. All subsequent citations to *Invisible Friends* are to this edition. In the 1939 film version of Frank Baum's *The Wizard of Oz* Dorothy, upset that Auntie Em and Uncle Henry ignore her, as Lucy is ignored, when she complains about Miss Gulch's treatment of Toto, attempts to run away. Her fantasy world, the result of being hit on the head by a window loosed from its hinges by a tornado, has elements as sinister as those experienced by Susan and Lucy, both of whom suffer head injuries. Dorothy's journey to Oz is a journey to adulthood, an understanding of self and the world. Lucy too learns to make an accommodation with a less-than-perfect world as a result of her fantasy experience. In the gentle, charming *Dreams from a Summer House* (1992), a musical play, with composer John Pattison, Ayckbourn again contrasts the real world with a magical fairyland. In a variation of the "Beauty and the Beast" legend, sweet, lovely Belle, who can only communicate through song, and daunting, tone-deaf Amanda must exchange worlds to finally realize themselves as they guide hesitant Robert and awakening Mel to an acknowledgment of their love.

12. McAfee, "Alan's invisible asset," 24.

13. Hemming, "Children in mind," 19.

14. McAfee, "Alan's invisible asset," 5.

15. Heather Stoney, letter to Kalson, 17 May 1991. Ayckbourn fulfilled the promise with *Time of My Life,* presented in Scarborough in 1992. In a program note Ayckbourn again acknowledged a debt to J. B. Priestley: "I am hardly the first dramatist to be fascinated by time . . . as an aid to dramatic story telling. . . . A great deal of my interest, I confess, was first fueled when I encountered the work of the father of the twentieth century Time Play, J. B. Priestley. It was largely thanks to his adventurous experiments with stage time that I became aware of its huge narrative potential. Nearly a quarter of a century on, I'm still fascinated." *Time of My Life* involves three couples. One couple play out their relationship in constant, linear, present time; the second couple travel back in time over a period of months; the third travel forward in years.

16. Alan Ayckbourn, *Wildest Dreams,* unpublished manuscript.

17. Luigi Pirandello, *Henry IV,* English version by Edward Storer, *Naked Masks,* ed. Eric Bentley (New York: E. P. Dutton & Co., 1952), 208.

18. John Peter, "A nightmare in no man's land," *Sunday Times,* 12 May 1991, 5:13.

19. Mike Nichols, quoted by Mervyn Rothstein, "Mike Nichols Tries to Put the Fun Back into 'Godot,'" *New York Times,* 13 September 1988, 17.

20. Arthur Miller, quoted by Nigella Lawson, "The Exorcism of Arthur Miller," *Sunday Times,* 3 June 1990, 5:1.

Select Bibliography

Anouilh, Jean. *Dinner with the Family*. Translated by Edward Owen Marsh. London: Methuen, 1958.

——. *Five Plays*, Vol. 1; *Five Plays*, Vol. 2; *Seven Plays*, Vol. 3. New York: Hill & Wang, 1958, 1959, 1967.

Ayckbourn, Alan. *A Chorus of Disapproval*. London: Faber & Faber, 1986.

——. *Confusions*. London: Samuel French, 1977.

——. "Ernie's Incredible Illucinations." London: Samuel French, 1969.

——. *Henceforward . . ..* London: Faber & Faber, 1988.

——. *How the Other Half Loves*. London: Evans Plays, 1972.

——. *Intimate Exchanges*. 2 vols. London: Samuel French, 1985.

——. *Invisible Friends*. London: Faber & Faber, 1991.

——. *Joking Apart and Other Plays*. Harmondsworth, Middlesex, England: Penguin Books, 1982.

——. *Man of the Moment*. London: Faber & Faber, 1990.

——. *Mr A's Amazing Maze Plays*. London: Faber & Faber, 1989.

——. *The Norman Conquests*. New York: Grove Press, 1979.

——. *Relatively Speaking*. London: Evans Plays, 1968.

——. *Season's Greetings*. London: Samuel French, 1982.

——. *Sisterly Feelings* and *Taking Steps*. London: Chatto & Windus, 1981.

——. *A Small Family Business*. London: Faber & Faber, 1987.

——. *Suburban Strains*. London: Samuel French, 1982.

——. *Three Plays: Absurd Person Singular, Absent Friends, Bedroom Farce*. New York: Grove Press, 1979.

——. *Time and Time Again*. London: Samuel French, 1973.

——. *Way Upstream*. London: Samuel French, 1983.

——. *Woman in Mind*. London: Faber & Faber, 1986.

——, John Bowen, Lyndon Brook, David Campton, George Melly, Alun Owen, Harold Pinter, James Saunders, and Fay Weldon. *Mixed Doubles: An Entertainment on Marriage*. London: Samuel French, 1977.

Billington, Michael. *Alan Ayckbourn*. 2d ed. London: Macmillan, 1990.

Bishop, Thomas. *Pirandello and the French Theatre*. New York: New York University Press, 1960.

Bull, John. *New British Political Dramatists: Howard Brenton, David Hare, Trevor Griffiths, and David Edgar*. London: Macmillan, 1984.

Campton, David. *Laughter and Fear: Nine One-Act Plays*. London and Glasgow: Blackie & Son, 1969.

Cave, Richard Allen. *New British Drama in Performance on the London Stage: 1970–1985*. New York: St. Martin's Press, 1988.

Chambers, Colin, and Mike Prior. *Playwrights' Progress: Patterns of Postwar Drama*. Oxford: Amber Lane Press, 1987.

Chekhov, Anton. *Plays*. Translated by Elisaveta Fen. Hardmondsworth, Middlesex, England: Penguin Books, 1976.

Childs, David. *Britain since 1945: A Political History*. London: Methuen, 1986.

Coward, Noël. *Play Parade*. 6 vols. London: Heinemann, 1934–1962.

Davis, Jessica Milner. *Farce*. London: Methuen, 1978.

DeVitis, A. A. and Albert E. Kalson. *J. B. Priestley*. Boston: G. K. Hall, 1980.

Dukore, Bernard F., ed. *Alan Ayckbourn: A Casebook*. New York: Garland Publishing, 1991.

Esslin, Martin. *Brecht: The Man and His Work*. Garden City, NY: Anchor Books, 1961.

———. *The Theatre of the Absurd*. rev. upd. ed. Woodstock, NY: Overlook Press, 1973.

Feydeau, Georges. *Three Boulevard Farces*. Translated by John Mortimer. Harmondsworth, Middlesex, England: Penguin Books, 1985.

File on Ayckbourn. Compiled by Malcolm Page. London: Methuen Drama, 1989.

Frayn, Michael. *Benefactors*. London: Methuen, 1984.

———. *Look Look*. London: Methuen Drama, 1990.

———. *Noises Off*. London: Methuen, 1983.

Gay, John. *The Beggar's Opera*. Woodbury, NY: Barron's Educational Series, 1962.

Hall, Peter. *Peter Hall's Diaries*. Edited by John Goodwin. London: Hamish Hamilton, 1984.

Harvey, John. *Anouilh: A Study in Theatrics*. New Haven: Yale University Press, 1964.

Hayman, Ronald. *British Theatre since 1955: A Reassessment*. Oxford: Oxford University Press, 1979.

Ibsen, Henrik. *Eight Plays*. Translated by Eva Le Gallienne. New York: The Modern Library, 1982.

———. *Peer Gynt*. Translated by Rolf Fjelde. New York: Signet Classics, 1964.

Joseph, Stephen. *New Theatre Forms*. London: Sir Isaac Pitman & Sons, 1968.

———. *Theatre in the Round*. London: Barrie & Rockliff, 1967.

Kerensky, Oleg. *The New British Drama*. London: Hamish Hamilton, 1977.

Kopit, Arthur. *Wings*. New York: Hill & Wang, 1978.

Lahr, John. *Coward: The Playwright*. New York: Avon Books, 1982.

Laing, R. D. *The Divided Self*. New York: Pantheon Books, 1960.

Marwick, Arthur. *British Society since 1945*. Harmondsworth, Middlesex, England: Penguin Books, 1982.

Nightingale, Benedict. *An Introduction to 50 Modern British Plays*. London: Pan Books, 1982.

Nineteenth-Century British Drama. Edited by Leonard R. N. Ashley. Glenview, Illinois: Scott, Foresman & Company, 1967.

Pinter, Harold. *Old Times*. New York: Grove Press, 1971.

Pirandello, Luigi. *Naked Masks: Five Plays*. Edited by Eric Bentley. New York: E. P. Dutton & Co., 1952.

Priestley, J.B . *The Art of the Dramatist, A Lecture*. London: Heinemann, 1957.

————. *An Inspector Calls*. London: Heinemann, 1947.

————. *The Plays of J. B. Priestley*. 3 vols. London: Heinemann, 1948–50.

Redmond, James, ed. *Themes in Drama 10: Farce*. Cambridge: Cambridge University Press, 1975.

Sheridan, Richard Brinsley. *Plays*. Oxford University Press, 1975.

Sinfield, Alan. *Literature, Politics, and Culture in Postwar Britain*. Berkeley and Los Angeles: University of California Press, 1989.

Sked, Alan, and Chris Cook. *Post-War Britain: A Political History*. 2d ed. Harmondsworth, Middlesex, England: Penguin Books, 1984.

Taylor, John Russell. *Anger and After: A Guide to the New British Drama*. London: Methuen, 1962.

————. *The Second Wave: British Drama for the Seventies*. New York: Hill & Wang, 1971.

Travers, Ben. *Five Plays*. Harmondsworth, Middlesex, England: Penguin Books, 1979.

Watson, Ian. *Alan Ayckbourn: Bibliography, Biography, Playography; Theatre Checklist No. 21*. London: TQ Publications, 1980.

————. *Conversations with Ayckbourn*. London: Macdonald Futura, 1981; 2d ed. London: Faber & Faber, 1988.

Weintraub, Stanley, ed. *Dictionary of Literary Biography: British Dramatists Since World War II*. Vol. 13. Detroit: Gale Research Co., 1982.

Weiss, Peter. *The Persecution and Assassination of Jean-Paul Marat as Performed by the Inmates of the Asylum of Charenton under the Direction of the Marquis de Sade*. English version by Geoffrey Skelton. New York: Atheneum, 1966.

White, Sidney Howard. *Alan Ayckbourn*. Boston: G.K. Hall, 1984.

Index